CYBERWAR

KATHLEEN HALL JAMIESON

CYBERWAR

How Russian Hackers and Trolls
Helped Elect a President

What we don't, can't, and do know

OXFORD
UNIVERSITY PRESS

OXFORD
UNIVERSITY PRESS

Oxford University Press is a department of the University of Oxford. It furthers
the University's objective of excellence in research, scholarship, and education
by publishing worldwide. Oxford is a registered trade mark of Oxford University
Press in the UK and certain other countries.

Published in the United States of America by Oxford University Press
198 Madison Avenue, New York, NY 10016, United States of America.

© Oxford University Press 2018

CIP data is on file at the Library of Congress
ISBN 978-0-19-091581-0

3 5 7 9 8 6 4 2
Printed by Sheridan Books, Inc., United States of America

To Finnian, Sylvia, Ava, and Gabrielle Jamieson

CONTENTS

ACKNOWLEDGMENTS

Drawing on the rolling cross-sectional National Annenberg Election Surveys of 2000 and 2008, my colleagues and I were able to isolate the otherwise elusive campaign communication effects that we reported in *The 2000 Presidential Election and the Foundations of Party Politics* (Cambridge University Press, 2004) and *The Obama Victory: How Media, Money, and Message Shaped the 2008 Election* (Oxford University Press, 2010). With no urgent communication questions on the horizon, I packed away all but the PROSE award that *The Obama Victory* had won, sunset the National Annenberg Election Survey, and stepped away from the study of presidential elections. By commissioning a *Washington Post* op-ed on the Russian interventions, Marisa Bellack drew me back to the subject of communication's role in vote choice and birthed the idea for this book. Over salads in Cambridge, Sherry Turkle persuaded me to write it. By finding reviewers who helped me rethink the structure and by directing me to experts able to critique my claims, my Oxford editor, David McBride, transformed a possibility into plans, plans into chapters, and chapters into print, with valuable help along the way from Emily Mackenzie, Liz Davey, and Christine Dahlin.

My thanks to Nicco Mele and Tom Patterson of the Kennedy School's Shorenstein Center and their colleagues (especially Matt, Nancy, Susan, and Tim), not only for licensing me to forsake my original sabbatical project for the tracking of trolls but also for providing a welcoming home-away-from-home. In sun and in snow, the other fall 2017 Shorenstein fellows expanded my horizons with insider knowledge about the Federal Communications

Commission (Tom Wheeler), the world of bots and Bitcoin (Wael Ghonim), Cape Cod and the Kennedy School's warrens (Tyler Bridges), the wonders of Cajun cooking (Donna Brazile), and European political communication scholarship (Claes H. de Vreese). Having Andy Rosenthal and Dan Balz within pestering distance and former Penn colleague Drew Faust walking the pond and sharing lunch rounded out four memorable months.

Two other gracious groups of colleagues opened opportunities for me to test ideas in progress. Thank you to both Marty Kaplan of USC's Norman Lear Center and to the Annenberg faculty, of what we at Annenberg-Penn fondly term "our sister school," for permitting me to honor the legacy of Everett Rogers by delivering a lecture about trolls and hackers as agents of malign diffusion. I am indebted as well to the professors at University of Indiana, Julia Fox in particular, whose classes of digital natives provided insights and geolocation as I wandered their campus as a Patten lecturer. For spotting and detonating land mines, I also owe special thanks to Siva Vaidhyanathan, Robert Jervis, John Lapinsky, and Matt Levendusky.

At the Annenberg Public Policy Center, which I direct, Lana Xu managed my ever-changing schedule while also tracking down references; Emily Garretson Maroni verified endnotes and formatted and re-formatted the manuscript; and Gary Gehman kept a lookout for all things troll-related while searching the platforms and archives for apt illustrations. Annenberg researchers Lauren Hawkins, Leo Page-Blau, Timothy McAuliffe, Charlotte Laracy, and Ghali Benlafkih systematically scrutinized troll Facebook ads for signs of their underlying strategy. On the home front, Patrick and Laura, Rob and Sarah are stalwarts; Bill, Jim, Rita, and Anita are better than best siblings; and our hundred-year-old mom, grandmother, and great-grandmother, Katherine, who cheered this project on while in hospice, is not only the family matriarch but also a model of what we all aspire to be.

When unexpectedly asked by a USC radio host to indicate my favorite word, without hesitation, and with a nod to my husband, Bob, I said, "Grandchildren." Finnian, Sylvia, Ava, and Gabrielle Jamieson, this book is lovingly dedicated to you in the hope that our country will have safeguarded its campaign and electoral processes long before you cast your first votes.

Kathleen Hall Jamieson
Philadelphia, 2018

PROLOGUE

"You would 'have to believe in unicorns' to conclude that Russian meddling changed the 2016 election results."[1]
Former Arkansas governor Mike Huckabee. December 12, 2016.

"We learned that the Russians are more involved in our election process than the League of Women Voters."[2]
Humorist Dave Barry. 2016 year-end review.

"When I decided, I said to myself, I said, 'You know, this Russia thing with Trump and Russia is a made up story.'"[3]
President Donald J. Trump on the context for his firing of FBI director James Comey. May 11, 2017.

"I haven't seen, even once, any direct proof of Russian interference in the presidential election."[4]
Russian President Vladimir Putin. June 2017.

"We do not know . . . how to place an advert on Facebook. We have never done this, and the Russian side has never been involved in it."[5]
A Kremlin spokesperson. September 2017.

"The Russia hoax continues, now it's ads on Facebook. What about the totally biased and dishonest Media coverage in favor of Crooked Hillary?"[6]

President Donald J. Trump. September 22, 2017.

"He [Putin] said he didn't meddle—I asked him again. . . . You can only ask so many times. I just asked him again. He said he absolutely did not meddle in our election. He did not do what they are saying he did."[7]

President Donald J. Trump. November 11, 2017.

In December 2017 *BuzzFeed* reported that in July 2017 Putin's Deputy Foreign Minister Sergei Ryabkov offered a State Department under secretary a pact under which neither country would interfere in the other's internal affairs. According to the *BuzzFeed* account, the Trump administration rejected the overture.[8]

"[T]he big emerging journalism story is the Russians, who, according to many unnamed sources, messed with the election. Nobody seems to know how, specifically, the Russians affected the election, but everybody is pretty sure they did *something*."[9]

Humorist Dave Barry. 2017 year-end review.

"Today, Sen. Jeff Flake gave a big speech on the Senate floor, and he compared President Trump to Russian dictator Joseph Stalin. Trump said, 'Why? Because we were both elected by Russians?' "[10]

Comedian Jimmy Fallon, host of *The Tonight Show*. January 17, 2018.

"Russia started their anti-US campaign in 2014, long before I announced that I would run for President. The results of the election were not impacted. The Trump campaign did nothing wrong—no collusion!"[11]

President Donald Trump. February 16, 2018. Response to the February 2018 Mueller grand jury indictment of thirteen Russians for their interventions in the 2016 election.

"Could anyone really believe that Russia, thousands of miles away . . . influenced the outcome of the election? Doesn't that sound ridiculous even to you?"[12]

Vladimir Putin to NBC's Megyn Kelly in a March 2, 2018, interview, aired in the United States on March 9, 2018.

"The Russians had no impact on our votes whatsoever, but certainly there was meddling and probably there was meddling from other countries and maybe other individuals." Asked about Russia interfering in the 2018 midterm election, he added, "No, because we'll counteract whatever they do."[13]

President Donald J. Trump. March 6, 2018.

On July 16, 2018, at the joint Putin-Trump press conference in Helsinki, Jeff Mason of Reuters asked the Russian president, "Did you want President Trump to win the election, and did you direct any of your officials to help him do that?" Putin responded, "Yes, I did. Yes, I did. Because he talked about bringing the US-Russia relationship back to normal." Mason later told NPR that "my suspicion is he heard the first part of my question and may not have heard the second part" (July 18, 2018).

After Chris Wallace of Fox News handed him a copy of the July 13, 2018 US indictment of twelve Russian military intelligence agents for hacking the Democratic accounts, Putin stated, "Was it rigging of facts? Was it some forgery of facts? That's the important…point…. Was there any false information planted? No, it wasn't. These hackers…hacked a certain e-mail account and there was information about manipulations conducted within the Democratic Party to incline the process in favor of one candidate and as far as I know the entire party leadership resigned…. Manipulation of the public opinion should stop and an apology should be made to the public at large instead of looking for those responsible or the party at fault."

Interview with Chris Wallace, Fox News, July 16, 2018.

CYBERWAR

Introduction

US Susceptibilities, Troll and Hacker Synchronies, and My Suppositions

Imagine a strategy memo forecasting cyberattacks by Russian hackers, trolls, and bots designed to roil social discontent and damage the electoral prospects of a major party US presidential nominee, or, if she winds up winning, sabotage her ability to govern. Guaranteed payoff. No fingerprints. No keystroke record. No contrails in the cloud. To ensure that Americans would believe that disparaging messages about her were made in the US, use bitcoin to buy space and set up virtual private networks (VPNs) on American servers. Distribute hacked content stolen from the accounts of her staff and associates through an intermediary, WikiLeaks. Use identity theft, stolen Social Security numbers, and appropriated IDs to circumvent Facebook and PayPal's demand for actual names, birth dates, and addresses. On platforms such as Instagram and Twitter, register under assumed names. Diffuse and amplify your attack and advocacy through posts on Facebook, tweets and retweets on Twitter, videos on YouTube, reporting and commentary on RT, blogging on Tumblr, news sharing on Reddit, and viral memes and jokes on 9GAG.[1] Add to the mix a video game called *Hilltendo* in which a missile-straddling Clinton figure vaporizes classified emails sought by the FBI.[2] Employ "online agitators" and bots to upvote posts from imposter websites such as BlackMattersUS.com to the top of such subreddits as r/The_Donald and r/HillaryForPrison.[3] Drive content to trend.

To maximize the impact of your handiwork, use data analytics and search-engine maximization tools built into the social media platforms. To test and fuel doubts about the security of US voter information, hack the election systems of states.[4] And, throughout the primary and general election season, seed the notion that if Hillary Clinton were to win, she would have done so by rigging the election, an outcome that would repay her assaults on the legitimacy of their leader's presidency with doubts about her own. Were she instead to lose, she would no longer be a thistle in the toned torso of the hackers and trolls' boss's likely boss.

Every result but one produces desirable results for the Kremlin. Outcome one: Clinton is off the international stage. Outcome two: she wins but can't govern effectively. Outcome three: the former Secretary of State is elected and the country simply moves on, but the sabotage nonetheless has magnified cultural tensions and functioned as a pilot from which to birth later success— perhaps when she runs for a second term. The only eventuality that damages the Russian cybersoldiers and their commander-in-chief is the fourth in which, in real time, the cyberattackers are unmasked by a vigilant intelligence community, condemned by those in both major political parties and around the world, characterized by the media as spies and saboteurs, the Russian messaging is blocked or labeled as Russian propaganda, and, when included in media accounts, the stolen content is relentlessly tied to its Russian origins and sources. None of that happened.

Instead, to the surprise of the Russian masterminds as well as both Hillary Clinton and Donald Trump, he won the Electoral College and with it a four-year claim on 1600 Pennsylvania Avenue. Although countrywide she bested him by almost 2.9 million votes,[5] he unexpectedly captured an Electoral College majority by running the table. By the end of the evening of November 8, Florida as well as Wisconsin, Michigan, and Pennsylvania were in his column. The ways in which Russian hacking and social media messaging altered the content of the electoral dialogue and contributed to Donald Trump's victory are the subjects of this book.

To begin my exploration, this overview chapter will highlight key findings of the US intelligence community; preview my focus on the hackers and trolls and the synergies between them; justify casting the Russian machinations as acts of cyberwar; outline ways in which susceptibilities in our system of government and media structures magnified their effects; and note five presuppositions that will shape my analysis of the Russian trolls' work and one that will guide my study of the effects of the hackers.

The Findings of the Intelligence Community

Forming the backdrop for my inquiry are three reports on the Russian intervention in the 2016 presidential election: the October 7, 2016, statement jointly issued by the Department of Homeland Security (DHS) and the Office of the Director of National Intelligence (ODNI) on election security; the January 2017 conclusions of the US intelligence agencies (i.e., the CIA, the FBI, and the National Security Agency [NSA]); and the February 2018 Robert Mueller indictment of thirteen of the Russians allegedly behind the social media intrusions.

On a day that will live in campaign lore, as much for what didn't happen as for what did (more on that in a moment), the first of the three revealed the following:

> The U.S. Intelligence Community (USIC) is confident that the
> Russian Government directed the recent compromises of e-mails
> from U.S. persons and institutions, including from U.S. political
> organizations. The recent disclosures of alleged hacked e-mails on
> sites like DCLeaks.com and WikiLeaks and by the Guccifer 2.0 online
> persona are consistent with the methods and motivations of Russian-
> directed efforts. These thefts and disclosures are intended to interfere
> with the U.S. election process. Such activity is not new to Moscow—
> the Russians have used similar tactics and techniques across Europe

and Eurasia, for example, to influence public opinion there. We believe, based on the scope and sensitivity of these efforts, that only Russia's senior-most officials could have authorized these activities.[6]

The next report put a name to one of those senior-most officials and specified an intended beneficiary. Specifically, after Donald Trump was elected but before he was inaugurated, the January 6, 2017, document declared:

> We assess Russian President Vladimir Putin ordered an influence campaign in 2016 aimed at the U.S. presidential election. Russia's goals were to undermine public faith in the U.S. democratic process, denigrate Secretary Clinton, and harm her electability and potential presidency. We further assess Putin and the Russian Government developed a clear preference for President-elect Trump. We have high confidence in these judgments.
>
> We also assess Putin and the Russian Government aspired to help President-elect Trump's election chances when possible by discrediting Secretary Clinton and publicly contrasting her unfavorably to him. All three agencies agree with this judgment. CIA and FBI have high confidence in this judgment; NSA has moderate confidence.[7]

Just over a year later, the third update on Russian intrigue was released on February 16, 2018, by the Justice Department and by Special Counsel Robert Mueller, the former FBI director appointed by the deputy attorney general, Rod J. Rosenstein, to oversee the investigation into Russian tampering in the 2016 presidential election. Among the charges in that grand jury indictment of thirteen Russians and three Russian organizations were conspiracy to defraud the United States, conspiracy to commit wire and bank fraud, and aggravated identity theft. As its object, the conspiracy had "impairing, obstructing, and defeating the lawful governmental functions of the United States by dishonest means in order to enable the Defendants to interfere with U.S. political and electoral processes, including the 2016 U.S. presidential election."[8] According to the brief, the conspirators' efforts were designed to "promote discord in the United States and undermine public confidence in democracy," and also support the presidential campaign of then-candidate Donald J. Trump and disparage that of Hillary Clinton.

For the sake of brevity, I will refer to this third document as the Mueller troll indictment and characterize the three declarations in combination as reports from the intelligence community. Two facts, central to my analysis, are included in the January 2017 report and elaborated on in the February 2018 indictment: there was a synergistic relationship between the WikiLeaks releases and Moscow-backed social media content, and the Kremlin-authorized efforts were designed to discredit Hillary Clinton and help elect Donald Trump. Accordingly, *Cyberwar* will concentrate on the actions of those discourse saboteurs, traditionally termed "trolls," as well as the spies or espionage agents conventionally called "hackers." As my subtitle—*How Russian Hackers and Trolls Helped Elect a President*—suggests, I will rely on those commonplace characterizations of both.

Introducing the Trolls, Hackers, and Noting the Synergies between Them

Unlike the otherworldly creatures in Norse mythology who live in rocks, caves, mountains, and forests, the Russian internet trolls of interest here assumed guises that shielded their true identity as they marauded about in cyberspace creating the illusion that they were grassroots activists while posting provocative, often inflammatory content. (A quick side note: because it is the *messaging* promulgated by bots and not their automated nature that is my focus, throughout the book I will engage in a shorthand that credits bot content to trolls.) Of central concern are operatives belonging to the Russian Internet Research Agency (IRA) "troll farm" in St. Petersburg, where, as a July 2016 article in the *New Yorker* revealed, "they produced blog posts, comments, infographics, and viral videos that pushed the Kremlin's narrative on both the Russian and English Internet."[9]

The timeline on which the trolls operated is telling. An analysis by the *Wall Street Journal* found that some of the Russian Twitter accounts with more than 10,000 followers "were created in late 2015 as the presidential primaries were in full swing."[10] According to an NBC News analysis of a database of 202,973 tweets sent by known Russian trolls, "Russian twitter troll volume increased significantly on July 21, two days after Trump became the official Republican nominee, and continued at the same intensity or higher for the rest of the year."[11]

To harness the fears and enthusiasms of US citizens to their cause, Russian discourse saboteurs crafted and placed ads on US platforms, organized rallies that would showcase cultural divisions, created imposter sites, and strategically messaged to millions on Facebook, Instagram, Twitter, YouTube, Tumblr, and Reddit, among others. With a focus on constituencies whom Donald Trump needed to mobilize, Russian messages stoked fears of the multicultural, multiracial, ecumenical culture that the Clinton Democrats championed and that unified her coalition of blacks, Hispanics, and northern, college-educated whites. At the same time, the trolls amplified accurate information disadvantaging Clinton and spread disinformation about her to discourage voting by key Democratic blocs. The impersonators' core appeals are evident in election-related hashtags such as #TrumpTrain, #MAGA, #IWontProtectHillary, #BlacksAgainstHillary, and #Hillary4Prison, the Twitter account "March for Trump," and Facebook accounts including "Clinton FRAUDation" and "Trumpsters United."[12]

Scholars and reporters have assembled suggestive swaths of the trolls' message streams. One of my tasks here is integrating their disparate results into an explanatory framework that permits us to map the Russian efforts and, to the extent possible, determine the likelihood that their hacking and social media machinations altered the 2016 presidential outcome.

Tied to Russian spy agencies that included the General Staff Main Intelligence Directorate (GRU),[13] the Russian hackers gained unauthorized access to stored Democratic emails, data, and memoranda. Initially the stolen content was released through the personas Guccifer 2.0 and DCLeaks. com. Then a more effective partner entered the scene. This helpmeet was WikiLeaks, a controversial organization described by its chief spokesperson, Julian Assange, as "an uncensorable system for untraceable mass document leaking and public analysis."[14] In January 2017, the US intelligence agencies assessed "with high confidence that the GRU relayed material it acquired from the DNC [Democratic National Committee] and senior Democratic officials to WikiLeaks."[15] The reason for this choice of distributor? "Moscow most likely chose WikiLeaks because of its self-proclaimed reputation for authenticity." Assange denied that Russia was the source of the released Democratic content.

The released Russian-stolen messages exposed Democratic oppositional research compiled about Trump, afforded the Republicans access to voting data in a number of states, altered the media agenda, and were used by the moderators to frame exchanges in two crucial presidential debates. Out of the hacked private conversations, Republicans, their allies, and the trolls fabricated scandals, among them the notion that Hillary's campaign CEO was part of a bizarre secret cult. Another distortion alleged that the candidate herself had employed a racially charged epithet to refer to a person of Muslim faith. Russian-hacked content and disinformation not only infected the news agenda but also tilted the balance of discourse in battleground states against the Democratic Party nominee.

Why *Cyberwar*?

The title of this book asserts that these Russian activities can fairly be characterized as cyberattacks launched as part of an undeclared cyberwar. Before making that case, let me note that candidate Trump was onto something when, at a town hall in September 2016, he told his future national security adviser (the now-indicted) General Michael Flynn that "cyber is becoming so big today. It's becoming something that a number of years ago, short number of years ago, wasn't even a word."[16] Big, yes. But also weaponized. Although politics as war is a conventional metaphor and words such as campaigning and battleground no longer automatically evoke the sounds of guns, in 2016 an adversary engaged in a decidedly nonmetaphoric attack in cyberspace on the US body politic and on a US candidate for president.

If by cyberwar one means "actions by a nation-state to penetrate another nation's computers or networks for the purposes of causing damage or disruption,"[17] the 2014 specification offered by Richard Clarke, the intelligence analyst who foresaw 9/11, then the findings of our intelligence agencies that the activities were state-authorized satisfies the first part of the definition (i.e., actions by a nation-state). Whether attempted disruption of an election, rather than, for example, the electrical grid or the digital workings of Wall Street, satisfies the second (i.e., "causing damage or disruption") is open to question. In 2017, Clarke did characterize it as warfare when he said of the trolls' infiltration of social media that it was "[p]sychological warfare on a grand scale. They conducted the largest psychological warfare campaign in history and they won. . . . They invaded our country. They invaded our political system and they won."[18]

Rhetorical analogues to the notion of "cyberwar on democracy" can be found in wars against poverty, drugs, and terror. The notion that a war can be ongoing even as its meaning evolves is evident in the label "Cold War," used to convey the post–World War II standoff between the Soviet Bloc countries and the West. Like that state of affairs, Russian cyberactivities are ongoing and evolving, having involved opposing the 2017 nomination of 2012 Republican presidential nominee Mitt Romney as Trump's Secretary of State[19] and amplifying discord after the 2018 killings in Parkland High School in Florida.[20]

Helpful in situating these moves in context is the insight of Alexander Klimburg of the Hague Centre for Strategic Studies who noted that the former Soviet Union envisioned that "a war could be waged and won without the other side's knowing that war had been declared." The weapons involved in such conquest included strategic psychological operations designed to dominate "an adversary's decision-making process through various tools, including . . . semantics and the choice of terms in public discourse." In a statement that aptly forecasts Russian efforts to affect voters, Klimburg explains that "[i]n every case, the goal is to deliver information to the target to incline it 'to voluntarily make the predetermined decision desired by the initiator of the action.'"[21]

The term "cyberwar" locates the sphere in which the attacks occurred; defines hacking, posting, impersonating, and strategic release of stolen content as weaponry; presupposes agents with ill intent; invites us to see the perpetrators as enemies; casts hackers and trolls as soldiers, saboteurs, and spies; sees the US president as commander-in-chief; creates the expectation that the attacked country will retaliate; and implies the value of inviting the public to arm itself. Employing the mealy-mouthed word "meddling," as leaders on both sides of the aisle as well as reporters are wont to do, and as *USA Today* did in a 2018 poll,[22] obscures the enemy's intent and circumscribes the invited response. Where "meddled" invites us to ask "in what," "cyberattack" elicits the questions "on what," "on whom," "with what weapons," "to what end," "with what effect," and "whether, when, and, if so, how should those attacked retaliate"? Where an appropriate response to an actor who "meddles" is "mind your own business," the expected reaction to cyberattack is a hardening of one's defense and a counterattack. In short, the nature, urgency, and extent of the invited response all change when one abandons "meddling" and "interfered" for "cyberattacked" and engaged in "cyberwar."

Characterizing the Russian actions as "cyberwar" is precedented. During the fall 2017 hearings on Russian exploitation of the tech platforms, Senator Dianne Feinstein (D-CA) insisted to the lawyers representing Facebook, Google, and Twitter, "You don't get it! This is a very big deal. What we're talking about is cataclysmic. It is cyber warfare. A major foreign power with sophistication and ability got involved in our presidential election."[23] "Cyberwarfare with Russia 'now greater threat than terrorism,' warns British Army chief," read a January 2018 headline in the *Independent*.[24] "Frankly, the United States is under attack," Director of National Intelligence Dan Coats told the Senate Intelligence Committee on February 13, 2018.[25] To Megyn Kelly's question "Can we contain Russia in cyber warfare?," Russian president Vladimir Putin responded, "I think it is impossible to contain Russia anywhere."[26]

The notion that we are engaged in a war is embedded in the title of Michael Isikoff and David Corn's *Russian Roulette: The Inside Story of Putin's War on America and the Election of Donald Trump*. The reactions to the Russian hack-and-release that the Obama administration considered and then shelved could accurately be called response in kind. They included actions to "unleash the NSA to mount its own series of far-reaching cyberattacks: to dismantle the Russian-created websites, Guccifer 2.0 and DCLeaks, that had been leaking the emails and memos stolen from Democratic targets; to bombard Russian news sites with a wave of automated traffic in a denial-of-service attack that would shut them down; and to launch an attack on the Russian intelligence agencies themselves, seeking to disrupt their command and control nodes."[27] Other sidetracked plans included "leaking snippets of classified intelligence to reveal the secret bank accounts in Latvia held for Putin's daughters.... Dump[ing] dirt on Russian websites about Putin's money, about the girlfriends of top Russian officials, about corruption in Putin's United Russia Party." Where the title of their book characterizes Putin's activities as war, the headline on the Yahoo! article about it ("The cyberwar that never happened . . .") suggests that war only exists at the point at which the United States launches a counterstrike.

Some may argue that because the United States has a history of insinuating disinformation, deception, and funding into the elections of other countries, including Russia, taking umbrage at the Russian attacks and categorizing them as an act of war are hypocritical. "Russia isn't the only one meddling in elections. We do the same," proclaims an essay in the *New York Times* Sunday review.[28] Here Russian president Vladimir Putin agrees, telling NBC's Megyn Kelly in a March 2018 interview,

> Please listen to me and take to your viewers and listeners what I am about to say. We are holding discussions with our American friends and partners, people who represent the government by the way, and when they claim that some Russians interfered in the U.S. elections, we tell them (we did so fairly recently at a very high level): "But you are constantly interfering in our political life." Would you believe it, they aren't even denying it. Do you know what they told us last time? They said, "Yes, we do interfere, but we are entitled to do so, because we are spreading democracy, and you aren't, and so you cannot do it." Do you think this is a civilised and modern approach to international affairs?[29]

The likelihood that the United States is engaging in comparable activities may explain why terms more benign than "cyberwar" have been a mainstay of US characterizations of the Russian interventions. Another rationale for avoiding the language of war and its invited actions is that the United States may be unprepared to deal with anticipated levels of possible escalation. By seizing Russian compounds in the States and imposing economic sanctions, the United States has to this point, publicly at least, responded to cyberattacks with economic penalties. Rather than warehousing the label "cyberwar," one alternatively could think of these economic responses as counterattacks with a different kind of weapon.

A sampling of the outward signs of the Russian cyberwar reveals its range. One hundred and twenty-six million Americans were exposed to

Russian-trafficked content on Facebook. At least 1.4 million Twitter users were subjected to the wiles of Kremlin-tied trolls and bots feigning allegiance to American values while, according to an assessment by the US intelligence agencies, bent on fomenting dissent among US citizens and defeating one of the two major party candidates. Among those conned by cyberspies cloaked in ball caps and team jerseys was a St. Louis, Missouri, hip-hop artist who thought he was creating videos for a group allied with Black Lives Matter. Instead, his work was posted to a Russian troll site. When they endorsed content originating with @TEN_GOP, an account exposed after the election as a Russian front, household names in conservative political circles became Russian pawns as well. The electoral systems of twenty-one states by one count and thirty-nine by another were hacked. In locales from Florida to Minnesota, individuals unwittingly helped the Russians organize rallies. Some of these efforts were laughably inept. Although there are no coal mines near Philadelphia, trolls attempted to organize a rally of coal miners there. Others were adroit. Two of the troll-generated Florida events were subsequently featured on the website of a Trump supporter in the Sunshine State.

Susceptibilities in Our System

In executing their plans, the Russians exploited the American system's protections of speech and press; its free-market disposition not to regulate forms of expression and channels of political communication; the platforms' capacities to shield identity, harvest personal data, facilitate sharing, and target advertising; and the dispositions of the press to focus both on campaign tactics and supposed scandals and on ferreting out differences between the public pronouncements and private actions, views, and the undisclosed plans of political leaders.

Jujitsu-like, the Russian game plan capitalized on deeply held American values, such as those embodied in the First Amendment. These prized strengths of our system of government made the United States more vulnerable than the one in France, where the 2017 election-eve Russian attempt to undermine Emmanuel Macron with hacked content was met with a statement by France's electoral regulatory body, the Commission Nationale de Contrôle de la Campagne Électorale en Vue de l'Élection Présidentielle

(CNCCEP), asking the media not to report on or publish the contents, and reminding them that diffusing false information "is likely to fall ["susceptible de tomber"] under the scope of the law, particularly criminal law."[30] "It is worth noting," writes Jarred Prier, "that the French press did not cover the content of the Macron leaks; instead, the journalists covered the hacking and influence operation without giving any credibility to the leaked information."[31] Importantly, Emilio Ferrara, a researcher at the University of Southern California, has shown that the "nearly 18 thousand bots deployed to push #MacronLeaks and related topics" failed to either mobilize or produce significant discussion of the leaked documents among French users more likely to vote for Macron.[32]

The Kremlin's 2016 efforts also were facilitated by the United States' free-market impulse to minimize government regulation of new communication technologies. Unlike US political ads on radio and TV, those appearing online in 2016 were not required to carry a "clear and conspicuous" disclaimer indicating who authorized the ad, a reality that would be changed if the proposed Honest Ads Act were to become law. And in 2016, US campaign finance regulations did not require digital platforms to disclose who was funding campaign ads on them.

By making it possible for users to not only consume but also create, share, and comment on content with those in their networked community, the web revolutionized communication. Russian hackers, trolls, and bots worked their wiles in a media ecosystem susceptible to foreign intrusion, its architecture ready-made for productive engagement with family and friends as well as with those we know less well, if they are known at all. Because the geographic location of the communicator is not evident to those viewing posts and tweets, in a single sitting, a troll in St. Petersburg could masquerade as a housewife in Harrisburg, Pennsylvania; a black nationalist in Atlanta, Georgia; and a disaffected Democrat in Ripon, Wisconsin. Accordingly, @TEN_GOP was not in Tennessee, as its inhabitants alleged, but continents away. Likewise, there were no longhorns named Bevo or Boris anywhere near the Heart of Texas account's authors.

Counterfeiting location was not the only deception abetted by social media. By feigning following, liking, and sharing, automated accounts known as bots can affect media agendas by running up thousands of all-but-instantaneous "likes" to accelerate the trending of topics. Alternatively, to smother a topic not to their liking, their masters can overwhelm trending hashtags with unrelated ones.[33]

Misrepresenting the source, location, and identity of the communicator was a starting point for the Russians bent on exploiting the capacities of the big tech companies. They also benefited from the platforms' algorithms, which are designed to gain and sustain attention, a process that lends itself to user exposure to conspiracy theories and bogus allegations circulated by those of like mind. In 2016, the social media outlets not only were not programmed to privilege accurate, vetted information but also were and remain especially hospitable to fear-driven, anger-based, extreme content, particularly if it is visually evocative and congenial to the user's biases. The troll content that I will explore met those criteria.

The Russian desire to intravenously feed hacked Democratic "secrets" through WikiLeaks into mainstream media was abetted by two long-lived dispositions of US reporters. For decades, scholars, I among them,[34] have documented the tendency of the US press to explore campaign strategies rather than probe policy substance and also to feature the seeming disjunctions between the contenders' private selves and public personae rather than to examine the significance of either for governance. In a voracious twenty-four-hour-a-day news culture fascinated by polls, peccadillos, the personalities running campaigns and insider gossip about goings-on in the opposing political camps, hacked content has an importance it would lack were reporters' priorities elsewhere.

This book is not just about what the Russians did but also about how the US news media inadvertently helped them achieve their goals. The conclusions that the *Washington Post* columnist Anne Applebaum drew about the cyber thefts in August 2016 remained true for the rest of the campaign. "[M]ost of those covering this story, especially on television, aren't interested in the nature of the hackers," she noted, "and they aren't asking why the Russians apparently chose to pass the emails on to WikiLeaks at this particular moment, on the eve of the Democratic National Convention. They are focusing instead on the content of what were meant to be private emails."[35] Too often, the press served as a conveyor belt of stolen content instead of a gatekeeper.

Lacking the wherewithal to cover everything being leaked, reporters and editors prioritized supposed scandal over substance. So, for example, no one in a major news outlet comprehensively analyzed the leaked passages of Clinton's speeches that discussed trade. Had such scrutiny occurred, reporters would have learned that the Democratic Party nominee employed key themes in common with Trump, both in favoring "reciprocity" and in aggressively making the case for opening foreign markets to US goods. And they would have found as well that she was telling the truth in the final debate when she argued that the statement that she allegedly made about favoring "open borders" was taken out of context (as it was on most of the October 9, 2016, Sunday interview shows on the morning of the second debate as well). As Clinton contended, in the unfeatured second clause in the sentence, "open border" was referring to energy transfer, and, contrary to the meaning Trump superimposed on her statement, it was unrelated to immigration. Moreover, despite the fact that the purloined musings of Clinton's aides were gotten illegally, their Russian origin was not part of the dominant news frame enveloping the content. If, despite our best efforts, political hacking recurs, we need to know not only how 2016 media reporting on it affected the dialogue of that election but also how to thwart uncritical propagation of it in the next.

My Presuppositions

Before sharing what I've found, let me disclose five presuppositions. First, unlike Governor Huckabee,[36] I believe that it is more likely that Russian trolls changed the election's outcome than that unicorns exist. However, and this is my second supposition, any case for influence will be like that in a legal trial in which the verdict is rendered not with the certainty that $E=mc^2$ but rather based on the preponderance of evidence. "Beyond a doubt" is not a standard that works when as many different factors are simultaneously at play as they are here.

Nonetheless, we can know whether Russian interventions could have altered the outcome, and, if so, how plausible such an effect is. Here I am going to disagree, but only to an extent, with former CIA and NSA Director Michael Hayden, who argued in March 2017 that "[t]he Russian services not only messed with our heads (Goal 1), they also may have actually put their thumb on the American electoral scale. There's no telling the impact of the latter, though. It's not just unknown, it's unknowable."[37] Senate Intelligence Committee Chair Richard Burr made the second point as well when he argued, "What we cannot do, however, is calculate the impact that foreign meddling and social media had on this election."[38] My reservation about the notion that we cannot divine effects is that we can surmise the probable although not certain impact Russian shenanigans had on the balance of messages between the two major party campaigns, the options and decisions of key players, and the media and debate agendas. And we can know from past research whether, and if so, how changes in each are likely to affect voters.

Third, barring evidence of tampering with voting machines or vote tallies—and no credible proof of either has been forthcoming—Donald J. Trump is the duly elected president of the United States. (I will leave to others the question of whether that would remain the case if conclusive evidence were uncovered of a quid pro quo between the Kremlin and aspirant-turned-president Trump. My personal judgment is yes, even then Mr. Trump would be president. But probably not for long. As George Mason argued at the Constitutional Convention, procuring one's appointment by corruption should not escape punishment.) However, as far as we know at this point, the incumbent president's January 7, 2017, tweet was accurate when it stated, "Voting machines not touched!"[39] What was inaccurate was his contention that "Intelligence stated very strongly that there was absolutely no evidence that hacking affected the election results." Instead, the ODNI explicitly stated that it "did not make an assessment of the impact that Russian activities had on the outcomes of the 2016 election."[40]

Fourth, trolls did not elect Donald Trump. US citizens did. The Russian operatives' means of affecting the electoral context and the voters within it included:

- Creating visible signs of social disruption, including protests and counterprotests that could redound against the incumbent president and his heir apparent;

- Affecting the roles or behaviors of individuals such as Debbie Wasserman Schultz, who resigned her position as chair of the DNC;

Donna Brazile, who was fired by CNN after a leaked disclosure that she had shared a possible primary debate question with the Clinton campaign; and James Comey, the director of the FBI, whose decision to notify Congress and hence the public of the reopened Clinton investigation on October 28, 2016, may have been prompted in part by Russian disinformation or presumed Russian access to messaging subject to ready misinterpretation;

- Reweighting the climate of opinion against Democratic aspirant Hillary Rodham Clinton through targeted social media posts, tweets, videos, "news," and ads;

- Framing the news and debate agendas through release of hacked content.

My fifth presupposition is that regardless of whether the Kremlin propagandists swayed the attitudes and behaviors of enough voters to determine the election's outcome, if we are to thwart new attempts, we need to know as much as we can about how these foreign agents mucked around in our media systems and candidates' campaigns.

A Forecast of Things to Come

Before closing this chapter, let me outline the work to come. This introduction has provided a brief overview of the ways in which the Russians were able to exploit the dispositions of reporters, the capacities of the social media platforms, and our nation's respect for a free market and championing of freedom of speech and of the press. To examine what they did and whether it mattered, I have focused the book on four broad questions. Who did it, why, and what does research say about how it might matter? Did the Russian trolls do what was needed to plausibly affect the outcome? How did the Russian-hacked content alter the news and debate agendas in the final month and did those changes matter? And, what do we know and what can't we know about the effectiveness of the trolls and hackers? The first part has two chapters; the second, five; the third, three; and part four stands alone. A brief afterword asks what we should make of all of this.

In order to answer the questions "Who did it, why, and how did it matter?" Part I begins by detailing evidence for the conclusion that Russians were responsible for the activities of the trolls and the hackers. Chapter 2 argues that past research indicates that the kinds of messaging that Russians used and generated are capable of producing sizable-enough results to alter a close election. The chapters in Part II then focus on the five conditions the troll machinations would have had to meet to change the 2016 electoral outcome: (1) widespread messaging; (2) a focus on issues compatible with Trump's strategic needs; (3) addressing constituencies he needed to mobilize and demobilize; (4) persuasive content that was amplified in swing states, visually evocative, and magnified by sharing, liking, and commenting; and (5) well-targeted content.

Part III concentrates on the ways in which the hacked content could have altered the outcome by reweighting the message environment and altering the news and debate agendas in the final month of the campaign, from October 7 through November 8. The last part of the book telegraphs what we don't, can't, and do know about whether Russian hackers and trolls helped elect Donald J. Trump president of the United States. All of this is in service of exploring how and with what plausible effect Russian operatives capitalized on an already polarized political environment, manipulated susceptible social and mainstream media, and exploited the dispositions of a risk-prone, Putin-infatuated Republican contender and a wary, establishment-chained Democratic nominee.

Part One

Who Did It, Why, and What Research Says about How It Might Matter

As congressional committees probed the relationships between members of the Trump campaign staff and Russians and also asked how to forestall future sabotage of the US electoral process, lurking in the background was another question untreated in any of the three intelligence reports but asked of a Facebook attorney in the fall 2016 congressional hearings by Senator Mazie Hirono (D-HI): "[C]an you say that the false and misleading propaganda people saw . . . didn't have an impact on the election?"[1] The chief legal counsel for that media platform responded, "We're not well-positioned to judge why any one person or an entire electorate voted as it did."

Among those who are positioned to understand the likely effects of Russian infiltration of social media and WikiLeaks' strategic release of stolen content are researchers who study campaign communication. For more than forty years, I have been part of that community. One goal of my long nights in archives and days hunched over spreadsheets has been making sense of the effects of ads, debates, and news on both the outcome of presidential campaigns and the capacities of the winners to govern. In pursuit of those ends, I've authored or co-authored books ranging from *Packaging the Presidency, Presidential Debates,* and *Dirty Politics* to *The 2000 Election and the Foundations of Party Politics* and *The Obama Victory: How Media, Money, and Message Shaped the 2008 Election.* My conclusions here are based on what I have learned both from that work and from the excellent sleuthing done by others on Russian intrigue in the 2016 campaign.

How Do We Know That Russian Spies and Saboteurs (aka Hackers and Trolls) Intervened in the 2016 Presidential Election?

From former governor Mike Huckabee and the humorists to Putin and Trump, what those I quoted in the prologue are contesting about is the activity that General Michael Hayden, a former director of the CIA and National Security Agency (NSA), characterized as "just about the most successful covert influence campaign in history": the Russian cyberattacks designed to influence the 2016 US presidential election. Among other subversions, Hayden noted that the Kremlin-backed effort involved "the theft of Democrat [*sic*] National Committee [DNC] data and John Podesta's emails, washed through WikiLeaks and DCLeaks and launched by internet trolls to pull the data forward so that it appeared to be 'trending.' "[1] In classic whodunit fashion, let's begin by asking whether the suspect fingered by Hayden and the US intelligence agencies had the motive and the means. Then we should ask how we know that they've identified the actual culprit.

In a bipolar world in which China is the ascendant player, and Russia, at least on the economic front, an also-ran, that latter nation gains a psychological boost—at home as well as abroad—by showcasing discordances between the ideals and principles that the United States proclaims and its realities. Evidence of social fissures and citizen dissatisfaction with those in power accomplishes that end. In 2016 Putin also had issues with both the Democratic incumbent and his Secretary of State, Hillary Rodham Clinton. Among his grievances were US meddling in his own election as well as verbal slings, slights, and subversions.

When massive protests erupted in Moscow in response to his 2011 decision to seek a third term, reported *Politico*, and protesters were charging that Putin had rigged recent elections, "the Russian leader pointed an angry finger at Clinton, who had issued a statement sharply critical of the voting results. 'She said they were dishonest and unfair,' Putin fumed in public remarks, saying that Clinton gave 'a signal' to demonstrators working 'with the support of the U.S. State Department' to undermine his power."[2] "They heard this signal," he asserted "and, with the support of the U.S. State Department, started actively doing their work."[3] In a part of a 2014 speech at the University of Connecticut released by WikiLeaks, Clinton recalled that she said of that situation in Russia, "[W]e're concerned by what we see as irregularities in the voting in Russia, et cetera. And then he [Putin] attacked me personally, and people were pouring into the streets in Moscow and St. Petersburg to protest. . . . And he basically said I had made them go out and protest against him."[4]

Megyn Kelly's June 2017 NBC interview with the Kremlin chief not only contains this revealing précis of his suppositions about the United States' election-finagling in other countries but also hints at a Russian response in kind:

PUTIN: Put your finger anywhere on a map of the world and everywhere you will hear complaints that American officials are interfering in internal election processes.

KELLY: That sounds like a justification.

PUTIN: It doesn't sound like a justification. It sounds like a statement of fact. Every action has an equal and opposite reaction.[5]

A number of acerbic statements by the incumbent Democratic president also rankled the Russian leader. Speaking at The Hague in March 2016, Barack Obama had acknowledged that "Russian President Vladimir Putin's annexation of Crimea would be difficult to reverse."[6] In response to a question, the forty-fourth president of the US then observed that "Russia is a regional power that is threatening some of its immediate neighbors—not out of strength but out of weakness." In his September 2014 speech to the UN, Obama even sandwiched Russian aggression in Europe between Ebola and terrorism as global threats.[7] The state-owned Russia Today (RT) reported, "Following the U.S. President's speech at the UN, Russian FM Sergey Lavrov was puzzled with Barack Obama's ranking of international threats: deadly Ebola virus top, followed by so-called Russian aggression and ISIS in Syria and Iraq only third? . . . 'We earned the second place among the threats to international peace and stability,' Lavrov told journalists on the sidelines of the UN assembly."[8]

Putin also blamed Obama and his Secretary of State for the spring 2016 publication of the so-called Panama Papers that revealed that his close associates had secreted hundreds of billions of dollars into accounts outside Russia. "A $2bn trail leads all the way to Vladimir Putin," reported the *Guardian*.[9] "The Russian president's best friend—a cellist called Sergei Roldugin—is at the centre of a scheme in which money from Russian state banks is hidden offshore. Some of it ends up in a ski resort where in 2013 Putin's daughter Katerina got married." So we have motive as well as the means outlined in the introduction.

During the 2016 campaign, the Republican nominee contested the conclusion that the Russians were the ones who hacked the Democrats' accounts. When, in the second presidential debate, Democratic Party nominee Hillary Clinton claimed that "cyberattacks" on Democratic email accounts, including that of the DNC, "come from the highest levels of the Kremlin and they are designed to influence our election," her counterpart challenged that statement, and with it, the October 7 joint conclusion of the

Department of Homeland Security and Office of the Director of National Intelligence (ODNI) on election security that she was paraphrasing. "She has no idea whether it's Russia, China, or anybody else," the Republican nominee asserted, and "our country has no idea."

As the litany of quotations in the prologue suggests, those casting doubts on Russian election interference include two current presidents: one Russian, the other, American. In the case of the former, the denial asserts that "he" did not meddle, a phrasing that holds open the possibility of delegation. And, of course, believing the denials of a former KGB agent requires a heroic suspension of disbelief. Trump too dismissed the notion that Putin directed the intervention in the US election but on different grounds. "Somebody did say if he [Putin] did do it you wouldn't have found out about it," he noted. "Which is a very interesting point."[10]

Instead of a confession, Putin has offered up a boxcar-full of alternative suspects including the US intelligence services, patriotic Russians untied to the state, a non-Russian state actor, and a perpetrator inside the United States. To support the notion that the CIA and its intelligence community colleagues confected the Russian meddling story, Putin invoked a long-in-the-tooth conspiracy. "There is a theory that Kennedy's assassination was arranged by the US intelligence services," he said in a June 2017 interview, "so if this theory is correct and can't be ruled out, then what could be easier in this day and age than using all the technical means at the disposal of intelligence services . . . [to point] the finger at Russia?"[11] In a move that lends new meaning to the word "irony," Maria Zakharova, identified by the *New York Times* as "the spokeswoman for the Russian Foreign Ministry," also aimed a laser pointer at US operatives by posting under her own name on Facebook(!) her opinion that "[t]his tale of 'hacks' resembles a banal brawl between American security officials over spheres of influence."[12]

Another deflection is one that Putin and Trump share. "As President Trump once said," Putin told *Le Figaro*, "and I think that he was totally right when he said it could have been someone sitting on their bed or somebody intentionally inserted a flash drive with the name of a Russian national, or something like that."[13] The Russian president also informed NBC's Megyn Kelly that "IP addresses can be invented—a child can do that! Your underage daughter could do that. That [the existence of Russian IP addresses] is not proof."[14] Confronted by Kelly with the specific indictment by Mueller of thirteen named Russians, Putin responded in early March 2018, "Maybe, although they are Russian, they work for some American company. Maybe one of them worked for one of the candidates. I have no idea about this, these aren't my problems."[15]

Also advanced by both Trump and Putin is the view that allegations of Russian election intrigue are an attempt by Democrats to rationalize their standard-bearer's failed campaign. "They . . . prefer deluding themselves and others into thinking it was not their fault," argued the former KGB agent, "that their policy was correct, they did all the right things, but someone from the outside thwarted them. But it was not so. They just lost and they have to admit it."[16] Trump was "closer to the people and better understood what ordinary voters want."

The death of Seth Rich, a twenty-seven-year-old DNC staffer who was murdered on his way home from a DC bar in the early-morning hours of July 10, 2016, has also been shrouded by Trump apologists, Russian propaganda outlets, and Kremlin-tied trolls in suspicions that he was the one who stole the DNC content and passed it to WikiLeaks. By putting up a $20,000 reward for information leading to a conviction of the young aide's killer, that organization's founder, Julian Assange, fueled the notion that Rich was the thief. "A conspiracy theory that began on pro–President Trump message boards—a theory that Rich was actually a mole who wanted to expose corruption at the DNC—was fed by Russian news outlets including RT and Sputnik," noted a story in the *Washington Post*. "The Daily Mail, Fox News's website and several other mainstream outlets with large audiences churned through false information and leading questions."[17] "If Seth was wiki source, no Trump/Russia collusion," Fox's Sean Hannity tweeted on May 21, 2017.[18] "This story is now starting to get legs, that Seth Rich was murdered, it was a contract hire killing because he was leaking to WikiLeaks," the conservative radio host Rush Limbaugh told his listeners.[19]

In late May 2017, Newt Gingrich, the former Speaker of the House and a failed 2012 presidential aspirant, claimed that the DNC staffer "apparently was assassinated" after "having given WikiLeaks something like . . . 53,000 [DNC] emails and 17,000 attachments."[20] His extended claim reads:

> At the same time, we have this very strange story now of this young
> man who worked for the Democratic National Committee, who
> apparently was assassinated at 4 in the morning, having given
> WikiLeaks something like 23,000—I'm sorry, 53,000 emails and
> 17,000 attachments. Nobody is investigating that. And what does
> that tell you about what was going on? Because it turns out, it wasn't
> the Russians. It was this young guy who, I suspect, was disgusted by
> the corruption of the Democratic National Committee. He's been
> killed, and apparently nothing serious has been done to investigate
> his murder. So I'd like to see how Mueller is going to define what his
> assignment is, and if it is only narrowly Trump the country will not
> learn what it needs to learn about foreign involvement in American
> politics.

As FactCheck.org noted when it labeled this concoction a conspiracy theory, there was no evidence for Gingrich's conclusion. The Washington Metropolitan Police Department's review of the contents of Rich's laptop located "no apparent communications with anyone who was associated with WikiLeaks."[21] D.C. police surmised that Rich, whose wallet was not taken but whose body showed signs of a struggle, had been killed in a botched robbery.

My interest here is not in detailing the byways through which the conspiracy theory traveled in alt-right and legitimate conservative media outlets, trails that included a retracted Fox News story and a related lawsuit,[22] but rather in noting that the ways in which Russian English-language "news" outlets RT and *Sputnik* as well as a Kremlin-tied troll account promoted it. These included an RT video on the topic that has attracted 114,535 views[23] and a May 2017 *Sputnik* article that asked, "Why does the former DNC staffer attract so much attention?"[24] The answer:

> The crux of the matter is that he [Seth Rich] is believed to be an
> alleged whistleblower who leaked nearly 20,000 DNC emails to
> WikiLeaks, exposing Hillary Clinton's conspiracy against her

counterpart—former Democratic presidential candidate Bernie Sanders.

Back in August 2016, WikiLeaks founder Julian Assange dropped a hint that Rich could have been behind the leak. If that is true, the Democrats' narrative that Russia had "meddled" in the U.S. 2016 presidential election will fall apart like a house of cards.

Before it was shut down by Twitter, the Russian troll account @TEN_GOP contributed to this effort when in May 2017 it urged its followers to retweet "the hell out of" a video promoting the theory that it was the young murder victim who hacked the DNC.[25] That site's effort was a concerted one. "In May 2017," according to research by a fellow at the Atlantic Council's Digital Forensic Research Lab, @TEN_GOP "repeatedly tweeted a link to an online petition on the White House's *We The People* platform calling for the appointment of a special prosecutor to investigate the murder of DNC staffer Seth Rich."[26]

Figure 1.1 @TEN_GOP tweet about Seth Rich investigation.

Nonetheless, Trump and Putin have over time conceded that Russian intervention in the election existed. Following his January 2017 briefing by the intelligence agencies, the president-elect told assembled reporters, "As far as hacking, I think it was Russia. But I think we also get hacked by other countries and other people."[27] The same press conference contained an exchange that could be read to say that, if Putin directed the hacking to help Trump, that action foreshadowed an improved US-Russian relationship under the new incumbent.

QUESTION: On that intelligence report, the second part of their conclusion was that Vladimir Putin ordered it because he aspired to help you in the election. Do you accept that part of the finding? And will you undo what President Obama did to punish the Russians for this or will you keep it in place?

TRUMP: Well, if—if Putin likes Donald Trump, I consider that an asset, not a liability, because we have a horrible relationship with Russia. Russia can help us fight ISIS, which, by the way, is, number one, tricky. I mean if you look, this administration created ISIS by leaving at the wrong time. The void was created, ISIS was formed. If Putin likes Donald Trump, guess what, folks? That's called an asset, not a liability. Now, I don't know that I'm gonna get along with Vladimir Putin. I hope I do. But there's a good chance I won't. And if I don't, do you honestly believe that Hillary would be tougher on Putin than me? Does anybody in this room really believe that? Give me a break.

Responding to specific information in the Mueller February 2018 troll indictments, Trump conceded Russian involvement when he declared, "Russia started their anti-US campaign in 2014, long before I announced that I would run for President. The results of the election were not impacted. The Trump campaign did nothing wrong—no collusion!"[28] Additionally, in March 2018, he noted, "The Russians had no impact on our votes whatsoever, but certainly there was meddling and probably there was meddling from other countries and maybe other individuals."[29]

On the other side of the globe, the Russian leader tacitly acknowledged that the sabotage occurred when he hypothesized sui generative action by patriotic nationals in his country who might "start making their contributions—which are right, from their point of view—to the fight against those who say bad things about Russia."[30] A related concession occurred in an interview with NBC's Megyn Kelly on March 2, 2018:

KELLY: But [you are saying] it was not the Russians.
VLADIMIR PUTIN: Well, all right, Russians, but they were not state officials. Well, Russians, and so what? There are 146 million Russian people, so what?[31]

The Russian president's disavowal of responsibility was even clearer later in that interview when he declared that "[a]t the level of the Russian Government and at the level of the Russian President, there has never been any interference in the internal political processes in the United States." However, Putin contended as well that "no interference from the outside, in any country, even a small one, let alone in such a vast and great power as the United States, can influence the final outcome of the elections. It is not possible. Ever."[32]

The publicly disseminated October 2016 and January 2017 US intelligence reports that confirmed Russian involvement also have been subject to two serious challenges: the agencies lack the credibility to have their conclusions taken on faith, and they have failed to disclose the evidence required to warrant their inferences. The first reservation is rooted in the assumption that the credibility of the US intelligence community remains tainted by its legitimation of the unfounded notion that Saddam Hussein's Iraq harbored weapons of mass destruction. "These are the same people that said Saddam Hussein had weapons of mass destruction," read a statement by those guiding the Trump transition. "The election ended a long time ago in one of the biggest Electoral College victories in history. It's now time to move on and 'Make America Great Again.' "[33] The second reservation is that the unredacted parts of the assessments are more reliant on assertion than on traditional forms of proof, a point Putin exploited when he noted that "[t]here is no specific evidence, no facts, just assumptions, allegations and conclusions based on those allegations, nothing more."[34] The sections of the two intelligence assessments that I quoted in the introduction are more consistent than not with that view.

The evidentiary lacunae in the January 2018 assessment were detailed by Masha Gessen, a Russia expert and Putin biographer and critic, who noted, "On Friday [January 2017], when the report appeared, the major newspapers came out with virtually identical headlines highlighting the agencies' finding that Russian president Vladimir Putin ordered an 'influence campaign' to help Donald Trump win the presidency—a finding the agencies say they hold 'with high confidence.'"[35] Yet, she added, "A close reading of the report shows that it barely supports such a conclusion. . . . There is not much to read: the declassified version is twenty-five pages, of which two are blank, four are decorative, one contains an explanation of terms, one a table of contents, and seven are a previously published unclassified report by the CIA's Open Source division." Gessen's concerns aren't unique. "Like any orthodoxy worth its salt, the religion of the Russian hack depends not on evidence but on ex cathedra pronouncements on the part of authoritative institutions and their overlords," argued historian Jackson Lears in the *London Review of Books*:

> Its scriptural foundation is a confused and largely fact-free "assessment" produced last January by a small number of "hand-picked" analysts—as James Clapper, the director of National Intelligence, described them—from the CIA, the FBI and the NSA. The claims of the last were made with only "moderate" confidence. The label Intelligence Community Assessment creates a misleading impression of unanimity, given that only three of the 16 U.S. intelligence agencies contributed to the report. And indeed the assessment itself contained this crucial admission: "Judgments aren't intended to imply that we have proof that shows something to be a fact. Assessments are based on collected information, which is often incomplete or fragmentary, as well as logic, argumentation and precedents."[36]

Press reports took note of the "take it on faith" nature of the January assessment. "The unclassified January, 2017, report, made public by the O.D.N.I., included only the thinnest of evidence, leaving many people wondering if it were true," observed Dana Priest in the *New Yorker*.[37] "[T]his report is unlikely to change the minds of skeptics who, like the president-elect, remember the intelligence agencies' faulty assessments on Iraqi weapons of mass destruction and fear being misled again," wrote the *New York Times'* Scott Shane.[38] I agree with all four sets of observations.

The factors affecting acceptance, rejection, or agnosticism about the January update of the October assessment aren't only evidentiary, as Priest, Shane, Lears, and Gessen suggest, but also psychological. On that front, motivated reasoning disposes Clinton supporters to believe and Trump defenders to question or dismiss assertions that the Russians were involved. For Hillary loyalists, Kremlin intrigue not only rationalizes their candidate's loss but also sets up a premise that supports the narrative that her ne'er-do-well opponent or his allies colluded with the Russians in a quid pro quo for election help. The same form of confirmation bias disposes Trump champions either to ignore evidence of Russian involvement or to question the conclusion that Moscow's intent was affecting the outcome of the 2016 election. Falling into the latter category are the April 2018 claims advanced by the Republican majority on the House Intelligence Committee that the intelligence agencies failed to use "proper analytic tradecraft" and employed an "unusually constrained review and coordination process which deviated from established CIA practice" in reaching their conclusion that Putin intended to undercut Clinton's candidacy and advance Trump's.[39]

Intelligence analysts argue that proof of Russian culpability exists, albeit in classified form. As the headers of the January 2017 assessment note, "This report is a declassified version of a highly classified assessment; its conclusions are identical to those in the highly classified assessment but this version does not include the full supporting information on key elements of the influence campaign."[40] That leaves those not privy to the documentation with appeals to authorities whose record is mixed. Our recourse is trusting the details in the Mueller troll and hacker indictments and the integrity of individuals who not only have seen the classified evidence but also are temperamentally or ideologically disposed to view it skeptically.

If one assumes that Republicans on the relevant congressional committees have a vested interest in challenging conclusions not in the political interest of the incumbent president, then it is noteworthy that neither the Democratic nor the Republican members of the Senate Intelligence Committee who have seen the unredacted January 2017 report dispute that Russian hackers and trolls were involved in the US election. "There is consensus among members and staff [of the Senate Intelligence Committee] that we trust the conclusions of the ICA [the intelligence community's assessment]," Senator Richard Burr (R-NC), the committee's chairman, declared at an early October 2017 press conference.[41] The chair of the House Intelligence Committee didn't deny Russian interference either. Instead Representative Devin Nunes (R-CA) blamed the Democrats for not heeding his warnings about it.[42] Consistent with these positions by Nunes and Burr, Senate Majority Leader Mitch McConnell (R-KY) confirmed that he had "the highest confidence in the intelligence community, and especially the Central Intelligence Agency." That statement elicited one headline that read "McConnell, Differing with Trump, Says He Has Highest Confidence in Intel Agencies."[43] Importantly, in a joint statement issued in May 2018 with Senate Intelligence Committee chair Burr, vice chair Senator Mark R. Warner (D-VA) declared that, "The Russian effort was extensive, sophisticated, and ordered by President Putin himself for the purpose of helping Donald Trump and hurting Hillary Clinton."[44]

Near-unanimous House and Senate support for sanctions against Russia also suggests that the classified evidence is compelling. As a response to that intelligence, Barack Obama had among other actions ordered the seizure of two Russian compounds, one in New York and the other in Maryland. Despite the active opposition of the Trump administration, in summer 2017, the Republican-controlled Congress expanded the range of punishments by passing the Countering America's Adversaries through Sanctions Act (CAATSA) in the House 419–3, and in the Senate 98–2. Among the enacted punishments for Russian annexation of Crimea and meddling in the US election were "restrictions on the extension of credit to Russian entities . . . [and] sanctions on those deemed to be undermining cybersecurity, as well as those engaging in significant transactions involving the Russian defense and intelligence sectors."[45] Included in the larger bill were sanctions against North Korea and Iran for their weapons development as well. Despite his stated belief that it encroached on his constitutional prerogatives as president, Trump acquiesced to the reality that a veto could easily be overridden and signed the bill into law. His objections centered on Congress's imposition of a thirty-day review window in which it could thwart any changes the president might try to make in the Russian sanctions.

Exercising the authority in that legislation, on March 15, 2018, the Trump administration announced sanctions against nineteen people and five organizations, numbers that included those named in the Mueller troll indictment. Among other actions, the sanctions barred these individuals from traveling to the United States, froze any US assets they had, and prohibited US nationals from engaging in transactions with them. "The administration is confronting and countering malign Russian cyber activity, including their attempted interference in U.S. elections, destructive cyberattacks, and intrusions targeting critical infrastructure," said Treasury Secretary Steven Mnuchin in a statement detailing the sanctions. "These targeted sanctions are a part of a broader effort to address the ongoing nefarious attacks emanating from Russia."[46]

In summer 2017 Trump himself more obliquely granted that Russian intervention had occurred when, in a statement released upon signing CAATSA, he noted, "I also support making clear that America will not tolerate interference in our democratic process and that we will side with our allies and friends against Russian subversion and destabilization."[47] The acknowledgment was more specific in Section 211 of the legislation itself, which premised the enhanced sanctions on the "finding" that[48]

[o]n January 6, 2017, an assessment of the United States intelligence community entitled, "Assessing Russian Activities and Intentions in Recent U.S. Elections" stated, "Russian President Vladimir Putin ordered an influence campaign in 2016 aimed at the United States presidential election." The assessment warns that "Moscow will apply lessons learned from its Putin-ordered campaign aimed at the U.S. Presidential election to future influence efforts worldwide, including against U.S. allies and their election processes."[49]

Also bolstering confidence in the conclusions of the intelligence agencies are events that include: Facebook's confirmation in April 2017 that "our data does [sic] not contradict the attribution provided by the U.S. Director of National Intelligence in the report dated January 6, 2017";[50] Facebook's announcement in September 2017 that ads placed on its platform had been linked to the Russian Internet Research Agency;[51] the February 13, 2018, acknowledgment of the ongoing Russian threat by all six of the intelligence directors named by Trump;[52] the February 16, 2018, thirty-seven-page Justice Department indictment issued by Special Counsel Robert Mueller against thirteen Russian individuals and three organizations for their three-year effort to disrupt the 2016 election, undercut Clinton, and support Trump;[53] and the declaration the following day by the president's national security adviser, Lt. Gen. H. R. McMaster, that, "with the F.B.I. indictment, the evidence [that the Russians meddled in the election] is now really incontrovertible and available in the public domain."[54] Reinforcing that conclusion was the specificity of the twenty-nine page July 2018 Mueller indictment of twelve Russian intelligence officers for the 2016 hackings.[55] Days after that revelation, Trump contended at the Helsinki press conference with Putin that he saw no reason "why it would be" Russia who intervened in the election, a statement that he amended the following day to say "why it wouldn't be."

Importantly, in response to the announcement of the Mueller grand jury troll indictments, as I noted a moment ago, Trump granted the existence of Russian election meddling when he tweeted, "Russia started their anti-US campaign in 2014, long before I announced that I would run for President. The results of the election were not impacted. The Trump campaign did nothing wrong—no collusion!"[56] Using more forceful language, Paul Ryan, the Republican Speaker of the House, responded to the Mueller indictments by stating, "These Russians engaged in a sinister and systematic attack on our political system. It was a conspiracy to subvert the process, and take aim at democracy itself."[57]

Based on these affirmations and on the assumption that persistent press pursuit of possible Pulitzers has incentivized reporters to ferret out any evidence undermining the various intelligence community findings, throughout the following pages I will assume that Russian trolls and hackers are responsible for the messaging that is the subject of this book. The evidence that I will marshal includes content hostile to Clinton's candidacy and favorable to Trump's. None of my analysis requires that Putin personally ordered or masterminded the operation. Also off my plate here are questions about whether there was collusion between Donald Trump's campaign and Russians, whether Kremlin-tied sources funded messaging by Trump allies such as the National Rifle Association (NRA),[58] and whether the allegations about illegal and suspect Trump activities in the so-called Steele Dossier are accurate in whole or part or were instead planted Russian disinformation. Because there is simply too little publicly available data to integrate these interventions into a larger analysis, I also have set aside questions both about the uses of material hacked from the Democratic Congressional Campaign Committee (DCCC) in 2016 congressional races in a dozen states[59] and about Russian efforts to break into election systems, including Pennsylvania's, and success in gaining access to voter records in Illinois.[60]

To this point, I have suggested that we can credit the Russians with both hacking and insinuating substantial amounts of content into our social media stream with an intent, during the post-convention period at least, of defeating Hillary Clinton and electing Donald Trump. Whether the Russian interventions affected votes is more difficult to determine than whether they "meddled." Knowing if the effect was significant enough to change the outcome is even more challenging. But what we can know is whether past research indicates that the kinds of messaging that they used and generated are capable of producing sizable enough results to alter a close election. In the next chapter, I will lay out a theory of interpersonal and media influence that will inform my answer to those questions.

2

A Theory of Communication
That Posits Effects

Some dismiss out of hand the notion that Russian interventions affected citizens' decision making in 2016. Others assert outright that without the Russian trolls' and hackers' subversions, Hillary Clinton would have been elected and the Republican Party nominee returned to life as a CEO of enterprises branded "Trump." By instead suggesting that the likely impact of the troll trickery was negligible, a claim that sidesteps the possibility that the cyberthefts elicited effects, others have taken a more nuanced position. "The Russian propaganda activities detailed in Robert Mueller's indictment last week [February 16, 2018] had less impact on the election," argues *Wall Street Journal* columnist Holman W. Jenkins Jr., "than 20 seconds of cable TV coverage (pick a channel) of any of Mr. Trump's rallies."[1]

Lost in this highly charged wrangle are years and terabytes of research speaking to the ways in which communication can affect knowledge, beliefs, and even ballots. From the contest between FDR and Wendell Willkie in 1940 to the one between Romney and Obama in 2012, researchers have observed campaign-created changes in attitudes and behaviors: most ephemeral but some enduring, most small but some substantial. The instigators of central interest in past years were interpersonal influence and mass communication, with the latter usually assuming the form of news, ads, and debates. As the sophistication of research methods grew, so too did the realization that mass media and the more personal forms of exchange interacted not only with each other but also with the dispositions of audiences in ways that could magnify or minimize the effect of communication.

Despite dead ends and wrong turns, and occasionally because of them, these seventy-five-plus years of study have revealed when and, if so, how, at some times but not others, each of us is affected by the news, ads, debates, and other forms of communication within our ken. In the process of this sleuthing, our vocabularies have expanded to include such concepts as reinforcement, priming, framing, agenda setting, two-step flow, heuristics, contagion, the spiral of silence, and micro-targeting. Along the way, scholars have refined their ability to identify the characteristics and circumstances that increase audience susceptibility to influence. When the existence of the presumed cause reliably predicts the hypothesized effect in contest after contest, experiment after experiment, study after study, our confidence that a finding is not idiosyncratic grows. So too when convergent conclusions are reached by different ways of knowing (e.g., surveys, panels, and experiments). Hypotheses become principles when we understand how stimulus x produces response z, and we can specify the conditions under which that sequence occurs.

Because fear appeal was a key feature of troll messaging, let me telegraph what we know about how that use of emotion works and how I will use such knowledge in this book. Interpolating the troll strategy (which in the next sentence I will synopsize and insert in brackets) into the findings of a state-of-the-art meta-analysis will illustrate the nexus I will posit between past research and my hypotheses about the 2016 troll and hacking effects. That meta-analysis of what is known about fear in messaging found that "the effectiveness of such appeals increased when the message included efficacy statements [the trolls called for liking and sharing this message], depicted high susceptibility and severity [among other uses, the trolls cast "illegal" immigrants as resource-draining, job-stealing criminals], recommended one-time-only (vs. repeated) behaviors [vote against Hillary Clinton or for

Donald Trump], and targeted audiences that included a larger percentage of female message recipients [women in the social media stream may have been more susceptible to fear appeal]."[2]

As this exercise hints, despite a few stumbles that I will treat at greater length in the next chapter, the Russians' messaging was strategically adept. Their skill at impersonation and misdirection is evident both in their social media posts and in their reliance on a credible front group to inject hacked content into the election. The legacy media were complicit in this effort. By routinely crediting the purloined content to WikiLeaks, not St. Petersburg, for example, the news media deflected attention from Russia's role. The success of the St. Petersburg masking was also on display when duped Americans shared Russian-generated posts within their networks and "unwittingly"[3] helped organize their rallies.

Awkward grammar aside (more on this in a later chapter), the troll messaging employed tried-and-true persuasive gambits. Using classic means of constructing an enemy,[4] they cast the electoral choice in "us-versus-them" zero-sum-game terms ready-made to harness fears of cultural change. To that frame they soldered a causal one, blaming the anxieties plaguing the target audience on cultural and economic changes created by and benefiting "them." At the same time, the Russian hacks and posts stressed issues and traits more favorable to Trump than his Democratic counterpart and weighted the communication climate with anti-Clinton messaging. Each form of subversion—the social media messaging and the hacking—discernibly altered the communication available to at least some deciding whether and, if so, for whom to vote in the election's final weeks.

Those alleging that Kremlin-tied trolls, bots, and hackers could not have affected enough voters to swing a close election are paddling against currents of scholarship showing that audiences are influenced by agenda setting, framing, and priming. Commentators who contend that the imposter content could not have mobilized or demobilized voters are flying into headwinds created by research confirming that voters can be influenced by the relative weighting of messaging in news and ads. Never all voters. And in most cases, not even most. But there were greater numbers of susceptible citizens in 2016 than in past years for three overlapping reasons: (1) an unusually high level of voter disaffection with both major party nominees;[5] (2) a higher than average percentage of self-identified independents in the voting population,[6] with 39 percent making that claim in 2016;[7] and (3) a larger than ordinary proportion of the population—by one calculation, as many as one in eight[8]—making a decision in the last week before the election.

Those three categories are of course interrelated. When they vote at all, the Hamletic citizens in that late-deciding category tend to be less attached to a political party and hence more persuadable than those who make up their minds earlier.[9] On average, they also are less attentive to the ins and outs of politics[10] and less politically sophisticated,[11] factors that heighten the power of persuasion in general and of message framing and weighting in particular. Moreover, one reason that there were so many late deciders was dissatisfaction with the available options. Whatever the sources of their reluctance, last-minute deciders figured importantly in 2016. The 14 percent of the Wisconsin electorate that selected a candidate in the last week broke for Trump over Clinton, 59 percent to 30 percent.[12] In Pennsylvania, the Republican carried those who made up their minds in the final days by seventeen points and in Michigan by eleven.[13]

The goal of this chapter is telegraphing what scholars know about how campaign-related messaging affects votes and voters. In subsequent chapters, I argue that Russian-originated or stolen communication could have elicited the same kinds of effects as those we have seen in past elections by: shaping the agenda and framing of the news media; reweighting the message environment in news and social media; priming and reinforcing anti-Clinton content; capitalizing on timing consistent with short-term effects; and relaying and creating content designed to mobilize and demobilize key constituencies. But before offering a number of generalizations about the ways in which messaging can influence voters, let me both outline a few of the psychological processes that help explain how they achieve their ends and note how interpersonal and mass communication can affect voter intentions.

The Role of Basic Psychological Processes in Political Persuasion

Citizens don't ballot on the basis of systematic assessment of all available evidence. Nor do they necessarily focus on the same issues or attributes election after election or, in some cases, even week after week. Moreover, different voters may weigh the importance of a given issue differently as well. Defined as exposure that increases cognitive accessibility, the process known as priming plays a role in determining which issues, candidate traits, and language are at play when voting decisions are being forged. Both agenda setting, a media effect that shapes what audiences think about, and framing, a message effect that influences the ways that they think about a topic or issue, involve priming, a phenomenon that increases the cognitive accessibility and hence awareness of the existence of the primed language, topic, frame, or emotion. In a social media age, it is important to add that contagion (i.e., the infection-like spreading of an emotion, belief, or idea from person to person, group to group) plays a key role in the diffusion of primed content. Before showing that messaging can affect votes and voters, and specifying the conditions that limit or boost those effects, let me note a few of the ins and outs of priming, framing, agenda setting, and contagion.

Priming Increases the Cognitive Accessibility of the Primed Issues, Traits, and Language

Priming occurs when exposure to a stimulus produces an effect on memory and hence on subsequent responses. By making them more cognitively accessible, priming is able to make some issues, candidate characteristics, or concepts more salient or focal than others in decision making. Whereas Social Security preservation and reform were top of mind for the presidential candidates and voters in 2000, the economy was focal in 2008. In both elections these issues were prominently featured and as a result primed in news, ads, debates, and speeches. "Lockbox" was the term Democratic nominee Al Gore primed in 2000 to say that he would safeguard Social Security revenue. "Fuzzy math" was the language that his Republican counterpart, George W. Bush, primed to dispute Gore's calculations of the relative merits of the tax plans of the two. Whereas in 2004 Bush surrogates primed the notion that the incumbent was "resolute," Democratic standard-bearer John Kerry cast his opponent as "stubborn." The attitudinal effects of each of these moves have been documented.

The content that is primed matters because voters adopt criteria for assessment of candidates on the basis of accessibility—how quickly and automatically such criteria come to mind. If a criterion has been the subject of a lot of attention, it will be more accessible. Accordingly, when discussions of immigration dominate one's newsfeed and other issues receive less attention, that issue will become more salient to that person and more likely to be used in her assessment of candidates than less prominently featured issues or than those ignored altogether. When media produce this effect by concentrating attention on some issues rather than others, they set an agenda. Because some issues, traits, and language advantage one candidate more than the other, the content that is primed can be consequential. It matters even more when audiences are already disposed to regard the topic as of interest. Micro-targeting makes it possible to heighten the salience of different issues with different constituencies.

Agenda Setting Primes What We Think About

Captured in Bernard Cohen's memorable axiom, the press "may not be successful much of the time in telling people what to think, but it is stunningly successful in telling its readers what to think about,"[14] agenda setting's power has been confirmed in studies demonstrating the relationship between the most-often-covered issues and what the audience considers important. Such effects lurked in the famous 1940 Erie, Pennsylvania, data, where, near the end of the Roosevelt-Willkie campaign, the topics on which the media had been focusing increased in salience to some voters.

Consistent with that early finding, after correlating issues that undecided Chapel Hill, North Carolinians considered important with those featured in the media in 1968, journalism scholars Maxwell McCombs and Donald Shaw found that the press agenda guided what susceptible voters thought about.[15] The agenda-setting effect between the media (here the *New York Times*) and the public (reflected in a Gallup measure of public opinion) persisted as the United States moved from a few dominant news channels in 1956 to a proliferation of them in 2004. As press scholars Yue Tan and David Weaver showed, the average agenda-setting correlation (i.e., the association between the issue featured in news and the audience's assessment of its relative importance) was .51, which indicates that 26 percent of the variance was explained by the theory.[16] In other words, the issues highlighted in news help determine the ones prioritized by the citizenry.

Because candidacies benefit from different issues, media agenda setting can advantage one aspirant over another. Not only does research verify that mainstream media produce agenda-setting effects, but so too do their social media competitors. In the former case, in 1987, political scientist Ben Page and his colleagues demonstrated that the content of network television accounted for "a high proportion of aggregate changes (from one survey to another) in U.S. citizens' policy preferences."[17] In the latter, when Facebook scientists shuffled hard news articles being shared by friends to the top of newsfeeds, occasional Facebook users who saw more news in their feeds reported paying more attention to government and, after the election, also were more likely to say that they voted.[18] These findings suggest that when stories reporting on WikiLeaks content captured news attention throughout the last month of the election, media agenda setting increased their salience and with it the likelihood that voters would use that content and the frames within it in assessing Clinton's candidacy. More on frames in a moment.

By setting news agendas, topics trending on social media can affect voters indirectly. The content that is trending can influence them directly as well. "Regardless of who follows whom on a given social media platform," notes internet expert Lt. Col. Jarred Prier of the US Air Force, "a trending topic can bridge the gap between clusters of social networks. A malicious actor can quickly spread propaganda by injecting a narrative onto the trend list."[19] By using automated accounts called bots to increase the likelihood that some topics would trend, the Russians helped propel anti-Clinton themes into news.

When they increased the likelihood that anti-Clinton content would trend, the trolls elicited agenda setting. If you saw news segments in 2016 about those self-identifying as deplorables, it is likely that the belief that the topic was popular played some role in reporters and editors' decisions to promote those stories. Observe the time clock underlying the following report of a now-famous Clinton statement in the *New York Times*:

"You know, to just be grossly generalistic, you could put half of Trump's supporters into what I call the basket of deplorables. Right?" she said to applause and laughter. "The racist, sexist, homophobic, xenophobic, Islamaphobic—you name it. And unfortunately there are people like that. And he has lifted them up."

By Saturday morning, #BasketofDeplorables was trending on Twitter as Mr. Trump's campaign demanded an apology.[20]

Hillary made this remark on a Friday night. By the next morning the hashtag was trending. And as it was doing so, the Republican campaign demanded an apology. The reporter's account provides evidence that "trending" was a factor in understanding what's going on here.

We know that Russian trolls helped make that hashtag trend because Prier tracked the identity change that one poseur underwent in the process of joining the troll chorus. "Before the 'basket of deplorables' comment," he writes, "the trolls primarily used an algorithm to rapidly respond to a tweet from Donald Trump. . . . However, after the Clinton speech, a 'people search' on Twitter for 'deplorable' was all one needed to suddenly gain a network of followers numbering between 3,000 and 70,000. Once again, [the Russian troll] FanFan's name changed—this time to 'Deplorable Lucy'—and the profile picture became a white, middle-aged female with a Trump logo at the bottom of the picture. The FanFan follower count went from just over 1,000 to 11,000 within a few days." Observing "Deplorable Lucy," Prier finds that "tracing his follower trail again led to the same groups of people in the same network [as past trolling efforts], and they were all now defined by the 'Deplorable' brand. In short, they were now completely in unison with a vast network of other Russian trolls, actual American citizens, and bot accounts from both countries on Twitter. With a large network consisting of Russian trolls, true believers, and bots, it suddenly became easier to get topics trending with a barrage of tweets."[21]

The agenda-setting effect of trending topics is produced because journalists use that phenomenon as a sign that a subject is newsworthy. When reporters spend a lot of time online—with "more than half (53.8 percent) . . . regularly [using] microblogs such as Twitter for gathering information and reporting their stories"[22]—they create a "symbiotic relationship" between the agendas in Twitter posts and news.[23] Among the common uses to which journalists put social media are "check[ing] for breaking news (78.5 percent) and seeing what other news organizations are doing (73.1 percent)."[24] If a trending topic or meme shows up in one news outlet, journalistic attention to that source increases the likelihood that other stories will follow suit. The power of social media to affect mainstream news agendas is reflected in segments titled "What's trending" and notations about trending topics in the chyron on the bottom of the TV screen.

Framing

Like agenda setting, framing is central to my explanation of how Russian machinations affected votes. Frames are organizing structures that "through the use of selection, emphasis, exclusion and elaboration"[25] tell audiences how to think about issues.[26] A framing effect occurs when "salient attributes of a message (its organization, selection of content, or thematic structure) render particular thoughts applicable, resulting in their activation and use in evaluations."[27] Frames affect the likelihood that a particular way of seeing something will be selected by audiences.[28] In the process, they increase the importance of some arguments and evidence over others.[29] Put simply, agenda setting focuses our attention on some topics rather than others, and frames tell us how to make sense of them.

For Trump, "open borders" was a linguistic frame that encompassed disadvantageous trade, illegal immigration, menacing refugees, and Muslims who should be banned from entering the country. For Clinton, "open borders" was not preferred campaign language for a number of reasons: among them the contrast between her husband's presidential positions on trade and her own in 2016. Unsurprisingly, when she used the phrase in speeches delivered out of press view in 2015 and 2016, she was not disposed to tie it to immigration or trade writ large but rather to working with other countries toward goals such as preventing the spread of infectious disease and incentivizing cross-border energy transfer. By adopting the Trump-primed language of "open borders" and associating it with immigration, reporters featured language and a frame native to Trump's attacks on his general election opponent.

The terms in which journalists cast the Russian involvement in the election also penalized the Democratic nominee. As I noted in the introduction, they framed the Russian cyberactivities as "meddling" or "interference," not as "cyberattacks," "cyberstrikes," or "cyberwar." In the parlance of the legacy media, the materials siphoned from Democratic email accounts by hackers were "leaks," not "thefts," and sourced to "WikiLeaks," not the Russians. These choices obscured the perpetrator as well as that culprit's intent.

The issues such as illegal immigration that the trolls magnified in the social media stream advantaged Trump with his target constituencies. So too did the trolls' use of a "we/they" or "us/them" conflict frame. In dichotomous fashion, this structure embeds the assumption that "they" threaten "us." In the imposter-created world, those who are endangering "us" include Muslims, illegal aliens, Black Lives Matter activists, atheists, demanding women, those who oppose gun rights, and Hillary Clinton, to name a few. Among those cast as "we" were white males, Donald Trump, Christians, veterans, and workers whose jobs are threatened by bad trade deals and job-stealing "illegals."

Because both framing and priming work by making concepts salient, a natural advantage goes to the camp better able to weight the message environment inhabited by susceptible voters with messages discrediting the opponent. (Attack is not only more readily recalled than advocacy but also more likely to go viral.[30]) By directing messages to susceptible audiences, targeted media can magnify priming and framing effects. The trolls did all of that.

In the framing process, audience receptivity matters. Consistent with the sorts of press effects Joseph Cappella and I found in *Spiral of Cynicism*, communication scholar Dietram Scheufele and political scientist Shanto Iyengar argue that "the mode of presentation of a message or piece of information will be significantly more likely to have an impact if it resonates (or is applicable) to an audience member's mental schemas [i.e., cognitive organizational categories]."[31] When the audience hasn't developed the relevant schema, "framing effects are unlikely to occur." As I will argue in a later chapter, the media and debate framing of the hacked Clinton speech segments fit the appearance versus reality and public versus private schemas regularly invoked by the press and the candidates throughout the campaign. Such alignments increase the likelihood of persuasion.

Voters Rely on Issues Primed by Messages

By influencing our sense of the importance or salience of the topics they feature, media increase the likelihood that these issues will be on the minds of their readers and viewers when they assess candidates. In *News That Matters*, experiments by political scientists Shanto Iyengar and Donald R. Kinder demonstrate that "by priming certain aspects of national life while ignoring others, television news sets the terms by which political judgments are rendered and political choices made."[32] Work that my colleagues and I did on the 2000[33] and 2008[34] elections isolated such effects on voters' evaluations of candidates as well. In 2000 our finding went like this: Fearful that doing so would link him to incumbent Bill Clinton's impeachment liabilities, in 2000 Democratic Party nominee Al Gore failed to make the healthy economy focal to voters. Neither on the stump nor in interviews or debates was the phrase "Clinton-Gore economy" part of the vice president's working vocabulary. Because the orphaned concept went unprimed in 2000, the Democratic ticket did not get the level of advantage from the strong economic indicators that political science models anticipated.

Since increasing our awareness of some issues over others (or in the jargon of psychologists "increasing their cognitive accessibility") can prioritize them in voters' assessments of candidates,[35] messaging that focuses the news and campaign agenda on topics congenial to one contender or uncongenial to the other can affect ballots. The missives of Russian trolls were designed to increase the salience of illegal immigration; encourage a fear of Muslims and supposed assaults on religious liberty; magnify worries about lack of respect for police, veterans, and traditional morality; heighten white voters' awareness of civil unrest; increase black voters' awareness of black nationalism and abuse at the hand of those in power; underscore perceptions that Clinton was dishonest and corrupt; and foster the belief that she was unconcerned about veterans, the enemy of Christians, responsible for high rates of incarceration of blacks, aligned with Wall Street, and had rigged the primaries against her Vermont rival. By priming these topics, the trolls increased the likelihood that they would be used by targeted voters to judge the relative merits of the candidates.

Our 2000 work also showed that messaging can influence perceptions of candidate traits, which can in turn affect votes. In Gore's case in 2000, Republican ads coupled with press framing degraded public perception of his trustworthiness. We found effects on the Republican side as well. The ad-driven perceptions that George W. Bush was a "strong leader" shifted support to him in 2000. Messaging suggesting that Barack Obama "shares my values" produced the same sort of advantage for the Democratic nominee in 2008. As his Democratic ads reiterated that theme, from June 7 to November 3, 2008, a perception that Obama shared voters' values increased by .002 points a day for an overall increase of .3 on a 10-point scale. In 2016, the press framing of WikiLeak'd content primed the notion that Clinton was scandal-plagued and disingenuous. In Part III, I make the case that Russian-hacked content affected the decisions of both key players and voters.

Language Can Be Primed

After being made more cognitively accessible through priming, words can shape how we think about issues, events, people, and even ourselves. So, for example, "death tax" elicits more hostility than "estate tax."[36] And when individuals are primed to think of themselves as voters rather than as simply engaging in voting, they may be more likely to cast a ballot. In one study, voting increased by 10.9 percentage points among those in that first condition.[37]

Linguistic priming was notably at play in the troll and Trump characterizations of both those in the country illegally and Muslims. Because I will illustrate the Russians' messaging about each group in subsequent chapters, here let me simply note that the language through which we think about immigration matters. Specifically the label "illegal aliens" summons greater prejudice than "undocumented workers," an effect some researchers attribute to heightened perceptions of threat conveyed by allying two pejorative terms.[38] Enwrapping immigration in a crime frame as both Trump and the trolls did elicits negative cognitive responses, increases reports that immigration is a problem, and erodes perceptions that immigration produces positive consequences.[39]

Contagion

Agenda setting and framing can only affect voters exposed to them. By incentivizing interaction among networks of individuals, some from distant locales, social media platforms increase the spread of content with resulting effects on attitudes and behaviors. One process involved in this chain is termed "contagion."[40] We know that Facebook content can create a contagion effect,[41] because those whose newsfeeds were manipulated to include positive or negative emotion in one large study were more likely to mirror that feeling in their own subsequent posts.

Importantly, negative emotion produces more powerful contagion effects than does the positive kind.[42] All of this should be read in the context of Facebook investor Roger McNamee's observation that the platform's "algorithm exists to maximize attention, and the best way to do that is to make people angry and afraid."[43] His insight draws support from evidence that emotionally arousing[44] and intense[45] content is more likely to be shared. By increasing social bonds and cohesiveness,[46] sharing content creates a positive feedback loop that drives additional distribution. Put another way, Facebook is a contagion machine built to order for many good ends but also for fake pages and posts bent on inciting and then harnessing economic anxieties and fears of cultural change. In 2016 those fears were channeled against Clinton and for Trump by the trolls.

This quick overview of priming, agenda setting, framing, and contagion does not exhaust the processes at play in political persuasion. I've treated them here because they play an outsized role in my model of how Russian efforts produced effects. (Readers seeking more detail on each and an expansive menu of other forces and factors affecting citizen choices might turn to the chapters by leading scholars found in the *Oxford Handbook of Political Communication*.) Pivotal to my larger argument is the supposition that such phenomena help explain why, under some circumstances, consequential communication effects do occur in US presidential elections. Accordingly, we turn next to some of the evidence that both interpersonal and mass communication can affect voters. At issue is the question: Do interpersonal and mass communication ever change votes and, if so, under what circumstances?

Interpersonal and Mass Communication Can Affect Voters and Votes

Interpersonal Communication Can Shape Voting Decisions

As the country was deciding between FDR and Wendell Willkie in 1940, the residents of Erie, Pennsylvania, were the focus of the first of the classic

Columbia multiwave panel studies of vote choice.[47] A key finding from this pioneering work has particular relevance to the social media age. The interpersonal influence that proved powerful occurred through an indirect process termed "two-step flow." Step one involved "ideas flowing from radio and print to opinion leaders."[48] In step two, those influentials dispatched the ideas "to the less active sections of the population." Data from the Columbia research suggested that word-of-mouth information from trusted individuals (i.e., opinion leaders) was more likely to change the views of late deciders than was mass communication. Linking and sharing constitute the twenty-first-century version of two-step flow. Although the media reinforced existing predispositions in that 1940 study, it was the trustworthy personal communication of "opinion leaders" that affected votes. So influential was the two-step flow paradigm that one scholar proclaimed in 1968 that "few formulations in the behavioral sciences have had more impact."[49]

Fast-forward to the twenty-first century and two-step flow explains the effects of partisan as well as social media. Where the media set the agenda by featuring an issue and providing a context or frame through which to view it, opinion leaders play a key role in shaping and diffusing attitudes and behaviors about it.[50] So, for example, Fox and MSNBC influence not only those who watch them,[51] but those viewers in turn function as opinion leaders who, through two-step flow, affect others with whom they interact. They do so by shaping the structure and arguments in the conversation.[52]

Social media produce two-step-flow effects as well, including increased voting among both recipients and those in their networks. In an experiment asking whether posts on Facebook could affect turnout, researchers found that "the messages not only influenced the users who received them but also the users' friends, and friends of friends."[53] Moreover, "[t]he effect of social transmission on real-world voting was greater than the direct effect of the messages themselves." Those who were influenced were nearly all "'close friends' who were more likely to have a face-to-face relationship." This research opens the possibility that, in addition to their targets, the trolls may have influenced the friends of those whose newsfeeds their messages reached. In Part II, I will explore the notion of indirect troll effects, including those on news, in greater depth.

Ads and News Can Change Vote Intentions

At first blush, at least, the 1940s Erie results seemed to confirm that the impact of mass communication was minimal and largely indirect. Although the campaign stimulated both interest and information seeking, the Columbia sociologists found that rather than altering dispositions, it reinforced them.[54] Moreover, for most of the citizens who were tracked throughout that campaign, political communication did not initiate "new decisions" but instead solidified original intentions. Reinforcement effects can be durable. Once voters have made up their minds, most rationalize the decision. But importantly, some do shift from a once-favored candidate. Eight percent did just that in the 1940 Erie study,[55] a percentage large enough, if uniformly distributed, to change the outcome in an election as close as the Electoral College one in 2016.

Interestingly, some cross-party shifts in the Erie study were attributable to voter exposure to channels featuring the views of the other side. "Among persons with Republican predispositions *and* predominantly Republican media exposure, only 15 per cent voted for the Democratic candidate," noted a subsequent analysis by press scholars Lee Becker, Maxwell McCombs, and Jack McLeod, "but the Democratic vote among Republicans with predominantly Democratic exposure is 47 per cent."[56] That finding from 1940 foretells results from an ingenious study that capitalized on the natural experiment that occurred as the Fox News channel was making its way into the menus of local media markets from 1996 to 2000.

Adding that conservative outlet to the local news menu changed the media mix in these communities. It also gave conservative voices a niche in an existing media environment in which Reagan conservatism was being heralded on radio by talk-show host Rush Limbaugh and in print on the editorial page of the *Wall Street Journal*. Importantly, the arguments of Limbaugh, Fox commentators, and the *Journal* aligned.[57] This threesome created "a self-protective enclave hospitable to conservative beliefs" that "enwrap[ped] them in a world in which facts supportive of Democratic claims are contested and those consistent with conservative ones championed." Conservative social media streams add to and amplify the messaging in legacy media as well as in newer outlets such as *Breitbart*. And as I argued in chapter 1, they do so in a structure that increases the amount of like-minded content available to feed their audiences' basic disposition to seek out information that reinforces their existing beliefs.

The scholars studying the introduction of the Fox messaging located significant effects. After comparing the Republican vote share in 9,256 towns, divided into locales with and without access to Fox News, economists Stefano DellaVigna and Ethan Kaplan concluded that "Republicans gained 0.4 to 0.7 percentage points in the towns that broadcast Fox News."[58] Presumably Fox and other conservative outlets had the same sort of effect in 2016. But add to it the impact of being flooded with social media content reinforcing anti-Clinton themes and you open the possibility that Trump got a boost from the trolls over and above the one resulting from US-based messaging.

Notably, the researchers who studied the effects of inserting Fox News into the local media mix also found that doing so affected both "voter turnout and the Republican vote share in the Senate."[59] That impact on balloting is important because the trolls' messaging focused in part on mobilizing veterans and evangelicals and shifting Clinton votes to Stein. If changing the communication climate can increase the vote share of the favored candidate and increase turnout, and the trolls incremented up the weight of anti-Hillary, pro-Trump content, then they could have produced a similar effect.

Before proceeding, it is important to note that whether sponsored and characterized as "advertising" or not, a message is a message. What scholars describe as ad effects are actually message effects produced by a form of communication that is constrained by some legal and technical rules. These include the requirement that ads in broadcast and cable indicate a sponsoring source, be presented in preset lengths (i.e., 30 seconds, 60 seconds, etc.), and meet the technical standards of the medium.

The notion that messaging affects decision-making also draws support from political scientist Daron Shaw's study of statewide ad effects in the presidential campaigns of 1988–1996.[60] That idea was supported as well when scholars randomly altered the timing and volume of televised political ads in a gubernatorial race and then tracked voter response. Here too the ads had a discernible but short-lived impact.[61]

The effects of increasing the amount or weight of messaging also are clear. Using our 2000 Annenberg data, political scientists Gregory Huber and

Kevin Arceneaux found that increased exposure to ads for either Bush or Gore changed the likelihood that the National Annenberg Election Survey (NAES) panelists would support the candidate with the messaging advantage.[62] (I will return to the notion that communication effects tend to dissipate relatively quickly, in a moment.) Similar, substantively important and statistically significant persuasion effects exist in both the cross-sectional and NAES panel data from 2000.

The evidence of impact doesn't end there. Our Annenberg study of the 2008 election not only found comparable ad effects to those isolated by these other scholars but also showed that Obama's paid messaging increased the salience of a number of messages that affected votes. These included: Obama shares voters' values, McCain was allied with unpopular incumbent George W. Bush, and Sarah Palin was unqualified to be the president. In short, campaign communication can produce agenda-setting and framing effects. Our findings also confirm that messaging not only can change the standards of judgment that voters use in evaluating the candidates but also can frame voters' understanding of the contenders, their stands on issues, and their character and temperament. In short, the amount and relative weight of messaging matter.

Mass-Mediated Debate Exposure Can Affect Votes

Although most of the time, for most viewers, debates simply reinforce existing preferences,[63] these face-offs play a role in my theory of Russian influence as well. Magnifying the likelihood of debate effects are three advantages that these encounters have over other forms of campaign communication: they attract a sizable number of voters from across the ideological spectrum; they give these viewers the chance to see the candidates for a lengthy period side-by-side; and, to a considerable extent, the candidates are able to frame their own messages without press mediation.

Importantly, as Nate Silver argues, "[T]here were two debates that reversed the leader in the race. Mr. Reagan, in 1980, moved ahead of Jimmy Carter following their first and only head-to-head debate on Oct. 28, and then he won overwhelmingly. In 2000, George W. Bush moved ahead of Al Gore in the polls after their first debate, and Mr. Bush won the election, although he lost the popular vote."[64] As political communication scholar Steven Chaffee concluded after reviewing data from the 1960 and 1976 presidential encounters,[65] debates are most likely to affect the votes of individual viewers and hence alter electoral outcomes when at least one candidate is relatively unknown, when many voters are undecided, when the contest is close, and when party ties are weak. Unsurprisingly, the contests in which some, if not most, of these conditions occurred—1960, 1976, 1980, and 2000—are the ones to which scholars turn when making the case for the electoral impact of debates.[66] As I noted earlier in this chapter, three of Chaffee's four conditions were operative in 2016: a large number of undecided voters, a close election, and voters less loyal to party than they once were. In a later chapter, I will make the case that the second and third general election debates in 2016 shifted voters' attitudes in a fashion consistent with the agenda and frame set by hack-reliant moderator questions.

Factors Blunting and Bolstering Communication

Although messaging can affect votes, three factors reduce the likelihood that it will alter an election's outcome: the short-term nature of most effects, the existence of impervious audiences, and campaigns characterized by counterbalanced amounts of messaging. However, for reasons I will note, none of the three undercuts the proposition that the Russian interventions influenced votes. Here's why.

First, as thousands of experiments have demonstrated, unless reinforced, communication effects tend to be short-lived. But short-term influence on voters who are about to ballot can matter and some effects on perception of candidate character have proven durable. Moreover, the anti-Clinton messages were consistently reinforced.

Second, most citizens are relatively impervious to campaign communication. Before the first nominating convention has been gaveled open, their party identification, sense of the economy, and evaluation of the incumbent will reliably forecast the Election Day behavior of most voters. But independents, those who are conflicted about the choice they face, and late deciders are susceptible to mobilization or demobilization and persuasion. As I argued earlier, the 2016 election had ample numbers of all three groups to swing the outcome.

Third, the impact of campaign messaging is not usually reflected in shifts in electoral outcomes because the efforts of the alternative sides cancel each other out. However, imbalances in news or decision-relevant content can produce effects. Notably, in the closing weeks of the 2016 election the social media and news communication climate in key states and national news was weighted against Clinton. With that as a preview, let me relate each factor to the 2016 landscape.

Short-Term Effects

When exposure to communication produces direct effects, they are usually short-lived. Although Shaw's study of presidential voting in statewide races found an impact that persisted for more than ten days,[67] that survival rate is the exception. In the 2000 election, political communication scholars Seth J. Hill, James Lo, Lynn Vavreck, and John Zaller drew on Annenberg data to conclude that "[t]he half-life of persuasion effects . . . is about four days. Over the six-week period of [one] study, about half of the advertising effects that survived to Election Day were due to ads from the last week of the campaign and the other half were due to the accumulation of all surviving effects from the previous five weeks."[68]

Because message effects decay relatively quickly—within five weeks for some but in a matter of days for most—messaging that happens shortly before a wavering person votes has the greatest chance to shape that decision. In projecting effects, the length of time between exposure to the message and voting is crucial. Complicating matters further is the fact that, from early October through the second Tuesday in November, any day in that time frame can be Election Day in states that permit early voting. As a result, for those who have not yet made up their minds, communication during that five-or-so-week window is more consequential than that which was sloshing around the body politic at earlier points.

This state of affairs means that a ballot I cast on Thursday may be shaped by different communication than the one my husband casts a few hours or days later. A conflicted voter at noon on Friday, October 7, en route to a postal box with an absentee ballot in hand, may have been influenced by the news breaking that morning that the Department of Homeland Security had concluded that the Russians were behind the hacking of Democratic emails. Were the same voter to delay until 4:10 that afternoon, her vote may take into account the *Access Hollywood* tape. By 6 p.m. the news agenda had reshuffled to focus on WikiLeaks' release of segments of the Clinton speeches that Bernie Sanders had tried unsuccessfully to wrestle into public view during the primaries. Were our hypothetical voter a Sanders supporter, the revelations about the hacked Democratic National Committee content may have prompted her to tear her ballot up before leaving on a long cross-country camping trip. By Sunday, the morning interview shows had created another communication context by casting the Trump *Access Hollywood* tape and the supposed Clinton speech segments as parallel breaches of public trust.

All of this matters because the widespread use of early voting means that short-term media effects potentially affected votes throughout the last month of the campaign when Russian-hacked, WikiLeak'd content was featured in the news. I will make a case for its influence in a later chapter. The same short-term effects window also means that the headlines and stories focused on FBI Director James Comey's reopening of the Clinton server investigation on October 28 occurred within the period in which media agenda setting and framing could have altered Election Day behavior. In Part III, I will make the case that Comey's behavior affected media agenda setting in those final days. We know, as I reported earlier, that the late deciders in key states split decisively for Trump.

Importantly, not all message impacts come with an imminent expiration date. Instead, communication cues about candidate character may elicit lingering alterations in voters' perceptions. One long-lived change that occurred in 2000 was exactly the sort that plagued the Clinton candidacy in 2016. Prior to the first general election debate between Bush and Gore, Republican ads created a first effect by driving up the impression that the Democrat was dishonest. Among the messages whose influence we tracked was one that focused on a TV set on a kitchen counter, Gore on the screen. Delivered by a female voice-over, the ad's core message alleged that the Democratic Party nominee was "reinventing himself on television again." To underscore that assertion, Gore is shown saying, "I took the initiative in creating the internet," after which the unseen woman adds, "Yeah, and I invented the remote control."

Consistent with those ads, in the hours and days after the first general election debate of 2000, news framed two of Gore's misstatements as evidence of an "honesty" or "trustworthiness" deficit. The synergy between the Republican ads and that news coverage created a sustained effect. Interestingly, the perceptions of debate watchers were not the ones that changed. Instead, the persistent drop occurred among non-debate viewers exposed to media framing of the debate.[69] The shift in voter perception was consequential. "Where in September character considerations added between two and three points to his [Gore's] share of vote intentions," we concluded, "in October, they subtracted a like amount, perhaps more."[70] We noted as well that "shifts in trait perceptions were the most important single story of the campaign. They produced a dramatic reversal of fortune, induced a transition between campaign phases, and put Al Gore well behind his opponent. The reversal was largely attributable to the collapse of his reputation as a person of character."[71] And in this reversal, news exposure and attention made a big difference. Richard Johnston, Michael G. Hagen, and I concluded that the change in perceptions of Gore proved resilient because they were not anchored to voters' party biases. The ability of voters to disassociate character attributions from party loyalty also was evident in 2016. In that contest, a majority of the electorate, reliable Democrats and Republicans included, held both major party candidates in relatively low regard.

A Largely Impervious Audience: Messaging Doesn't Change the Votes of Most

The second factor blunting the effects of messaging on electoral outcomes is the limited susceptibility of the voting population. No matter the message or the nominee, rock-ribbed Republicans are likely to vote their party. Diehard Democrats are no different. In 2016, the strongest predictor of a vote for Trump was self-identification with the GOP. The most reliable forecaster of a ballot for Hillary was considering oneself a Democrat.[72]

Party is a good predictor for a number of reasons. Most voters are armed to resist messages that counter their existing beliefs and self-identities. From the earliest decades of serious scholarship about campaigns,[73] scholars have "documented cognitive bias in perception of candidates' issue positions, bias motivated by voters' own prior partisan commitments."[74] Partisan stereotyping can also deflect an otherwise persuasive message.[75] These mutually reinforcing phenomena help prompt those with strong party identification to vote for their party's candidate.

As a result of factors such as these, in most elections, so much of the vote is locked in by the end of the conventions that there aren't enough persuasible individuals left to change the outcome. Not so in 2016. For reasons I will detail in a later chapter, it was not a foregone conclusion that two reliable Republican voting blocs—evangelicals and those in military families— would turn out for Trump. Also possible was a scenario in which the rhetoric of the Republican standard bearer would incentivize turnout for Clinton by a key Democratic constituency—blacks—that gave Barack Obama a margin of safety in both 2008 and 2012. Just as Trump carried liabilities with some traditional Republican blocs of voters, so too did Hillary Clinton on the Democratic side. As an establishment candidate, she had defeated a challenge from the left by Democratic Socialist Bernie Sanders but at the cost of disaffection by his young liberal and black base. Unsurprisingly, then, as I noted earlier, in 2016 the citizenry included higher-than-average numbers of independents, conflicted voters, and late deciders—groups susceptible to agenda setting, framing, priming, the weighting of the discourse in their environment, and contagion.

Messages' Effects Cancel Each Other Out: Imbalances Create Impact

Another reason that presidential campaign communication does not alter outcomes is that the efforts of the professionals on one side blunt those on the other.[76] Because, before the era of micro-targeted communication, members of the public were exposed to messages from both sides, each message "has its effects," notes political scientist John Zaller, "but the effects tend to be mutually canceling in ways that produce the illusion of modest impact."[77]

In years past, when candidates had roughly comparable access to audiences through news and debates, differentials in messaging occurred largely in advertising in mass media and, as such, were reflected in spending gaps between the campaigns. "In five cases," Larry Bartels finds, "[Republican candidates'] popular vote margin was at least four points larger than it would have been, and in two cases—1968 and 2000—Republican candidates won close elections that they very probably would have lost had they been unable to outspend incumbent Democratic vice presidents."[78] The same research found that "[s]ince Republican candidates spent at least slightly more money than their Democratic opponents did in each of those elections, it is not surprising to find that they did at least slightly better in every election than they would have if spending had been equal."

The clearest evidence that it is the relative balance in messaging that matters comes from the 2000 contest where we were able to isolate messaging effects by marrying our Annenberg rolling cross-sectional survey to exposure to ads and news. The results revealed that in the final week of the 2000 election, while Democratic nominee Al Gore was widening his popular-vote advantage by having the network news almost all to himself, Republican George W. Bush secured the presidency in the critical state of Florida by dominating the airwaves with ads reassuring seniors that he would safeguard Social Security.[79]

At the same time, the popular vote advantage for Gore was increased by the synergy between his Social Security message in the third debate and his unrebutted reiteration of it in news in the election's final week. That breakthrough argument alleged that Bush would shortchange Social Security by siphoning part of an individual's payroll tax into a personal savings account. As the nightly news featured the Democrat hammering home his claim that his counterpart would reduce the solvency of a program on which seniors rely, Bush was ducking such venues to avoid questions about a just-disclosed DUI conviction in his past. In nonbattleground states, the resulting message imbalance in news advantaged Gore. Meanwhile, in the battleground, Bush's team blunted the news effect by outspending the Democrat on ads reassuring seniors and those approaching retirement age that their Social Security benefits were safe in his hands.

The same sort of ad effect was evident in the 2008 Obama-McCain contest. After integrating a comprehensive data set of radio, TV, and cable buys into our rolling cross-sectional NAES, we confirmed that what our political science colleagues call fundamentals—specifically, an unpopular incumbent, a faltering economy, and a party-identification advantage for the Democrats—had impressive predictive power. Indeed, these variables explained three-fourths of the variance in vote disposition. But Obama's capacity to significantly outspend McCain on advertising also produced effects. In particular, a "100 gross ratings point (GRP) advantage for Obama in local TV advertising increased by 1.5 percent the probability that a person with a baseline probability of 50 percent would say that if the election were held on the day of the interview she would cast an Obama vote, cable produced a 4.1 percent impact, and radio, a 5.5 percent one."[80] So, for example, the extent by which Barack Obama outspent John McCain on ads predicted voters' belief in a central Democratic ad claim: electing the Arizona Republican meant a third Bush term. Agreeing with that conclusion significantly increased the likelihood of an Obama vote.[81] Here too, as Zaller predicted, the effects of the advertised messages were related to the relative amount of messaging offered on behalf of each candidate. Of special relevance to my analysis of 2016 is the 2008 finding that the most highly micro-targeted of the three media—radio—produced the greatest effect on vote intention.

Through social cues about community sentiment, reweighting the messaging in our social environment can influence our attitudes, beliefs, and behaviors as well. So for example, a high number of views for a YouTube video signals those who are sensitive to social cues that the issue is important.[82] Likes and comments also function as a surrogate for community sentiment. In a similar fashion, a trending item is laden with cues that suggest its acceptability. Trending topics also are more likely to elicit news coverage, a subject that I treated earlier.

By activating or suppressing our disposition to communicate, our networks, peers, and communities can shape what we share. As Elisabeth Noelle-Neumann's theory of the spiral of silence posited, a person who embraces views that she believes are antipathetic to those widely held by others is unlikely under most circumstances to proselytize family, friends, or peers about them.[83] Instead that individual will probably fall silent. This tendency persists when we move online where "encountering agreeable political content predicts speaking out, while encountering disagreeable postings stifles opinion expression."[84] The importance of this phenomenon will become clear in later chapters, which will argue that by amplifying anti-Clinton and pro-Trump messages in swing states, the Russian impersonators and hackers helped create a communication climate more hostile to Clinton than it otherwise would have been.

How Russian Machinations Could Have Affected Voters

By noting consistencies between the trolls' activities and what scholars know about effective fear appeal, I foreshadowed the way in which I will use past research to inform my analysis of the plausible impact of the Russian operatives. My inference that the Russian interventions mattered is grounded in the fit between their messaging (and its demonstrable impact on the media, debates, and behaviors of key actors) and the relationships between similar stimuli and effects found in scholarship about past contests. Where this chapter telegraphed what scholars know about campaign effects, in subsequent ones I will argue that Russian-originated or stolen communication affected media agenda setting and framing, reweighted the message environment in news and social media, primed and reinforced anti-Clinton content, capitalized on timing consistent with short-term effects, and relayed and created content designed to mobilize and demobilize key constituencies. Here let me briefly weave these central concepts into a preview of the narrative I will advance in later chapters.

1. *Agenda setting and framing.* Not only did media reports on the hacked content set in place topics and frames antipathetic to Clinton's interests, but they also primed attributes damaging to her candidacy. Moreover, as I will show in detail in a later chapter, two days before a presidential debate when the *Access Hollywood* tape briefly was colonizing the media agenda and Trump's lewd language on it was initiating a contest to see whether his remarks would be framed as a "confession of sexual assault" or as "boys-will-be-boys locker-room banter," WikiLeak'd Russian hacking redirected the media agenda. Displaced in the process was the DHS and ODNI conclusion that the Russians were behind the hacking. In place of coverage that would have juxtaposed the intelligence report against the *Access Hollywood*

tape was framing that counterposed the tape against the newly released stolen speech segments. In short, the release of Russian-stolen Clinton speech segments shifted the media landscape from one focused on Trump's proclivities and the reasons the Russians might be happy to see him elected to one concentrating on the vulnerabilities of both candidates. From October 28 to November 6, the reopened Comey investigation had a similarly powerful effect on the media agenda. Reporting on WikiLeak'd stolen emails and press speculation about what Comey would find on the laptop of the estranged husband of a top Clinton aide matter for the same reason. Primed content affects voters' assessments of candidates.

2. *The weighting of the message environment.* By injecting negative information into the discourse stream through WikiLeaks, the Russians weighted the informational environment with topics (e.g., disclosure of possible inconsistencies, suspect dealings, and wrongdoing), framed in a language of "revelation" that primed negative attributions to which Clinton was susceptible. Contributing to the tilted message environment was the news' and debate's crediting of the hacked content to "WikiLeaks" or to leaks rather than to Russian espionage, cyberattack, or theft. Adding to the mix was the assumption that the "leaked revelations" were newsworthy, even scandalous. Moreover, reporters' truncation of a hacked speech segment advantaged Trump in a key debate. By driving the trending of topics, Russian trolls also increased the likelihood that anti-Clinton hashtags and memes would infiltrate mainstream news coverage.

　　Meanwhile, in social media, Russian trolls and bots reweighted the communication environment in their networks by increasing the visibility of existing anti-Clinton messages and heightening perceptions that content congenial with their aims was "liked" and "shared." If past research provides an accurate forecast, these amplifications increased the likelihood that nontrolls would post stories (some accurate, others not) that were hostile to the Democrat. Meanwhile, the recipients of the trolls' posts would overestimate the extent and extremity of anti-Clinton sentiment in their communities. One predicted result would be increased communication against Clinton and a drop in messaging supporting her. Because people who are frequently exposed to a piece of information tend to accept it as true, another effect of increasing exposure to content is increasing belief in its accuracy.[85] (Although scholars have called this phenomenon "illusory truth," when mentioning it in later chapters, I will refer to it simply as a familiarity effect.)

3. *Reinforcement.* When an indictment is a persistent part of the communication stream, burnishing it and boosting its weight in decision making are easier tasks than trying to create a new impression. Reinforcement ups the likelihood of effects. When fresh WikiLeak'd "disclosures" kept Clinton "revelations" in the news and coverage of the reopened FBI investigation elicited multiday coverage and conjecture, the suspicions and negative attributes that each primed were reinforced. The trolls and the Trump campaign then harnessed the WikiLeaks and Comey agenda setting and the framing of each to their appeals to both "lock her up" and to spread hashtags and memes urging "Hillary4Prison." Because the social media platforms are built to create and sustain like-minded communities, the Russian trolls were more likely to reinforce than change minds. Mobilization is, of course, a process built on reinforcement.

4. *The effects window was open.* As this chapter's brief journey through studies of past campaigns suggests, if it matters at all, most communication is likely to elicit small, short-term effects. Unsurprisingly, central to my model of Russian influence is the fact that the messaging on which I am focusing occurred during the period in which early voting was taking place. Election Day also fell within the window in which reinforced priming of negative attributes has produced shifts in vote intention in the past. We know that on Election Day the trolls urged the users whose sympathies they had cultivated to ballot against Clinton or

for Trump. Short-term stimuli aside, recurrent priming of negative candidate traits is able to produce longer-term influence. This is the case because such evaluations are more likely to be made apart from party considerations. At the same time, negative information is more readily recalled. And, of special note, it is difficult to restore personal credibility. Attack was the trolls' modus operandi.

5. *Susceptible voters existed.* A sufficiently large number of susceptible voters were making up their minds during the last month to affect the outcome of a close election. In key swing states, the results were driven by late deciders. Those who were the object of troll attempts to mobilize and demobilize were potentially susceptible during this window as well.

Importantly, two signals that could have elicited an anti-Russian backlash went unsent in 2016. Confident that his heir apparent would be elected and reportedly concerned that voters would see a public presidential condemnation as election meddling of his own, incumbent President Barack Obama did not speak out. Nor did the media cast the October 7, 2016 confirmation by the Department of Homeland Security (DHS) and Office of the Director of National Intelligence (ODNI) that the Russians were behind the hacking in a "we-they," "democracy vs. enemy state," or "cyberattack" news frame. Had the press reports on WikiLeak'd content focused public attention on the source of the stolen content and its probable electoral intent, its negative effects on Clinton's candidacy would have been minimized if not blunted entirely.

Before asking what we don't, can't, and do know about the plausible effects produced by the Kremlin-tied spies and saboteurs, I will outline the hurdles that the trolls and hackers had to jump to influence the electorate. The trolls needed to diffuse social media content that was consistent with Trump's message, aligned with his electoral needs, persuasive, and well targeted. By contrast, the challenge for the Russian hackers was shaping the media and debate agendas as late deciders were making up their minds in the final month of the election. The two efforts were of course interlaced. Determining how and how well they succeeded are my tasks in Parts II and III of this book.

Part Two

The Prerequisites of Troll Influence

T he questions that I will ask in the following pages are foundational. How did the trolls and hackers affect the election's message streams? Were the extent and virality of Russian social media content and the nature, coverage, and exposure to Russian-hacked Democratic materials sufficient and sufficiently persuasive to plausibly affect the outcome of an election decided in three states by about 78,000 votes? To thread that needle, the Russian troll efforts would have needed to be

- extensive enough to make a difference in an environment surfeiting with other campaign content;

- consistent with Trump's messages and interests;

- focused on constituencies whose mobilization or demobilization was critical to a Trump victory;

- persuasive; and

- well targeted.

Or alternatively, release of the hacked content would not only have had to have reshaped press coverage and debate focus, but also have altered the balance of messaging against Clinton during the period in which late deciders were determining whether to vote and, if so, for whom.

Most, but not all, of the first five conditions addressed in this second part of the book are more relevant to the activities of the trolls than the hackers. Trump's strategic need to mobilize some constituencies and demobilize others is the exception. Since hacked content was used both to rally evangelicals and depress Clinton support among Sanders's base, chapter five of Part II will draw on evidence from both of the Russian interventions. Part III will then be devoted to the role hacked content played in setting the media and debate agendas and influencing the actions of those able to affect one or the other.

It is possible that the troll activities detailed in the five chapters that comprise Part II were of themselves able to decisively affect voting. Alternatively, the effects of reporters' use of the hacked content explored in Part III could have achieved that end. For practical purposes, the two sets of activities were mutually reinforcing. Before beginning this exploration, let me note that, since we can only understand the Russian machinations and their plausible effects if we focus on the synergies between the hacker-gotten content and the troll messaging, I will flag those throughout the following chapters.

3

The First Troll Prerequisite
Widespread Messaging

In November 2016, Facebook chief executive Mark Zuckerberg employed a twofold justification to dismiss the idea that his social media platform's content influenced the outcome of the 2016 election: "Voters make decisions based on their lived experience" and "fake news on Facebook . . . [is] a very small amount of the content."[1] His inference was wrong on both counts. As I argued in chapter 2, campaign-related messages can matter. And even in an environment awash in appeals, targeted missives from a trusted source can persuade. After all, to change the outcome, Clinton only needed to capture 78,000 additional votes in three key states in an election in which 139 million ballots were cast.[2]

Before turning to the trolls' hijinks in social media, we should note that not all of the Russian propaganda that insinuated election-related substance into US homes, hotels, and onto YouTube operated out of public view. Although the acronym RT signals an appeal to retweet in social media, those two letters also camouflage the identity of a source once known as Russia Today. Some viewers may be familiar with this state-sponsored English-language "news channel" because they have seen it on their cable menus at home or in hotels. Others may recall that RT's December 2015 tenth anniversary party in Moscow was the location mentioned in the credit line of a photo of retired Lieutenant General Michael Flynn, seated next to Vladimir Putin. That image not only punctuated reporting on Flynn's firing as Trump's national security advisor but also appeared alongside coverage of his guilty plea in the Mueller probe.

RT broadcasts in English within the United States, and, in 2016, employed journalists such as Larry King and Ed Schultz, who, respectively, once called CNN and MSNBC home. The outlet boasts a sizable audience. In 2003 it was the first news outlet to reach one billion views on YouTube,[3] and it now claims 2.2 million subscribers.[4] That viewership potential adds importance to the fact that, in 2016, RT prominently featured WikiLeak'd content as well as segments arguing that Clinton was funded by ISIS supporters,[5] was in poor health,[6] and was corrupt. In the final week of the election, for example, an RT interview with WikiLeaks founder Julian Assange, which elicited 115,000 Facebook likes, was headlined "Assange: Clinton and ISIS Funded by Same Money, Trump Won't Be Allowed to Win."[7]

On Facebook and Twitter, these stories were amplified by Russian-generated ads, posts, and troll-controlled computer bots. Specifically, "three RT accounts targeting an American audience—with a combined following of roughly six million users— . . . spent $274,100 to promote tweets in 2016."[8] Moreover, in a study of more than 36,000 Russian tweets, one scholar not only located a conservative bias to the top news links, with *Breitbart News*, the *Daily Caller*, Fox News, and the *Gateway Pundit* among them, but also found that RT ranked nineteenth.[9]

In an atypical September 2016 moment, in an interview carried on RT, candidate Trump told Larry King, "I don't know who hacked [the Democratic National Committee, or DNC]. You tell me: Who hacked?"[10] Asked about reports that Russia had launched a covert operation to affect the 2016 election, the Republican Party's standard-bearer noted, "I think it's probably unlikely. Maybe the Democrats are putting that out—who knows." Trump then added: "If they are doing something, I hope that somebody's going to be able to find out so they can end it. Because that would not be appropriate at all." In a sign of the migratory nature of media content, a campaign aide told reporters that his boss would not have accepted the invitation had he known that the interview would be carried not simply on King's podcast but also on RT. That outlet's role in the 2016 election earned it an appendix in the January 2017 intelligence assessment. In fall 2017, the US government required RT to register as a foreign agent, a move that, according to Putin, rendered it "unable to do its work properly."[11]

Whereas the reach and viewership of RT are an open secret, scholars and the platforms took more than a year to determine the extent of the trolls' covert social media messaging. The first clear signal that the amount may have been large enough to matter came in the October 31 and November 1, 2017, congressional hearings.[12] "It's clear that they were able to drive a relatively significant following for a relatively small amount of money. It's why this activity appears so pernicious," Facebook's general counsel, Colin Stretch, told the House Intelligence Committee.[13] Facebook was not the only platform that funneled notable amounts of Russian messaging to its users. As I observed in the introduction, Instagram, Twitter, YouTube, Tumblr, Reddit, and 9GAG were also hijacked by trolls. Before detailing the extent of their work, we should take note of the fact that exposure or reach do not mean that the content was read. But even if some of it was not, the impact of simply registering a message in passing should not be dismissed out of hand. Decades of scholarship have confirmed that even momentary exposure to a stimulus can produce effects.

By November 2017, a number of the tech giants had confirmed Russian activity on their platforms. At the 2017 hearings, Twitter initially reported that 1.4 million automated, election-related tweets were generated by Russian operatives reaching approximately 288 million Twitter users.[14] Importantly, US news organizations shared links to Russian-generated tweeted content.[15] Moreover, nearly 150 million American Facebook and Instagram users were exposed to Russian-generated content, which consisted of paid ads, free posts, and event notices. The more than three thousand ads purchased by the Russian Internet Research Agency (IRA)-tied accounts were "seen by 11.4 million people,"[16] with 5.6 million of those views occurring after the election.[17] Kremlin-tied messengers loaded over one thousand videos to Google's YouTube.

As information released in mid-January 2018 signals, the extent and reach of Moscow-tied social media propaganda took time to confirm. Whereas

Twitter originally reported that it had uncovered 1,062 accounts traceable to the Russian IRA, in January 2018 that figure was updated to 3,814.[18] At the same time, that platform revised its number of Russian-run automated accounts from about 36,000 bots to upward of 50,000 and reported that "Russian-linked Twitter bots shared Donald Trump's tweets almost half a million times during the final months of the 2016 election. . . . The automated accounts retweeted the Republican candidate's @realDonaldTrump posts almost 470,000 times, accounting for just more than 4 percent of the re-tweets he received from Sept. 1 to Nov. 15, 2016."[19]

As part of that January 19 statement, Twitter announced that email notifications were being sent to "677,775 people in the United States who followed" one of the accounts "potentially connected to a propaganda effort by a Russian government–linked organization known as the Internet Research Agency (IRA)" or who "retweeted or liked a Tweet from these accounts during the election period."[20] Less than two weeks later, on January 31, 2018, the tech giant more than doubled the number being notified from the original 677,775 to "approximately 1.4 million people." According to the social media platform, the alerted individuals consisted of:

. . . Twitter users with an active email address who our records indicate are based in the US and fall into at least one of the following categories:

- People who directly engaged during the election period with the 3,814 IRA-linked accounts we identified, either by retweeting, quoting, replying to, mentioning, or liking those accounts or content created by those accounts;

- People who were actively following one of the identified IRA-linked accounts at the time those accounts were suspended; and

- People who opt out of receiving most email updates from Twitter and would not have received our initial notice based on their email settings.

Knowing how many of these followers resided in key states would make it easier to determine the effectiveness of Russian troll strategizing. The

Mueller indictment, for example, revealed that ads placed on Facebook by the trolls to promote Florida rallies reached more than 59,000 users and were clicked on by over 8,300.[21]

Since the initial Facebook, Instagram, and Twitter revelations, scholars have compiled additional information about the reach of the trolls' messages. A study of six of the Russian-controlled sites—Blacktivists, United Muslims of America, Being Patriotic, Heart of Texas, Secured Borders, and LGBT United—by Jonathan Albright, research director at the Tow Center for Digital Journalism at Columbia University, concluded that "the content had been 'shared' 340 million times."[22] His analysis of "28 of the 170 accounts that Instagram removed from its platform after discovering that they had been created by the I.R.A." confirmed "2.5 million recorded interactions with posts from the accounts, as well as 145 million likely interactions with people who had passively viewed them."[23] It was Albright as well who, with *BuzzFeed*, revealed in February 2018 that "Tumblrs run by Russian trolls generated hundreds of thousands of interactions with anti–Hillary Clinton, pro–Bernie Sanders content."[24] Of these accounts, "4mysquad appears to have been the most successful . . . , racking up multiple posts that each generated hundreds of thousands of notes on Tumblr. (The number of 'notes' is the total of all reblogs, likes, replies, and answers that a post receives.)" In the fall of 2016, that account upped the level of circulating deception and "sparked a wave of outrage after it took a video of a black girl being sexually assaulted by a police officer, turned it into a set of GIFs, and propagated the false claim that the video showed an NYPD officer."

Also in the mix in 2016 were automated accounts known as bots that can increase the likelihood that hashtags, posts, and stories will trend. By creating the illusion that an action, position, or topic is popular, bots can feign public opinion and in the process influence it. At the same time, they can be programmed to attack and drive into silence those supporting an alternative candidate or position.[25] In 2016, "One pro-Trump bot, @amrightnow, [had] more than 33,000 followers and spam[med] Twitter with anti-Clinton conspiracy theories."[26]

The activities of Russian-associated bots did not end with the election. They also made their presence felt in late January and early February 2018, as the House Intelligence Committee and the US president were deciding whether to release a memo by the staff of that committee's chair, Devin Nunes (R-CA). That controversial document, which some in conservative media alleged contained evidence that the Trump-Russia investigation had been ginned up by Clinton supporters, focused on the process that led to surveillance of a former Trump campaign advisor.

Evidence that Russian-linked Twitter bots promoted release of the document was tracked by the German Marshall Fund's dashboard known as Hamilton 68, set up to monitor Russian disinformation. According to that project, #ReleaseTheMemo was "the top-trending hashtag among Twitter accounts linked to Russian influence operations." Among those accounts, WikiLeaks was the most-shared domain. "In total, they've easily shared more than 4,500 hashtags on the topic in the past two days, and our top URL is Assange's offer to pay for a copy of the memo."[27] The advent of such uses of bots prompted Stanford law professor Nathan Persily to observe that "[i]n many ways, the advent of campaign bots represents the final break-down in established modes and categories of campaigning."[28]

"The use of automated accounts was deliberate and strategic throughout the election," concluded researchers at the University of Oxford Computational Propaganda Project.[29] These accounts and their programmers "carefully adjusted the timing of content production during the debates, strategically colonized pro-Clinton hashtags, and then disabled activities after Election Day." Their content included "embarrassing photos . . . references to the Federal Bureau of Investigation inquiry into Mrs. Clinton's private email server" as well as "false statements, for instance, that Mrs. Clinton was about to go to jail or was already in jail."[30] The Oxford scholars also discovered that accounts supporting Trump "overwhelmed similar programs supporting Hillary Clinton five to one in the days leading up to the presidential election." How much of that bot content was Russian in origin is not yet clear. We do know that by January 2018 Twitter had identified 50,258 Russian-linked automated accounts.[31]

Calculating how many humans have sent, liked, or shared content is complicated by the fact that algorithmically driven social bots can effectively masquerade as actual users.[32] As a result, when news outlets reported on Trump's tweets during the campaign on the assumption that his 140-character bursts were influencing large numbers of followers, they should have factored the presence of bots into those totals. In June 2017, CNN reported that "[o]ne analytics tool, Twitter Audit, estimates that 11.6 million of Trump's 32 million Twitter followers are either dormant or accounts run by bots."[33]

Another phenomenon circumscribing troll electoral impact is the fact that not all of the US citizenry is on platforms such as Facebook, Instagram, or Twitter. A 2016 national survey by Pew of 1,520 adults conducted March 7 to April 4, 2016, concluded that "[o]n a total population basis (accounting for Americans who do not use the internet at all) . . . 68% of all U.S. adults are Facebook users, while 28% use Instagram, 26% use Pinterest, 25% use LinkedIn and 21% use Twitter."[34] Those not on the platforms can, however, as research I cited earlier indicates, be influenced by those who are.

As we explore the extent of Russian messaging, it is important to remember that, as I illustrated earlier, the Russian spies' goals extended beyond reaching susceptible social media users. They also urged some to hold and attend rallies. To create a dramatic visual for one public event, not only did the trolls pay one individual to construct a cage atop a flatbed truck but also paid another to don a costume "portraying Clinton in a prison uniform."[35] As a *Wall Street Journal* investigation confirmed, "At least 60 rallies, protests and marches were publicized or financed by eight Russia-backed Facebook accounts from Los Angeles to Washington, D.C."[36] Notably, "At least 22 of the 60 events actually took place." "Collectively," reported the *Journal*, "the eight accounts were 'liked' nearly two million times." In January 2018, a Facebook document submitted to the Senate Intelligence Committee revealed an even greater number than the *Journal* had found. Specifically, a "total of 129 events were created across 13 IRA Pages. Approximately 338,300 unique accounts viewed [announcements for] these events. About 25,800 accounts marked that they were interested in an event, and about 62,500 marked that they were going to an event."[37] That document added, "We do not have data about the realization of these events."

The authors of that Facebook statement have omitted human agents from these forgettably phrased sentences about what was done and what is known. In this Facebook report, it is "accounts," not people, that perform the "viewing" and "marking." And instead of saying "We don't know whether the events actually occurred," the tech giant employs language designed to anesthetize its audience (i.e., "We do not have data about the realization of these events"). Accountability dodging aside, the importance of Russian efforts to move disgruntled citizens to the streets should not be understated because, as Columbia University's Jonathan Albright told the *Washington Post*, "This shows the effort to create long-term relationships with segments of the American public.... This was also about measuring individual motivations to translate online signals into real-world behaviors."[38]

Events, rallies, and protests were not the only phenomena altering the persuasive terrain. In the mix as well were the hacked and strategically released stolen emails on which I will concentrate in the third part of this book. A count by the Associated Press (AP) concluded that "Guccifer 2.0, WikiLeaks and DCLeaks ultimately published more than 150,000 emails stolen from more than a dozen Democrats."[39] The results not only reduced Hillary's control over the message environment but also unsettled her staff. "It's clear," noted the *AP* report, "Clinton's campaign was profoundly destabilized by the sudden exposures that regularly radiated from every hacked inbox. It wasn't just her arch-sounding speeches to Wall Street executives or the exposure of political machinations but also the brutal stripping of so many staffers' privacy."[40] Indeed, Clinton herself was subjected to threats when, as a result of the October 7 WikiLeaks' dump of content from Podesta's private account, hostile individuals secured brief access to her private contact information.

The WikiLeak'd material added arguments to Trump's rhetorical arsenal, precipitated the resignation of a DNC chair, created a countervailing narrative to the one emanating from the release of the *Access Hollywood* tape, led to CNN's firing of articulate advocate Donna Brazile, changed the contour of two presidential debates, and, throughout the critical weeks of the general election campaign, fostered an anti-Clinton agenda and frame in news. Importantly, the leaked content also redirected press time and resources in ways that had only a downside for the Clinton campaign and an upside for that of her Republican counterpart. "The publications sparked a media stampede as they were doled out one batch at a time, with many news organizations tasking reporters with scrolling through the thousands of emails being released in tranches," noted the AP investigation I cited a moment ago.[41] "At the AP alone, as many as 30 journalists were assigned, at various times, to go through the material."

By shaping news and debate agendas, WikiLeak'd Russian-hacked Democratic content affected the mass audience. At the same time, by initiating, cross-promoting, and amplifying posts on Facebook, Instagram, Twitter, YouTube, Tumblr, Reddit, and 9GAG, the trolls reshaped the communication climate inhabited by potentially susceptible voters. And when the trolls succeeded in getting memes to trend, and reporters took note, what began as an interpersonal channel of influence became a mass-mediated one.

Because much of the troll messaging was consistent with content available elsewhere in the social media stream, its existence matters not so much for injection of new ideas into the campaign dialogue (although there are instances in which that was done) but rather to the extent that it increased the visibility of anti-Clinton and pro-Trump content (an amplifying effect); drove memes into traditional news outlets (an agenda-setting effect); signaled social media users that its sentiments were widely shared (a normative effect); helped the trolls identify users susceptible to subsequent mobilizing or demobilizing appeals (target identification); increased the likelihood that, rather than sitting out the election, a person would decide to cast a vote for Trump (a mobilizing effect); was shared by those not already exposed to the message (a two-step flow effect); changed the relative amount of anti-Clinton content or negative emotion in the feeds of susceptible individuals (with weighting, contagion, and spiral of silence effects); and increased perception of the accuracy of the messages (a familiarity effect). Past research and the available data suggest that all of these are plausible outcomes. But none is likely to matter if the messaging was not aligned with Trump's interests or against Clinton's. Hence the next chapter asks whether that prerequisite was satisfied.

The Second Troll Prerequisite

Messages Aligned with Trump's Electoral Interests

Any argument that the Russian content was aligned with Trump's messaging presupposes familiarity with his central themes and intended audiences. The identity of both was on display in his closing statement in the final debate of the general election, where he stated:

> We're going to make America great. We have a depleted military. It has to be helped. It has to be fixed. We have the greatest people on Earth in our military. We don't take care of our veterans. We take care of illegal immigrants, people that come into our country illegally better than we take care of our vets. That can't happen. Our policemen and women are disrespected. We need law and order, but we need justice too. Our inner cities are a disaster. You get shot walking to the store. They have no education. They have no jobs. I will do more for African-Americans and Latinos than she can do for ten lifetimes. All she's done is talk to the African-Americans and to the Latinos, but they get the vote and

then they come back, they say "we'll see you in four years." We are
going to make America strong again and we are going to make America
great again and it has to start now. We cannot take four more years of
Barack Obama, and that's what you get when you get her.

The electoral importance of messaging of this sort was confirmed when
a study by the Public Religion Research Institute (PRRI) revealed that fears
about cultural displacement were among the factors predicting whether white
working-class voters would ballot for Trump. Specifically, those in that demographic group "who say they often feel like a stranger in their own land and
who believe the U.S. needs protecting against foreign influence were 3.5 times
more likely to favor Trump than those who did not share these concerns."[1]
Findings relevant to the Russian strategy include that "[n]early two-thirds of
the white working class say American culture has gotten worse since the 1950s.
Sixty-eight percent say the U.S. is in danger of losing its identity, and 62 percent
say America's growing number of immigrants threaten the country's culture.
More than half say discrimination against whites has become just as problematic as discrimination against minorities."[2] These findings parallel those from a
panel study comparing the views of the same individuals in 2012 and 2016. It
attributed support for Trump not to economic hardship but instead to status
threat, specifically to "changes in the [Republican] party's positions on issues
related to American global dominance and the rise of a majority-minority
America: issues that threaten white Americans' sense of dominant group
status."[3]

However, there is also evidence that economic frustrations were a factor.
Consistent with that take on the election, roughly a third of the counties that
twice sided with Obama supported Trump in 2016. And, as an analysis by the
New York Times notes, "Forty years ago, workers in the flip counties earned 85
cents for every dollar earned by workers in the Democratic strongholds. By 2016,
the ratio had fallen to 77 cents."[4] Moreover, as economist Jed Kolko has shown,
at the county level the 2012–2016 shift toward Trump was "stronger where un-
employment was higher, job growth was slower and earnings were lower."[5]

A compatible view, which I share, sees economic and cultural anxieties as
mutually reinforcing. So, for example, sociologist Andrew Cherlin argues that
Trump "exploited voters' feeling that they were being left behind by a Democratic

Party that seemingly favored blacks and immigrants."[6] This integrated perspective draws support from analyses of survey and county vote data by political analysts Robert Griffin and Ruy Teixeira. "The economic concerns of voters made contributions to Trump's success, both directly and indirectly," they argue, "through promoting the cultural attitudes associated with Trump support."[7]

A Focus on Issues on Trump's Agenda

To those fearful of downward mobility and cultural dislocation, Trump's debate statement not only promised jobs, but also forecast that as president he would quash illegal immigration and restore "law and order," a phrase pregnant with past associations. Veterans should turn out to vote for him because he would restore respect for them, protect their interests, and build up the military. He stands with police and, by implication, not with those who protest against their actions. However, blacks and Latinos have no reason to turn out in large numbers for Hillary. He promises to do more for either than Clinton. And for those concerned about the revelations on the *Access Hollywood* tape, he asserts his respect for women.

As I noted in Part I, in 2016 Republican voters were more concerned than they had been in 2012 about topics such as immigration and groups such as Muslims. Driving that change, at least in part, was Trump's rhetoric amplified by Russian posts evoking fears of Sharia law and veiled women, messages aligned with a proposed Muslim ban. The trolls also urged protection from those "invading" from across the border, appeals consonant with building a wall to thwart entry. An illustrative troll post on September 15, 2016, declared in a "we/they" frame, "They are criminals, not American citizens. Why should they receive any benefits? The only thing they should be eligible for is deportation." On the imposter site Secured Borders, which lured in 133,000 followers, immigrants were referred to as "freeloaders" and "scum."[8]

In line with Trump's promise to "restore" Christians' "right" to campaign in churches and his pledge to protect religious prerogatives from the intrusions of the Affordable Care Act, one troll post, also embodying a "we/they frame," asked, "How can that be that wearing [sic] hijab or praying to Allah in public places is okay, while demonstrating you're a Christian is 'offensive'? This anti-Christian Governmential [sic] policy has to stop as soon as possible."

Other messages increased the centrality of the need to protect gun rights. On Twitter and Facebook, viewers saw a handgun in the foreground backed by a close-up of a young woman answering the question "Why do I have a gun?"[9] Her response: "Because it's easier for my family to get me out of jail than out of cemetery [*sic*]." Unstated was the assumption that an unidentified threat wished her dead. A complementary troll post featured Trump defending her preferred solution: "'The Second Amendment to our Constitution is clear. The right of the people to keep and bear Arms shall not be infringed upon [*sic*]. Period.'—Donald J. Trump."[10]

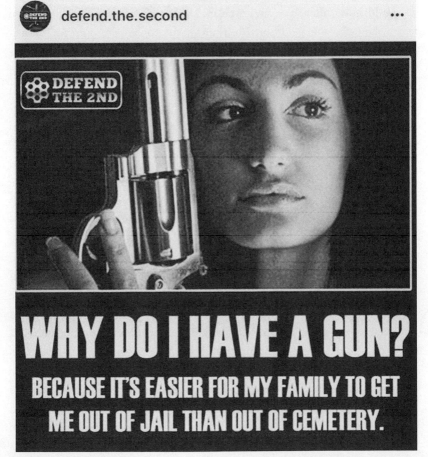

Figure 4.1 Instagram post from the "defend.the.second" account.

Heralding Trump's plans to restore US military greatness and champion the nation's veterans, an imposter lamented the fact that "[o]ur government spends billions of dollars on illegal aliens, while our brave Veterans are dying waiting for help. What the hell?"[11] As I noted in chapter 2, researchers have found that political messages such as these can increase the importance of the featured issues in voter evaluation of candidates, a finding that is particularly relevant in an election in which one in four disliked both major party candidates.[12]

From suggesting that the police and veterans are no longer valued and heightening fears of Islam and immigrants to increasing the salience of LGBTQ rights and black nationalism, the major Russian foci magnified fear of cultural change and, with it, antipathy toward both an incumbent Democratic president who launched his national career with ecumenical appeals and his anointed successor, whose inclusive view of Muslims, immigrants, and communities of color was telegraphed in her campaign slogan "Stronger Together."

The ostensibly disparate troll moves that advanced Trump's electoral interests included magnifying social tension and economic distress, allying the resulting anxieties with Clinton, suggesting that her presidency would exacerbate them and Trump's would eliminate them, and casting her as evil, a liar, and corrupt. Increasing the anxieties of those fearful of economic dislocation and cultural change and magnifying the sense that the country was under siege played to the advantage of a candidate pledging to "Make America Great Again." Exacerbating cross-group conflict also redounded against the incumbent president and his heir apparent. In the trolls' construction of reality as in Trump's, Hillary is the enemy, and Trump is the savior.[13] Importantly, whole swaths of the trolls' messaging simply changed the weighting of the targets' communication environment by amplifying existing anti-Clinton or pro-Trump communication, focusing on issues favorable to Trump and vilifying his opponent.

The groups with whom the trolls identified in their "we/they" message frames included veterans, Christians, those who are pro-life, crime-fearing citizens, the police, and those feeling left behind. Their targets for embrace were individuals threatened by those whose existence signaled a change in the culture—immigrants, the LGBTQ community, Black Lives Matter,

Muslims, and Hillary Clinton. The threat that "they" posed was telegraphed by the identities in which the trolls enwrapped themselves such as "Stop All Invaders." At the same time, their kinship with target audiences was conveyed in identities such as "Army of Jesus" and "American Veterans."

Accordingly, a troll-trafficked image identified by Twitter as "content which received significant engagement" pictured the T-shirt-clad back of a white male at a Trump rally whose shirt bore this message:

> Obama called me Clinger
> Hillary calls me Deplorable
> Terrorists call me Infidel
> Trump calls me
> AMERICAN!

Figure 4.2 Tweet from @Pamela_Moore13.

"Great shirt!" proclaimed the imposter, @Pamela_Moore13, as she relayed the image.[14] Because their telegraphy is powerful, the troll-amplified image and message invite examination here. But first, some background. In April 2008, Clinton condemned Obama's "demeaning," "elitist and out of touch" closed-door appraisal of those left behind in rural areas and manufacturing regions. In 2016, Trump and the trolls castigated her "deplorables" aspersion on the same grounds. Yet, despite its patronizing tone and inartful phrasing, Obama's diagnosis prefigures the part that economic and cultural anxiety would play in 2016's vote choices. In so doing, he anticipated the appeals that Trump would make to white working-class voters. At a closed-door 2008 event in San Francisco, the Democratic aspirant from Illinois had said:

> You go into some of these small towns in Pennsylvania, and like a lot of small towns in the Midwest, the jobs have been gone now for 25 years and nothing's replaced them. And they fell through the Clinton administration, and the Bush administration, and each successive administration has said that somehow these communities are gonna regenerate and they have not. So it's not surprising then that they get bitter, they cling to guns or religion or antipathy to people who aren't like them or anti-immigrant sentiment or anti-trade sentiment as a way to explain their frustrations.

Described by that digest was the constituency whose economic anxieties and fears of cultural displacement Trump would harness. In 2016, the t-shirt-clad Trump supporter and his candidate were not only expressing the same sentiments but also sending the same signal to small town, rural, and Rust Belt voters. Obama saw them as bitter, frustrated, fearful "clingers." Clinton viewed them as "deplorables." By contrast, the Republican standard-bearer celebrated their identity as gun-cherishing Christians. Not clingers. Not deplorables. True Americans. By making America great again, he would restore their jobs and standing in the nation and the world. To cast the contest as one between the elites and a populist, a globalist and a nationalist, the Republican campaign also appropriated the song "Do You Hear the People Sing?" from *Les Miserables* while projecting "Les Deplorables" and French flags on a back screen at his rallies.

The trolls' desire to cast Clinton as at odds with traditional values of a once-great America is evident in a post showing a widow grieving over the flag-draped casket of her husband as the message asserts that "we" know the difference his death made but "she" does not: "Hillary Asks 'What Difference Does it Make?' Follow Veterans_US If You Know The Difference."

At the same time, her identification with "Black Lives Matter" and Trump's with "law and order" made it possible for troll posts to invite audiences to invest messages with those meanings without mentioning either candidate's name. When voters integrate their own assumptions into content, they become accomplices in their own persuasion. As theorists since Aristotle have recognized, that process yields deeper conviction. "Another Gruesome Attack on Police by a BLM Movement Activist" reads an illustrative post depicting police officers paying tribute to a fallen colleague.

Figure 4.3 Instagram post from the "american.veterans" account.

The complementarity of the Trump and troll messaging is evident in a testosterone-oozing Russian post that ridiculed "political correctness" as it longed for restoration of male privilege. In it, the image of a cigarette-smoking, unshaven white cowboy is overlaid with the questions "LGBT? You Mean Liquor, Guns, Bacon And Tits?" The antagonisms being fueled and the reclamation being promised also were on display when "Stop All Invaders" juxtaposed a supposed picture of a homeless emaciated white veteran with one of a burly "undocumented unafraid unapologetic" male of color. "How come this veteran gets nothing while this illegal gets everything[?]" read the caption. By encouraging viewers to "[l]ike and share if you think this is a disgrace," the trolls located voters whose cultural and economic fears increased their susceptibility to the pro-Trump, anti-Clinton appeals that the Russian minions launched as Election Day approached.

In troll world as in his campaign, Trump stood with those longing for the country as it supposedly once was and against the cultural forces

Figure 4.4 "LGBT" Facebook post from the "Heart of Texas" account.

Figure 4.5 A "Stop A.I. (Stop All Invaders)" Facebook post.

represented by the first woman to head a major party ticket in the nation's history. To make their case, the trolls focused attention on issues central to the Trump candidacy and magnified his lines of personal attack against Clinton. They also stoked unrest among communities that caused unease in some segments of the white working-class population that Trump was intent on mobilizing.

The Russian desire to fan discord while also priming topics central to Trump's issue agenda is clear in the names adopted by troll Facebook accounts, which included "Fed-up with Illegals," and "Infidels against Islam." Seeding conflict between citizens and those in the country illegally and heightening concerns about Muslims worked to the Republican nominee's advantage by creating an enemy his presidency could promise to vanquish, in the first case by deportations and building a wall, and, in the second, by banning the entry of Muslims into the country. By contrast, the Clinton campaign defended the so-called Dreamers and opposed both the Muslim ban and barricading the southern border.

Sowing Discord Advantaged Trump

Not only are fomenting discord and defeating Clinton compatible activities, but one facilitates the other.[15] Dissension in the country hurts the prospects of a nominee who served in the cabinet of and is running on the argument that she will protect and extend the legacy of the incumbent. Moreover, if the Russians' goal was upping the heat in the US cultural wars in order to demonstrate discontent within a rival political system, advancing the candidacy of Donald Trump was a ready-to-order means.

To illustrate how their counterfeit content roiled intergroup conflict in the run-up to the 2016 election, let me briefly synthesize some of the moves the Russian impersonators made not only to exacerbate tensions within the black community but also to remind the larger audience of the existence of racial tension and its association with violence. Among these opportunistic Russian ventures was one in Maine recounted by its Republican Senator Susan Collins, who noted that, in response to racist remarks by that state's governor, the trolls manufactured two front groups: "one of African-Americans protesting the governor's comments and one of nationalists defending him."[16]

They also magnified conflicts between those in the black community and the police while priming forms of black identification with the Black Panther movement and aligning the police with the Ku Klux Klan (KKK). Were such efforts to result in violent clashes, media coverage would not only redound against the country's first black president and his preferred successor but also likely agitate and hence mobilize voters anxious about the increasingly multiracial and multicultural composition of the country.

Here the Russian understanding of both the political climate in the United States and its 1960s and 1970s history suggests political sophistication. In those earlier decades, those identifying as Black Panthers both killed and were killed by police officers. The tensions that the trolls magnified were reflected in news headlines, such as "Inside the Black Nationalist Groups That Captivated Killers

Figure 4.6 A "Blacktivist" Facebook post.

in Dallas, Baton Rouge."[17] Russian efforts to exacerbate discord included the following tweets:

- February 16, 2016: "The Black Panthers were originally created to help black community to survive in a racist country. The Black Panthers are gone but never forgotten.... The KKK was created to enforce discrimination and oppression. Somehow, they are still around us working in a police department."[18]

- February 23, 2016: "Trust me, underneath those KKK robes are cops, teachers, lawyers, judges, politicians, banker, [sic] etc. All positions of power. They just pretend caring [sic] about us."[19]

- May 18, 2016: "If Black Panthers, Malcolm X, Martin Luthern [sic] King could stand up to cops back then, why can't we get together and do it again together?"[20]

- June 27, 2016: "The KKK employed violence to obtain their objectives, in fact, this racial hate group was committed to maintain the status of white supremacy and suppress the activities of people of color. In contrast, the Black Panthers' goal was to elevate the oppressed black Americans and overthrow the racist political system."[21]

- July 11, 2016: "Today, KKK wear suits and blue uniform [sic] with a license to kill."[22]

- October 10, 2016: "Black Panthers were dismantled by [sic] U.S. government because they were black men and women standing up for justice and equality."[23]

Among the Russian-crafted messages magnifying community-police tensions was a YouTube channel titled "Don't Shoot" which garnered more than 368,000 views and contained "more than 200 videos of news reports, police surveillance tape and amateur footage showing incidents of alleged police brutality."[24] A report on CNN concluded that "Don't Shoot" may have had "the dual goal of galvanizing African Americans to protest and encouraging other Americans to view black activism as a rising threat."

Efforts to amplify conflicts between the Black Lives Matter movement and police also are evident in the Russian-tied "Being Patriotic," a Facebook page with 200,000 followers[25] that showed uniformed police officers saluting the flag-draped coffin of a colleague. Superimposed on the evocative image are the words "Another Gruesome Attack On Police By A BLM Movement Activist. Our Hearts Are With Those 11 Heroes." Priming interracial hostility were tweets such as one claiming, "Whites actually brought their children to watch planned lynching as a form of twisted entertainment. Today, police killing surpass [sic] the worst years of lynching."[26]

Another post, which Twitter identified as "content which received significant engagement," was tweeted on September 21, 2016, by an imposter

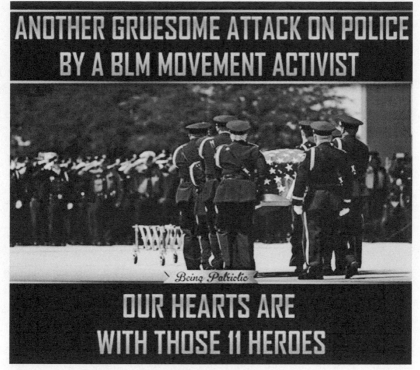

Figure 4.7 A Facebook post from "Being Patriotic."

identifying herself as Crystal Johnson. It read, "Cops have killed 68 people in 22 days since #Kaepernick started protesting. 68 in 22 days . . . have no words #KeithLamontScott."[27] Colin Kaepernick is, of course, the former San Francisco 49ers quarterback who in 2012 led that team to the Super Bowl. In 2016, the star athlete, who is black, elicited both imitation and attack when he protested racism and racial injustice by "taking a knee" instead of standing for the pregame singing of the national anthem. In August 2016 candidate Trump suggested that Kaepernick "find a country that works better for him."[28]

Forms of Kremlin-tied instigation were not limited to online messaging from St. Petersburg. Congressional investigators told ABC News that "two online groups—BlackMattersUS and BlackFist—were among those used by Russian operators to reach out directly to unwitting individual Americans engaged in political activism and . . . encourage them to help organize rallies, train in self-defense and create music videos."[29] The co-opted US artists were unaware that their work was being commissioned by Russians. Its ultimate home was BlackMattersUS, an imposter site that conflated its identity with that of the Black Lives Matter movement. Among those duped was a St. Louis, Missouri, hip-hop artist named Ronnie Houston, who performs under the name Rough the Ruler. Houston told ABC News that at the request of "someone claiming to be from BlackMattersUS [who] contacted him on the Facebook-owned photo-sharing platform Instagram in March of 2016," he created "a short music video featuring video clips from marches, graphics touting the BlackMattersUS website, and lyrics describing police as 'assassins' and protesters as 'avengers.' "[30]

Setting aside whatever they were up to before that point, we now know, thanks to the Mueller troll indictment, that in February 2016 the imposters were instructed to "use any opportunity to criticize Hillary and the rest (except Sanders and Trump—we support them)."[31] That intent was clear on Election Day, November 8, 2016, as well when they launched "a final push on Twitter to elect Donald Trump . . . us[ing] a combination of high-profile accounts with large and influential followings, and scores of lurking personas established years earlier with stolen photos and fabricated backgrounds" to dish out "carefully metered tweets and retweets voicing praise for Trump and contempt for his opponent, from the early morning until the last polls closed in the United States."[32] Details of the operation were pieced together by the *Daily Beast*, which "analyzed a dataset of 6.5 million tweets containing election keywords such as 'Hillary' and 'Trump' that was collected over 33 hours. . . Nov. 7–9 [2016] by Baltimore-based data scientist Chris Albon."

Russian-hacked emails and social media content also generated and reinforced central Trump lines of argument against Clinton personally and about key issues. Prominent among these was the notion that she was a corrupt liar who espoused positions antithetical to the interests of working-class and culturally anxious Americans.

Corrupt, Lying Hillary/Killary

Trump's preferred nickname for his opponent, "Crooked Hillary," and his assertion that she was a liar were reinforced and amplified by trolls who alleged in one ad that the former Secretary of State had delivered "decades of lies and scandal."[33] Such charges capitalize on the fact that, because candidates who are women are assumed to be more honest than their male counterparts,[34] they are especially vulnerable to allegations of unethical conduct, dishonesty, and corruption.[35] Claims about Hillary's duplicity or assertions that she belonged in jail also played on what political scientists call negative partisanship,[36] the notion that what binds citizens to one political party is aversion to or dislike of the other party rather than affection for their own.

The way in which the trolls amplified extreme anti-Clinton memes already circulating in US media is illustrated by their embrace of the label "Killary." For those drawn to travel, the word may summon images of a fjord west of Ireland. But to those on the extreme right it asserted that Clinton was responsible for the 2012 deaths at the Benghazi compound and the murder of DNC staff member Seth Rich, among others. "Killary's" alleged carnage put Lizzie Borden to shame. So, for example, the US blog post "Killary: The Clinton Body-Count," averred that "a large number of persons . . . have recently met their demise in suspicious circumstances who [sic] appear to have some connection to the Clintons."[37] (A linked blog post prompts visitors to access VK–VKontakte – a Saint Petersburg-based social media and social networking site.[38]) On YouTube, the "Killary Clinton Body Count Song"[39] (uploaded by a self-identified "independent journalist and Youtuber" who claims also to be "a sassy Canadian cat"[40]) elicited more than 20,000 views.

Like the rabbit-duck illusion, in which an ambiguous drawing can be seen to be either one, when spoken, the word "Killary" can betoken a predator ("Killer-y") or prey ("Kill-her-y"). Rather than the *agent* of violence, "Killary" became its *object* when t-shirts sold at Trump rallies superimposed "Killary Rotten Clinton" on a picture of her face set in a bull's-eye.[41] Here too the trolls adopted an existing meme. On the Heart of Texas page, the election of "Killary Rotten Clinton" was forecast to mean more "refugees, more mosques, and terrorist attacks."[42] Unless the assumption is that the former Secretary of State would welcome such attacks, that latter notion exists in tension with the photoshopped image of her shaking the hand of Osama bin Laden which appeared elsewhere on the same site.[43]

While virtually unmentioned in mainstream media, the aspersion "Killary" appeared on extreme websites and in the world constructed by the trolls. Not only did it grace US-based Facebook and Instagram pages in 2015, but it also appeared as the hashtag #Killary, and made its lyrical presence felt in the "[i]t's about Killary" political action committee (PAC) established by a Las Vegas resident who "told the FEC (Federal Election Commission) in a filing that 'Killary is a fictional character.'"[44] In a civics lesson gone awry, a handful of teenagers in Columbus, Ohio, even established their own "Killary Clinton" PAC.

In the last week and a half of the campaign, Heart of Texas took the verbal vilification of the Democratic nominee to a new level while also striking all of Trump's major themes. "The corrupt media does not talk about the crimes committed by Killary Rotten Clinton, neither does it mention the leaked emails but it would rather keep on kicking around some outdated tapes featuring Trump," it said.[45] Sentences later, the ad proclaims, "If Trump wins, there will be a possibility to secede peacefully but not without tension. What will happen if Hitlery becomes President? Higher taxes to feed undocumented aliens. More refugees, mosques, and terrorist attacks. Banned guns. Continuing economic depression. Let's re-mind them what Texas is made of and show that we're ready to SECEDE!" From the 26th of October through Election Day, three identical versions of that "Killary . . . Hitlerly" ad generated 36,399 total impressions. "Killary" also appeared mid-August in an American Veterans Instagram ad directed toward "Veterans/Military" that generated 17,654 impressions.[46]

Employing a form of ad feminam that I call "defaming by renaming," the act of transforming "Hillary" either into "Hitlery," as the Heart of Texas ad did, or into "Killary" subverts the candidacy of the first woman to be nominated for president by a major political party. It does so by displacing the notion that she is the protector and champion of the public in general or, in some cases, veterans, in particular, with one alleging that she is a pred-ator. These messages are potentially percolating in the background at Trump rallies as the crowd chants "lock her up." It is possible that T-shirts showing Hillary as a shooting target primed the response of the individual at a Trump rally who, according to CNBC reporter Christina Wilkie, shouted "kill her."[47]

Compared to "Killary," "liar" seems relatively tame. Unlike the former aspersion, which was reinforced by troll conspiracies, the latter made fodder of the hacked material, up on which Trump drew to claim that Clinton: was a liar (cf. "WikiLeaks: 'Clinton-Kaine Even Lied about Timing of Veep Pick'"[48]; "'WikiLeaks Drip-Drop Releases Prove One Thing: There's No Nov. 8 Deadline on Clinton's Dishonesty and Scandals'"[49]); had rigged the primaries against Sanders ("The Wikileaks [sic] e-mail release today was so bad to Sanders that it will make it impossible for him to support her unless he is a fraud!"[50]; "Leaked e-mails of DNC show plans to destroy Bernie Sanders. Mock his heritage and much more. On-line from Wikileakes [sic] really vicious. RIGGED"[51]); and was the beneficiary of an incestuous relationship with the "liberal" media ("So terrible that Crooked didn't report she got the debate questions from Donna Brazile if that were me it would have been front page news!"[52]; "WikiLeaks reveals Clinton camp's work with 'VERY friendly and malleable reporters' #DrainTheSwamp #CrookedHillary"[53]; "Very little pick-up by the dishonest media of incredible information provided by WikiLeaks. So dishonest! Rigged system!"[54])

Russian provocateurs reinforced the theme that Hillary was mendacious. So, for example, on April 1, 2016, one posted, "How ironic, Hillary accuses another candidate of lies! Those who live in glass houses should not throw stones, they say. 'I am so sick of the Sanders campaign lying about me. I'm sick of it,' Clinton said. . . . [A]t least he's got principles and honesty. Hillary, otherwise, lies as often as she breathes. And, by the way, the answer about her corruption ties [sic] with corporations was not given in that interview. America's sick of your lousy lies, Hillary!"[55] In a similar vein, on Election Day, @TEN_GOP tweeted a reminder of Republican vice presidential nominee Mike Pence's statement that "Hillary Clinton is the most dishonest candidate for POTUS since Richard Nixon."

Along the same lines, on June 18, 2016, Russian imposters tweeted images bearing the headline "Once a liar always a liar!"[56] The first photo, which was from Clinton's days as a young staffer on the Watergate committee, bore an inaccurate claim: "Hillary Clinton is fired from Watergate investigative committee, for lying, unethical behavior." Adjoining it was a second picture, this one of her testifying on State Department actions before, during, and after the deaths of four Americans in the US diplomatic and intelligence compound in Benghazi, Libya, in September 2012 at the hands of Islamic militants. To that image the trolls added, "Hillary faces Benghazi Investigative Committee for

Figure 4.8 An @TEN_GOP tweet on Hillary Clinton, claiming "once a liar always a liar!".

lying about the deaths of four Americans." At the bottom of that image, the message read, "Forty Years Later and She's Still a Liar."[57]

The troll attacks didn't end with branding the Democrat a corrupt liar, both claims central to Trump's indictment of her. They also infected the discourse stream with visuals too extreme for even the norm-breaking Republican nominee. So, for example, the troll account named "Heart of Texas ran an unflattering portrait of Mrs. Clinton with the tag 'Pure Evil'; posted a fake photo of her shaking hands with Osama bin Laden; and paired her with Adolf Hitler as a supporter of gun control."[58]

My focus here has been on showing the mutually reinforcing nature of the messaging of the Trump campaign and the trolls' efforts to fan social discontent, advance Trump's themes, and deploy anti-Clinton attacks. These moves were compatible with those I noted earlier that took the form of amplifying attacks on Clinton that originated on such conservative sites as Breitbart and Infowars. This alignment suggests that the trolls' understanding of Trump's communication needs was sound. So too does the evidence I will marshal in the next chapter showing that they focused messaging on constituencies Trump needed to mobilize, demobilize, and shift in order to best Clinton. It is to that analysis that we now turn.

5

The Third Troll Prerequisite

Mobilizing Veterans and White Christians, Demobilizing Blacks and Sanders's Supporters, and Shifting Liberals to Stein

A theory explaining how they will get their candidate to victory underlies campaign consultants' decisions about messaging and media strategies. But anchoring the game plans of all of the contenders are some common realizations. Specifically, they are all aware that not all who are eligible to vote will cast a ballot. The likelihood that an eligible voter will do so can be affected by access to the means and motivation.[1] Having ready access to an early ballot increases the odds that a person will vote.[2] So too do strong party identification, a past history of voting, enthusiasm for a candidate, and, if balloting in person, knowing the location of one's polling place and the date of the election. Weather is a factor as well, with rain reducing participation "by a rate of just less than 1% per inch, while an inch of snowfall decreases turnout by almost .5%."[3] Messaging matters too, and here social pressure increases participation. Being aware that others will know whether you balloted is a motivator, as are direct pleas to vote.[4] Voter turnout also can be increased by personal canvassing and by direct-mail appeals.[5]

Importantly, a ballot cast for Trump because the voter in question despises Clinton counts as surely for the Republican nominee as one cast by a citizen wearing a MAGA cap and an "Art of the Deal" T-shirt. And favoring one candidate over another only matters if that disposition translates into a vote. Consultants know the characteristics that predict likely vote choice. Among them are political party identification, race, ethnicity, gender, marital status, regular church attendance, educational level, military service, income, and occupation. If a male high school–educated veteran who is white votes, the Republican is his likely choice. An unmarried female elementary-school teacher who is black is likely to cast her vote for the Democrat. Consultants know which voters they need to mobilize and which they want to stay home. And they can figure out who the likely swing voters are.

Some campaigns focus on reconfiguring the electorate by mobilization and demobilization. Others concentrate on capturing the swing voters. Some do both. In 2012, although Romney carried Independents, Obama won by mobilizing blacks and creating a coalition that included northern white voters.[6]

Whatever the source of the insight, the troll messaging focused on five voting groups that Trump needed to influence. The Russians' efforts to affect three of these groups—blacks, Bernie Sanders's supporters, and those who could be shifted to Green Party candidate Jill Stein—were documented by the February 2018 Mueller indictment. The playbook apparent in the Russian-generated social media streams also reveals actions to increase participation by white working-class Americans in general and the evangelicals and veterans among them in particular.

Although in the United States the Electoral College decides which candidate becomes president, winning both it and the popular vote increases the capacity of the incumbent to claim a mandate to govern. Russian efforts in

Texas make sense in this context. As I noted in the last chapter, the Heart of Texas page was more venomous than the others fielded by the trolls. Apart from its "Killary . . . Hitlery" attacks, this was the page that brandished the "LGBT" assault featured in figure 4.4. That page's 253,862 followers suggest its reach. In this chapter, my focus is not on efforts to mobilize those in one specific locale, but rather on the general voting groups that Trump needed to activate or demobilize.

Two traditional Republican voting blocs—churchgoers and military families—required attention because they were unlikely supporters of a thrice-married candidate who confessed that his celebrity status permitted him to kiss and grope women at will, secured multiple deferments to avoid military service, dismissed the heroism of a prisoner of war, attacked Gold Star parents, and joked that dodging venereal disease was his personal Vietnam. While Trump needed high turnout from those otherwise reliable Republican groups, a decisive Electoral College victory for Clinton required turnout by black voters in numbers close to those achieved by Obama, heavy voting among Clinton leaners who supported Sanders in the primaries, and a minimal defection of liberals to the candidacy of Stein.

Interestingly, support for the notion that the Russian messaging had the potential to mobilize comes from Republican strategist Patrick Ruffini, who, after arguing that "the [trolls'] subject matter was designed to engage extremist voices on the political fringe, not persuadable voters undecided between Donald Trump and Hillary Clinton," also notes, "Where Russia appears to have made more headway—before and after the election—is in further animating partisans, capitalizing on their need to have their existing beliefs confirmed. It didn't matter that those confirming their beliefs were foreign adversaries."[7] That mobilizing goal is reflected in the ways in which Russian posts amplified anti-Clinton news. As we explore those efforts, it is important to keep in mind that, although traditional media remain the dominant source, 62 percent of US adults get news from social media.[8]

The messaging created by the Russian Internet Research Agency (IRA) upped the signal strength of news prominently featured on conservative websites. So, for instance, as Fox News carried the headline "Flag-Stomping Protesters Fueling Tensions at Trump, Other Events"[9] and the *Daily Caller* headline blared " 'F***K This Flag. F***K This Country'—BLM Protestors Spit and Stomp on American Flag,"[10] an April 5, 2016, imposter post said:

> Trump's rally in West Allis this Sunday faced a protest from BLM [Black Lives Matter] riots. Some of the "protesters" wore caps with "F*ck Yo Flag" signs and their slogans were the same. They kept on shouting "F*ck this flag, f*ck this country." ISN'T THAT ENOUGH FOR ARRESTING THEM AS ANTI-AMERICAN TERRORISTS? Later a couple of U.S. veterans appeared at the scene and called [sic] the black extremists to stop insulting the American flag. The BLM bastards' reaction was opposite [sic]: they started to spit on the flag they were stomping. The most disgusting thing in this story was its final [sic]: the police "calmed the scene." Not a single man was arrested. Well, arrests were are [sic] actually not necessary in such cases: such anti-Americans must be immediately shot! I'm sick of liberals and their media approving BLM and Black Panthers terrorists. I'm sick of the Authorities who forbid our policemen to arrest and shoot any sh*thead who dares to insult the [sic] Old Glory. I'm sick of the "right defenders" who raise the whole generation of black racists who believe they can do anything.[11]

Exposure to such evocative content increases our ability to recall it and, in the process, ups the likelihood that audiences will consider such activities to be more widespread than they actually are.[12] The underlying persuasion model can be thought of as a four-step process:

- Create, fabricate, or publicize cultural discord.

- Draw the attention of susceptible voters to it.

- Heighten their sense that the culture championed by the Democrats is out of touch with these voters' values.

- Translate their fears and feelings into a ballot against Clinton and, hence, unless sidetracked to a third-party contender, for Trump.

Mobilizing Evangelicals

Special insider knowledge is not required to infer that, in order to win the presidency, a Republican had to secure the votes of large numbers of white, conservative churchgoers, a category that includes evangelical Protestants and conservative Catholics. Because the distinctions between the two are unimportant for my purposes, unless otherwise indicated, I will refer to both simply as evangelicals. A cursory reading of the history of past elections shouted the need for a Republican to mobilize those identifying with this broadly defined faith community. So too did the Trump acceptance speech at the Republican convention, where an extended passage signaled his alliance with evangelicals and his commitment to name a like-minded replacement for recently deceased pro-life jurist Antonin Scalia:

> The replacement for Justice Scalia will be a person of similar views and principles. This will be one of the most important issues decided by this election. . . . At this moment, I would like to thank the evangelical community who have been so good to me and so supportive. You have so much to contribute to our politics, yet our laws prevent you from speaking your minds from your own pulpits. An amendment, pushed by Lyndon Johnson, many years ago, threatens religious institutions with a loss of their tax-exempt status if they openly advocate their political views. I am going to work very hard to repeal that language and protect free speech for all Americans. We can accomplish these great things, and so much else—all we need to do is start believing in ourselves and in our country again.

The trolls not only sang from the same hymnal as Trump but also, in the words of Senator Mark Warner (D-VA), "lured in" users with religious imagery and quotes from the Bible before posting anti-Clinton memes.[13] Kremlin-backed messaging moved from the benign expressions of respect for Jesus and the Bible to assertions that Clinton was evil and satanic.

In the process, the trolls not only assured targeted Christians that the ability to wish others a Merry Christmas would be protected by Trump but also promoted the unsupported claim that former president Bill Clinton had fathered an out-of-wedlock son with "a black prostitute." Reinforcing the message that the Clintons violated Christian norms was an RT video,[14] garnering 6 million views,[15] that spread the lie that 100 percent of the Clintons' charitable contributions "went to themselves." The trolls' interest in evangelicals and their monitoring of US conservative media personalities were both on display in a Heart of Texas post noting that two pastors had spoken with Sean Hannity. "[G]uess what top Evangelical leaders said about Hillary Clinton's positions?" asked the imposter. "They are wicked and evil [sic] I couldn't agree more with the Pastors. There is no way, [sic] a true Texan can vote for that lying murderer and criminal."

Russian hacking also shifted the message terrain against the Democratic nominee among white evangelical Protestants and Catholics (the latter group a key voting bloc in Philadelphia, Detroit, and Milwaukee) when WikiLeaks released, and conservative media touted,[16] the hacked email of Clinton communications director Jennifer Palmieri, who is herself Catholic, that seemed dismissive of both evangelical Christians and conservative Catholic Republicans. In that exchange, Palmieri responded to John Halpin, a senior fellow at the Center for American Progress (CAP), a person outside the Clinton campaign who subsequently confirmed the accuracy of the chain:[17]

HALPIN: Many of the most powerful elements of the conservative movement are all Catholic (many converts) from the [Supreme Court] and think tanks to the media and social groups. It's an amazing bastardization of the faith. They must be attracted to the systematic thought and severely backwards gender relations and must be totally unaware of Christian democracy.

PALMIERI: I imagine they think it is the most socially acceptable politically conservative religion. Their rich friends wouldn't understand if they became evangelicals.

"Emails Reveal Top Clinton Aide Mocked Evangelicals and Catholics" read a headline in the evangelical publication *Christianity Today*.[18] A half-million-member conservative group called Catholic Vote demanded Palmieri's resignation.[19]

The hacked Palmieri email was fodder for the Republican team as well. *Time*'s Elizabeth Dias reported that "[i]n a national conference call . . . , campaign manager Kellyanne Conway, who is Catholic, called on Clinton to apologize for 'hostility to religious liberty and to the beliefs we hold as Catholics.' Former House Speaker Newt Gingrich, who converted to Catholicism in 2009, added that 'now we know what Hillary meant by deplorables. It was people of faith.'"[20] Meanwhile, on the stump and in tweets,[21] Trump reminded voters about Palmieri's supposed sentiments.

As I noted in chapter 2, the messaging of Russian trolls was designed to increase the salience of illegal immigration, fear of Muslims, and supposed assaults on religious liberty; magnify worries about lack of respect for police and veterans; heighten white voters' awareness of civil unrest and blacks' awareness of black nationalism and abuse at the hand of those in power; polish perceptions that Clinton was dishonest and corrupt; and foster the belief that she was unconcerned about veterans, was the enemy of Christians, was responsible for high rates of incarceration of blacks, was aligned with Wall Street, and had rigged the primaries against her Vermont rival. By moving these topics up on the agenda of voters, the trolls increased the likelihood that they would elicit the kinds of preference shifts that Richard Johnston, Michael Hagen, and I documented in 2000. As I noted in chapter 2, by focusing attention on a flaw in George W. Bush's Social Security plan in the final weeks of the election, and having the platform of network news largely to himself to make that case, Gore increased the role of that issue in voters' decisions in the nonbattleground states.

Trump unquestionably faced a challenge in mobilizing some traditional Republican constituencies. For many churchgoers, for example, a vote for him was not automatically in the cards. A January 2016 Pew Research Center poll[22] found that 44 percent of white evangelical Republicans viewed the real estate mogul as "not too" or "not at all" religious. Their decision had not gotten easier by July. In a mid-summer 2016 Pew survey, 55 percent of white evangelical voters reported that they were dissatisfied with the choice of presidential candidates.[23] Forty-two percent of white evangelicals reported that "it will be difficult to choose between Trump and Clinton because *neither one* would make a good president." At the same time, the pollsters found that "white Catholics are evenly divided between those who prefer Trump and those who favor Clinton." If they voted, history suggested that white con-servative church-goers would support the Republican. So a risk for Trump was that they would stay home.

In 2016, they did not. Turnout among self-identified, white, born-again, evangelical Christians remained unchanged from 2012 and 2008 at about 25 percent of voters.[24] Trump actually outperformed prior Republican nominees with this group. Exit polls found that 81 percent of self-identified, white, born-again, evangelical Christians cast their ballots for Trump in 2016: compare that with 78 percent for Romney in 2012, 74 percent for McCain in 2008, and 78 percent for Bush in 2004.[25] In 2016, white Catholics also hewed to their past party preference with 60 percent supporting Trump. In 2012, 59 percent had backed Romney. In 2008, 52 percent supported McCain, and in 2004 56 percent cast their vote for George W. Bush.

Mobilizing Veterans

The signpost in his acceptance speech that signaled Trump's alignment with the interests of veterans was concise and clear. "We will take care of our great veterans like they have never been taken care of before," the Republican nominee declared. On the other side of the equation, Hillary's record on military affairs was enhanced by membership on the Senate Armed Services Committee, where she battled for special benefits for those suffering from post-traumatic stress disorder.[26] The trolls' alternative fact set consisted of a rich brew of fabricated numbers and fomented fear. "At least 50,000 home-less veterans are starving [sic] dying in the streets, but liberals want to in-vite 620,000 refugees and settle them among us,"[27] said one counterfeit missive. Another read, "Our government spends billions of dollars on illegal aliens, while our brave Veterans are dying waiting for help. What the hell?"[28] Employing an aspersion that I discussed in the last chapter, one Russian mes-sage on the account "american.veterans" proclaimed, "Killary Clinton will never understand what it feels like to lose the person you love for the sake of your country." Attached was the image of a grieving widow (see figure 4.3 in chapter 4), viewed 17,654 times.[29]

Not to be outdone, a September 8, 2016, post that engaged 737,178 users (the sum of "likes," "reactions," and comments) alleged without evidence[30] that "Hillary Clinton has a 69 percent disapproval rating among all veterans." Signaling approval or disapproval by respected peers is, of course, a potent means of persuasion.[31] Related posts impugned Clinton's patriotism. An October 15, 2016, one from Secured Borders contended, for instance, that "If Killary thinks that being American, loving your country and be [sic] concerned about ours [sic] and our children's future is deplorable then hell yeah count me in that basket."[32]

In mid-August, an NBC SurveyMonkey poll found Trump leading Clinton by only 10 points among military households,[33] a group that supported Romney over Obama by 20 points.[34] By Election Day, the spread between veterans' support for Trump and for Clinton had widened. Exit polls suggest that he bested Clinton among that group by a substantial 60 percent to 34 percent.[35]

The trolls mounted efforts to demobilize a number of pro-Democratic constituencies as well. Indeed, in the judgment of Senator Mark Warner, the senior Democrat on the Senate Intelligence Committee, "In many cases, it [the Russian effort] was more about voter suppression rather than increasing turnout."[36] If so, the citizens whose ballots Trump did not want cast were African Americans and Sanders's young supporters.

Suppressing the Black Vote

On February 16, 2018, the Mueller Russian intervention indictment confirmed that "In or around the latter half of 2016, Defendants and their co-conspirators, through their ORGANIZATION-controlled personas, began to encourage U.S. minority groups not to vote in the 2016 U.S. presidential election or to vote for a third-party U.S. presidential candidate."[37] These efforts were extensive. Of the forty troll-generated Facebook ads that garnered over 10,000 impressions in October 2016, twenty-eight sought out those in the black community. In November, twenty-seven of the twenty-eight ads that exceeded that number did the same. The ads' targeted "interests" reveal their intended audience. Among those the Russian minions selected were: "MLK, Police Brutality is a crime, African American culture, Civil Rights, African American History, Police Brutality in the US, Stop Police Brutality, Malcom X or Union of Huff Post writers,

Panafricanism, Black (Color), Black Nationalism, Police Misconduct, and Black Consciousness Movement." Some of the troll ads attracted sizable numbers. So, for example, one promoting the "Woke Blacks" page was viewed more than 307,000 times.[38] Another, sponsored by Blacktivist, earned just over 191,000 impressions for its "heart-piercing story about a racial bias that might cause law enforcement officers to shoot innocent and unarmed black people."[39]

The Kremlin's vote-suppression maneuvers were many and various. Prominent among them was not only priming a specific facet of Bill Clinton's record but also doing the same for remarks by Hillary Clinton that vexed liberals in general and black voters in particular. Days before the South Carolina primary, a BLM activist raised both when she demanded at a Clinton fundraiser that the candidate apologize for her husband's support of mass incarceration and for her own 1996 characterization of gang members as "super predators."[40] In late August (August 21, 2016), the Republican nominee retweeted the C-SPAN 2 video of Hillary Clinton's 1996 statement in support of sentencing reform that referred to "super predators" who need to be "brought to heel." In that speech she said,

> [W]e also have to have an organized effort against gangs. Just as in a previous generation we had an organized effort against the mob. We need to take these people on. They are often connected to big drug cartels, they aren't just gangs of kids anymore. They are often the kinds of kids that are called super predators—no conscience, no empathy. We can talk about why they ended up that way, but first, we have to bring them to heel.

When that statement was resurrected in 2016, Hillary responded with an expression of regret that said, "Looking back, I shouldn't have used those words, and I wouldn't use them today."[41] Importantly, as *PolitiFact* noted, "The full context of this incident does link children and superpredators, but nowhere in the speech does she directly label African-American youth this way."[42] If "super predator" was the phrase Clinton wanted black voters to forgive or forget, "harsher prison sentencing" was the policy. An article in *The Nation* put the indictment of the Clinton administration's actions this way:

> When [Bill] Clinton left office in 2001, the United States had the highest rate of incarceration in the world. Human Rights Watch reported that in seven states, African Americans constituted 80 to 90 percent of all drug offenders sent to prison, even though they were no more likely than whites to use or sell illegal drugs. Prison admissions for drug offenses reached a level in 2000 for African Americans more than 26 times the level in 1983. All of the presidents since 1980 have contributed to mass incarceration, but as Equal Justice Initiative founder Bryan Stevenson recently observed, "President Clinton's tenure was the worst."[43]

Russian tweets translated these concerns into statements such as "Black families are divided and destroyed by mass incarceration and death of black men. Facts don't lie"[44] and "U.S. prisons now hold more black men than slavery ever did."[45] Troll posts also claimed that "Black people continue to make up more than 30 percent of the people dying from police misconduct, though we make up only 13 percent of [*sic*] nation's population."[46] In early 2016 an IRA Tumblr account posted the video of Clinton using the term "super predators."[47]

(Parenthetically, let me note that some of the 2017 Russian efforts elicited ridicule, among them a Tumblr post from an account called "Hustle in a Trap," which included this claim: "While Afrikan [*sic*] people are increasingly DISTRACTED by issues pertaining to homosexuality and a government occupied with focusing on 'gay rights,' some one or some thing is stealing and consuming our children." Superimposed on snapshots of smiling black children was the appeal "Look Up Black Organ Harvesting." "The Beast is eating, sniffing & injecting us," read the message. "Melanin $158,144 a pound, 185 pounds in the Average Black mans [*sic*] body. Dead black man with 185 pounds of melanin worth $29,256,640."[48])

We know that the Russian operatives were not the only ones working to suppress the 2016 votes of blacks as well as those of young liberals (i.e., likely Sanders supporters), because late in October 2016, *Bloomberg*'s Joshua Green and Sasha Issenberg learned from Trump's digital operatives that his campaign had "three major voter suppression operations underway."[49] Their demobilizing moves involved dispatching anti-Clinton content to young white liberals, young women, and black voters. Among the attacks was "a *South Park*–style animation" showing "Clinton delivering the 'super predator' line (using audio from her original 1996 sound bite), as cartoon text popped up around her saying: 'Hillary Thinks African Americans are Super Predators.'"[50] The campaign relayed the animation "to certain African American voters through Facebook 'dark posts'—nonpublic posts whose viewership the campaign controls."[51] As Trump's digital director, Brad Parscale, put it, this content would reach "only the people we want to see it."[52] "We knew the 14 million people we needed to win 270," he told a postelection campaign managers' forum at Harvard's Kennedy School.[53] "We targeted those in over 1000 different universes with exactly the things that mattered to them. . . . We won exactly where we laid our money other than one state, Wisconsin, Michigan, Pennsylvania, Ohio. We pulled out of Virginia."

The Russian trolls also disseminated sponsored content with the potential to discourage or redirect minority voting. Fake ads (one featuring actor Aziz Ansari;[54] another showing a black woman in front of an "African Americans for Hillary" sign[55]) encouraged voters of color to "Avoid the line. Vote from Home." Viewers were instructed to text or tweet their support for Clinton instead. "This time we choose between two racists," proclaimed an ad posted by the troll page titled "Williams&Kalvin" on Election Day.[56] "No one represents Black people. Don't go to vote. Only this way we can change the way of things . . ." Data released in May 2018 revealed that that appeal to suppress the black vote was seen nearly 8,500 times.

Russian content also downplayed the threat of a Trump presidency. As the Associated Press study of the content of the imposter Twitter accounts noted: "One Russian account, 'Blacks4DTrump,' tweeted a Trump quote on Sept. 16 in which he declared 'it is the Democratic party that is the party of slavery, the party of Jim Crow & the party of opposition.' Meanwhile, TEN_ GOP asked followers to 'SPREAD the msg of [*sic*] black pastor explaining why African-Americans should vote Donald Trump!'"[57] Imposter bloggers self-identified as Williams and Kalvin, who supposedly lived in Atlanta, posted print and video messages declaring, "We, the black people, we stand in one [*sic*] unity. We stand in one to say that Hillary Clinton is not our candidate."[58]

Efforts to reduce voting by young blacks existed not only on Facebook and Twitter but also on the blogging site Tumblr. In February 2018, Jonathan Albright, research director of the Tow Center for Digital Journalism at Columbia University, working with *BuzzFeed*, revealed evidence of "a highly engaged and far-reaching Tumblr propaganda-op targeting mostly teenage and twenty-something African Americans."[59] It appeared, they noted, "to have been part of an ongoing campaign since early 2015." These IRA Tumblr and Twitter accounts had "the same profile image or linked to each other in their bios. Some IRA Tumblrs and Twitter accounts also cross-promoted content between platforms, further linking them together."

On Tumblr, noted Albright, "Russian trolls posed as black activists . . . and generated hundreds of thousands of interactions for content that ranged from calling Hillary Clinton a 'monster' to supporting Bernie Sanders and decrying racial injustice and police violence in the US." Drawing on leaked data, the *Daily Beast* identified Russian IRA Tumblr accounts bearing names such as "Ghetta Blasta," "Hustle In A Trap," and "Swag In The Rain." The accounts "uniformly pushed mostly relatable memes about being black in America, then filtered in invitations to protests by IRA groups like Blacktivist, along with conspiracy theories about Hillary Clinton."[60]

The vote-suppressing synergy between the Bannon-run *Breitbart* site and Russian social media dupers was evident when both featured the same still photo from an anti-Clinton ad sponsored by the "Defeat Crooked Hillary" political action committee (PAC),[61] backed, according to a report by *Time*,[62] by Bannon-championing billionaire Robert Mercer. The thirty-second broadcast spot,[63] which was slotted to air in Ohio and Pennsylvania, showed a young African American actress supposedly "hired to record a pro-Clinton ad, [who] cannot make it through a script calling her 'honest and trustworthy.' "[64] As she walks away, the actress notes, "I can't say these words. I just don't believe what I'm saying." When reminded by the off-screen producer that she's an actress, she responds, "I'm not that good of an actress. Honest and trustworthy? Give me a break."

"The ad, which has been dubbed as 'one of the most amusing' and effective ones of the election cycle, may stick in the minds of voters because they will have initially thought that they were viewing a pro-Clinton ad before the script was flipped on them," posited an article on Breitbart. "And it may convince just enough voters, especially young and minority voters, to not support Clinton in November."[65] Atop a still image from that ad the St. Petersburg trolls "@TEN_GOP" posted the claim that it was "brilliant." "Spread it far &wide!" read the imposters' appeal. Another ad said, "You know a great number of black people support us saying that #HillaryClintonIsNotMyPresident."[66] "[A] particular hype and hatred for Trump is misleading the people and forcing Blacks to vote Killary," argued another message. "We cannot resort to the lesser of two devils. Then we'd surely be better off without voting AT ALL."

The Russians also worked to suppress voting by Muslims, a fact documented by the February 2018 Mueller indictment, which read: "By in or around early November 2016, Defendants and their co-conspirators used the ORGANIZATION-controlled 'United Muslims of America' social media accounts to post anti-vote messages such as: 'American Muslims [are] boycotting elections today, most of the American Muslim voters refuse to vote for Hillary Clinton because she wants to continue the war on Muslims in the middle east and voted yes for invading Iraq.' "[67]

After the election, the victor acknowledged the important role that low turnout among blacks had played in his election. "The African American community was great to us," Trump noted at a December 2016 rally in Grand Rapids, Michigan. "They came through, big league. Big league. And frankly if they had any doubt, they didn't vote, and that was almost as good because a lot of people didn't show up, because they felt good about me."[68]

Consistent with Trump's needs, white turnout was up and black turnout down in 2016. According to the comprehensive source for examining the social and demographic composition of subpopulations in the electorate, the Census Bureau's November supplement to the Current Population Survey, in 2016, turnout increased to 65.3 percent for non-Hispanic whites, a natural constituency for Trump, but decreased to 59.6 percent for non-Hispanic blacks, a prime demographic for Clinton.[69] Overall, the "black voter turnout rate declined for the first time in 20 years in a presidential election, falling to 59.6% in 2016 after reaching a record-high 66.6% in 2012. The 7-percentage-point decline from the previous presidential election is the largest on record for blacks. . . . The number of black voters also declined, falling by about 765,000 to 16.4 million in 2016, representing a sharp reversal from 2012."[70]

Converting or Suppressing the Sanders Vote

In his acceptance speech at his nominating convention, the Republican standard-bearer explicitly appealed to the supporters of Bernie Sanders with a claim that shortly thereafter would draw additional strength from Russian-hacked Democratic content, "I have seen firsthand how the system is rigged against our citizens," said Trump, "just like it was rigged against Bernie Sanders—he never had a chance. But his supporters will join our movement, because we will fix his biggest issue: trade."[71]

Interestingly, the controversial dossier compiled for the Democrats by the former British intelligence officer Christopher Steele cites an unidentified Trump associate reporting that Democratic National Committee (DNC) email leaks were designed to switch Sanders's voters from Clinton to Trump.[72] As the July 2018 Mueller hacker indictments confirm, WikiLeaks timed the release to thwart Clinton's efforts to consolidate the support of Sanders's voters. "Released just before the DNC convention in Philadelphia kicks off on Monday, the emails come at a precarious time," noted an article in *Vox*, "just as Sanders tries to convince his supporters to come out and vote for Clinton."[73] The first batch of damaging content was leaked on July 22, the day after Trump concluded his convention and three days before the start of the Democratic one.[74]

"The WikiLeaks emails—written by a wide range of DNC staff from the top leadership all the way down to the lowest employees—were carefully chosen to reveal senior members of the DNC staff speaking disrespectfully of Bernie and his supporters," recalled DNC vice chair Donna Brazile, who would become that organization's chairperson after the resignation of Debbie Wasserman Schultz.[75] The offensive comments found in them read like a playbook designed to alienate the very voters Clinton needed to woo. "[O]ne staff member had made an anti-Semitic remark. They questioned his [Sanders's] faith and conjectured about ways to smear him for being an atheist in strongly religious states like Kentucky and West Virginia. They mocked him for being an outsider, the very thing that had energized his supporters, who were sick of establishment corruption. The emails showed the DNC staffers developing a story to plant in the press about how his campaign failed." Press uptake was immediate. "Suddenly," recalls Brazile, "you could not turn on cable news without hearing these shameful statements."[76]

Unsurprisingly, Republicans eagerly argued and pundits confidently opined that the disclosed content showed the DNC in the tank for Clinton. Speaking on Fox News, Stephen Hayes, a columnist at the *Weekly Standard*, reported that the emails "show a clear pattern of Wasserman Schultz and the DNC 'thumbing the scales' in favor of Clinton and scheming for ways to 'thwart' Sanders."[77]

In tweets and on the stump, Trump turned revelations from those hacked DNC emails into justifications for a Trump vote by Sanders's supporters:

- July 23, 2016: "The Wikileaks [*sic*] e-mail release today was so bad to Sanders that it will make it impossible for him to support her unless he is a fraud!"[78]

- July 23, 2016: "Leaked e-mails of DNC show plans to destroy Bernie Sanders. Mock his heritage and much more. On-line from Wikileakes [*sic*] really vicious. RIGGED!"[79]

- July 25, 2016: "How much BAD JUDGEMENT was on display by the people in DNC in writing those really dumb e-mails, using even religion, against Bernie!"[80]

The notion that Hillary stole the primaries from Bernie persisted in the general election debates. In the second one, for example, Trump declared that Clinton had lost the 2008 primaries fair and square "unlike the Bernie Sanders race where you won, but not fair and square, in my opinion and all you have to do is take a look at WikiLeaks and just see what they said about Bernie Sanders and see what Debra [*sic*] Wasserman Schultz had in mind, because Bernie Sanders, between superdelegates [*sic*] and Debra [*sic*] Wasserman Schultz, he never had a chance and I was so surprised to see him sign on with the devil."

Stolen content also was transformed by Trump into an attack in tweets, on the stump, and in the last debate implying that Clinton's own campaign chairman shared the Republican nominee's view that she was unqualified for the presidency. Near the end of that encounter, Trump asserted:

No, you're the one that's unfit. You know, WikiLeaks just actually came out. John Podesta said some horrible things about you, and boy was he right. He said some beauties. And you know Bernie Sanders, he said you have bad judgment. You do. And if you think going into Mosul after we let the world know we're going in and all of the people we really wanted, the leaders are all gone, if you think that was good, then you do. Now John Podesta said you have terrible instincts. Bernie Sanders said you have bad judgment. I agree with both.

"Bernie Sanders on HRC: Bad Judgement. John Podesta on HRC: Bad Instincts. #BigLeagueTruth #Debate," proclaimed a Trump tweet.[81]

After "WikiLeaks published internal DNC emails, some of which appeared to show DNC officials deriding Sanders and plotting ways to help Hillary Clinton,"[82] noted *Vox*, Congresswoman Debbie Wasserman Schultz resigned as head of the committee. Her resignation seemed to confirm the narrative that suggested that Sanders had been treated unfairly by a body that was supposed to remain impartial.

Use of WikiLeak'd content to dampen the enthusiasm of Sanders's supporters did not end with the disclosures of DNC material just before the Democratic convention. In October, *Breitbart* drew on it to imply that the *Access Hollywood* tape could be a form of Democratic sabotage akin to a supposed Clinton campaign plot to smear Sanders as a sexist whose supporters had harassed women. The charge read:

> The leak also contains opposition research on Clinton's main primary challenger, Senator Bernie Sanders, in which the campaign plotted to smear Sanders as a "sexist" with "extreme views on women," as well as accuse his supporters of harassing women on the internet. The "Bernie Bros" smear, which did exactly that, became a major narrative of the Clinton campaign during the Democratic primary.[83]

Imposter pages on Facebook also made appeals to those who had championed Sanders. So, for example, "Born Liberal" overwrote a picture of Sanders with his statement calling the Clinton Foundation a "Problem." Also relaying messages to Bernie's supporters were Ukrainian-based Facebook pages supposedly made up of his stalwarts. One ersatz pro-Sanders Facebook page that attracted "nearly 90,000 followers" was, according to the *Guardian*, "run by an Albanian IT expert who, when interviewed by the Huffington Post, appeared to speak very little English, although his page consistently published polished English prose."[84] An IRA Tumblr account "noted that Donald Trump had pointed out how unfairly Sanders was being treated by the 'establishment.' "[85] By February 2018, internet scholar Albright reports, it had 200,000 notes.

An analysis of the 2016 Cooperative Congressional Election Survey, a poll of about fifty thousand people, found that 12 percent of those who backed Sanders cast a vote for Trump and in "each of the three states that ultimately swung the election for Trump—Michigan, Wisconsin and Pennsylvania—Trump's margin of victory over Clinton was smaller than the number of Sanders voters who gave him their vote."[86] Demobilizing or converting Sanders's supporters was eased in states whose primaries the Vermont senator had won. Choosing an alternative to the eventual nominee in a state's primary raises the odds of a decision to stay home or vote for someone other than the party's standard-bearer in the general election. Sanders had bested Clinton in both Michigan and Wisconsin.

Although general election defection from the party's nominee by Sanders supporters was not unusually high,[87] it is difficult to know whether it would have been lower had the hackers and trolls not fueled antagonism toward Clinton. Some of the general underlying attitudes and party dispositions of Sanders voters particularly on trade and Wall Street did more closely align with Trump's views than Clinton's.[88] But others, such as support for improving rather than repealing the Affordable Care Act, backing a higher minimum wage, championing college tuition support, and keeping the power to nominate Supreme Court justices out of conservatives' hands, more closely paralleled Clinton's. Those commonalities would ordinarily have predicted a lower rate of defection than in past elections.

If the Russian effort was designed to demobilize individuals unwilling to support Trump, the obvious place to look for an effect is not on those who voted but those who didn't. Importantly, the black vote and Sanders vote are overlapping categories. In an article titled "Registered Voters Who Stayed Home Probably Cost Clinton the Election," *FiveThirtyEight*'s Harry Enten argues from postelection SurveyMonkey data that "Donald Trump probably would have lost to Hillary Clinton had Republican- and Democratic-leaning registered voters cast ballots at equal rates."[89] The reasons are clear. "Among white voters, voters 18–29 years old made up 30 percent of voters who did not participate in the November election. Among young Hispanic voters, that climbs to 43 percent. Among young black voters, it was an even higher 46 percent."[90] In the primaries, black voters under thirty had favored Sanders over Clinton.[91]

Drawing Liberals from Clinton to Stein

The Russian campaign also attempted to peel votes away from Clinton by urging balloting for Green Party candidate Jill Stein. Run from November 3 through Election Day, a Blacktivist Facebook ad garnered 18,888 impressions for its close-up picture of the Green Party candidate and its appeal, "Choose peace and vote for Jill Stein."[92] To that message, the trolls added, "Trust me, it's not a wasted vote.... The only way to take our country back is to stop voting for the corporations and banks that own us. #GrowASpineVoteJillStein." Targeted by the ad were those whose interests included "Pan-Africanism, African-American Civil Rights Movement (1954–68), African-American history or Black (Color)."

Among the odd links between Stein and the Russians are these, summarized in an essay in *Vanity Fair*:

> Stein met with Russian Foreign Minister Sergey Lavrov. Her running mate, Ajamu Baraka, has echoed Russian talking points about the crash of Malaysia Airlines flight 17, which U.S. intelligence sources believe was shot down by pro-Russian separatists in Ukraine. (Stein herself has suggested that Russia was entitled to invade Ukraine, that NATO should leave Russia alone, and that the overthrow of former Ukraine president Viktor Yanukovych was a C.I.A. coup.) During the campaign, Stein made multiple appearances on RT.[93]

Also, as Senator Warner has noted, Stein spoke in a complimentary fashion about Julian Assange, the founder of WikiLeaks, who, Warner noted, "clearly was being used by the Russians to take some of the hacked information and release [it] into our political system."[94] Interestingly, Assange addressed the 2016 Green Party convention, albeit from a remote location.

In her campaign account, titled *What Happened*, Clinton flags Stein's pro-Russian rhetoric and actions but does not raise the possibility that Kremlin-tied messaging may have benefited the Green Party nominee's candidacy. "[A] small but still significant number of left-wing voters may well have thrown the election to Trump," she writes. "Jill Stein, the Green Party candidate, called me and my policies 'much scarier than Donald Trump' and praised his pro-Russia stance. This isn't surprising, considering that Stein sat with Putin and Michael Flynn at the infamous Moscow dinner in 2015 celebrating the Kremlin's propaganda network RT, and later said she and Putin agreed 'on many issues.'"[95] An NBC analysis of the RT and Sputnik archives located "more than 100 stories, both on-air and online, friendly to Stein and the Green Party."[96]

Facilitating 2012 and 2016 comparisons of the Green Party vote in Michigan, Pennsylvania, and Wisconsin is the fact that Stein, a Harvard-educated physician, was that party's standard-bearer in both years.

- Whereas in 2012, she garnered 7,665 votes in Wisconsin,[97] in 2016, she received 31,072.[98] Trump's margin over Clinton was under twenty-three thousand (22,748).[99]

- In Michigan, she won 21,897 votes in 2012[100] and 51,463 votes in 2016.[101] In that state, Trump's margin was just under eleven thousand (10,704).[102]

- In Pennsylvania, Stein received 21,341 votes in 2012[103] and 49,941 in 2016.[104] Trump's margin in that commonwealth was roughly forty-four thousand (44,292).[105]

If one assumes for the sake of argument that the 2012 Green Party vote is that party's base level of support, and grants that the additional votes Stein drew in 2016 over and above that number go to Clinton, the results would have changed the Trump-Clinton outcome in Wisconsin and Michigan but not Pennsylvania.

The vote that Trump and the trolls needed to demobilize or shift was one that Obama activated in 2012. But, had they voted, would their ballots have gone to the Democrat? Using data from the Cooperative Congressional Election Study, a survey of over 64,000 adults, political scientists Sean McElwee, Jesse H. Rhodes, Brian F. Shaffner, and Bernard L. Fraga grouped eligible 2012 voters into one of five categories.[106] In order to determine whether a person voted, they used validated voting rather than self-reported turnout. Their analysis found that "while 9 percent of Obama 2012 voters went for Mr. Trump in 2016, 7 percent—that's more than four million missing voters—stayed home. Three percent voted for a third-party candidate." Of those who reported voting for Obama in 2012 but failed to vote in 2016, the scholars found that 51 percent were people of color, 23 percent were under thirty, and more than 60 percent made less than $50,000 a year. Had they voted, their votes would have overwhelmingly gone to Clinton. "Four out of every five Obama-to-nonvoters identify as Democrats, and 83 percent reported they would have voted for a Democrat down-ballot. A similar share of Obama-to-nonvoters said that they would have voted for Mrs. Clinton had they turned out to vote."

This chapter and the one before it have argued that the trolls' theory of the electoral needs of the Trump campaign was sound. Not only did their messaging align with his, but their efforts to fuel discontent could reasonably be expected to distance those feeling culturally displaced and anxious about their economic future from the Democratic Party nominee. At the same time, bringing the evangelical and veterans' votes up to their prior levels, depressing the voting of blacks to well below the Obama levels, and persuading some young Sanders supporters that Clinton was unworthy of their ballots were metrics Trump had to meet to win the Electoral College. Directing the attention of young liberals to Stein was a smart move as well. In each focal group the numbers on the board on election night had moved in the direction of the Republican standard-bearer.

If, as the evidence in chapter 2 suggests, increasing the relative amount of strategically adept messaging increases its impact on vote intention, and the trolls were simply upping the volume and reach of legitimate pro-Trump campaign communication to these groups, then their efforts should have increased whatever effects those other efforts were already producing. And if, as the scholarly work I cited at the beginning of this chapter suggests, personal appeals to vote are able to increase turnout, then the endgame ones that we know the trolls launched to activate the Trump vote could have paid dividends as well. Of course efforts to demobilize, mobilize, and shift votes matter only if the messages are persuasive, and appropriate voters are influenced in consequential states. Accordingly, we now turn to assessing the sophistication of the trolls' posts and other activities.

6

The Fourth Troll Prerequisite
Persuasive Appeals

I f the trolls' message itself was unpersuasive, its thematic alignment with Trump's appeals and its precision delivery to the right voters were for naught. Moreover, if the content was alienating, history and common sense tell us that the candidate would be better off if it were left unsent. Although rare, such missteps have occurred. So offensive was the Goldwater film titled *Choice* in 1964 that supporters of the incumbent Democratic president Lyndon Johnson bootlegged a copy for use as a fund-raiser. In a similar vein, a number of political aspirants have been burned by supportive independent expenditure and political action committees that misunderstood the dynamics on the ground. Fearing just such an effect, in 2002 Republican Norm Coleman officially disavowed the message of one such group that was alleging that his opponent, incumbent Minnesota senator Paul Wellstone, was a pot-smoking alcoholic communist. Hence prerequisite four. To create an effect, a message must be persuasive.

As the activating and suppressing appeals I cited in recent pages suggest, the Russian messaging played effectively to the fears and concerns of decisive voting blocs in a fashion designed to magnify the sense of cultural and economic anxiety that was a key factor driving a Republican vote. Although sometimes more extreme than his, these Kremlin-backed appeals complemented messages advanced by Trump and his campaign. Additionally, as I noted in my discussion of the efforts to mobilize white evangelicals and shift or suppress the Sanders vote, the strategic release of damaging hacked content created an anti-Clinton news frame, with its seeming confirmation not only that the Democratic National Committee (DNC) had disadvantaged the Vermont Independent but also that some on that organization's staff disparaged Bernie and that a key Clinton aide was dismissive of evangelicals and Republican Catholics.

As I noted earlier, the Russians began their courtship of kindred spirits with benign appeals that signaled that they and their target audiences shared common values. More extreme ones followed. The Albright study of six sites describes the progression well by observing that on Facebook the Russians identified issues of concern for voters through organic posts, sorted voters into groups, and then addressed the cached audience with paid ads.[1] To his list I would add a final stage: the trolls urged the cached audience to vote on Election Day.

Three complementary factors were at play as well. In the national and social media streams cascading into key battleground states, the Russians helped create a communication climate more hostile to Clinton and hospitable to Trump than it otherwise would have been. When those who directly received Russian content made it their own by sharing it with their friends, imposter messages were amplified in credible ways. And finally, although, as I noted earlier, the Russian statements contained off-putting misuses of English, their visual content was evocative and powerful. Because it had the potential to alienate the intended audience, let me begin by examining the trolls' sometimes badly broken English.

Sophisticated Audiences Could Have Been Put Off by Cues That the Russian Materials Were Created by Those Whose Native Language Was Not English

Although the reach and strategic alignment of the Russian-created materials had the potential to influence the outcome of the presidential election, as some of the content I have already quoted suggests, a major factor diminishing their power was their sometimes glaring misuse of the English language, an unsurprising lapse since the trolls reportedly were told to school themselves in the idioms of US politics by watching the Netflix series *House of Cards* and were expected, as one told a liberal Russian TV channel, "to be a redneck from Kentucky and then later you had to be some kind of white dude from Minnesota.... And then in 15 minutes, you need to be from New York, writing something in black slang."[2]

Linguistic mismatches matter because speaking like others confirms both a respect for local conventions and a communal bond. So, for instance, in 2003, when Democratic presidential hopeful John F. Kerry ordered a cheese-steak with Swiss cheese[3] (as opposed to "Wiz [Cheese Wiz] with or widdout [onions])," his lapse prompted a Philadelphia reporter to observe that "[t]he Massachusetts Democrat may as well have asked for cave-aged Appenzeller."[4] Likewise, the Russian troll content contained jarring cues that its authors were raised in a community whose native language was not English.

So, for example, odd usages recur in a "Miners for Trump" event post, which noted, "The state of Pennsylvania rose owing to multiple enterprises mining coal, producing steel, and creating the need for other jobs...," followed by this sentence fragment: "As far as Mr. Trump pursues the goal of creating more jobs and supports the working class." In a postelection analysis, Philadelphia reporter Will Bunch noted that the Russian appeals to join Miners for Trump for an October rally in Philadelphia were written "in a kind of Boris-Badenov-'Is-moose-and-squirrel' pidgin English that reeked of a close encounter with Google Translate."[5] The trolls also displayed an idiosyncratic preference for punctuating their sentiments by asking, "What the Hell?"

A revealing characteristic of the Russian language, the absence of the definite and indefinite article, is evident in odd expressions such as "out of cemetery" and "burqa is a security risk." This pattern stands out in other instances as well, including "American army has never felt such a humiliation. Let's hope Trump will amnesty [*sic*] Miller when he becomes the next President," and "'Religious' face coverings are putting American people [*sic*] at huge risk!"

Punctuation errors provide additional cues (e.g., "You cannot enter a foreign country and set up your own set of laws and regulations that contradict most of the worlds [*sic*] moral stands"). Misspellings also convey dissonant signals. In one post, for example, Martin Luther King became "Martin Luthern [*sic*] King." (Some of these oddities may have been Freudian slips, a phenomenon possibly at play when, seeming "to momentarily break character,"[6] the day after Donald Trump was elected the forty-fifth president of the United States, a Russian troll styling herself Jenna Abrams shared the popular vote tallies while tweeting "See how *your* democracy works [emphasis added]?")

Given the frequency with which errors in grammar, punctuation, and spelling appear on social media, however, those mistakes may not have stood out to everyone. If likes are any indication, the disfluencies didn't matter to some. The Russian page "Don't Shoot" elicited 249,372 expressions of approval for its picture of an assault rifle overwritten with a red slash in a circle and the message "We aren't against police [*sic*], we [*sic*] against police brutality!"

Importantly, a number of the more widely viewed messages, including the videos produced by the Russian state-owned RT (formerly Russia Today) and the tweets generated by @TEN_GOP were fluent, a fact evident in retweets, in the case of @TEN_GOP, by Trump campaign manager Kellyanne Conway, Trump national security advisor Michael Flynn, Donald Trump Jr., and conservative firebrands such as Ann Coulter[7] and right-wing commentator Jack Posobiec, who was described in *Rolling Stone* both as "a well-known alt-right troll whom Trump himself has retweeted" and a "special-projects director for Citizens for Trump, a never-officially-organized voter-fraud prevention group."[8] In a tweet he subsequently removed, Posobiec initially questioned Twitter's deletion of the @TEN_GOP content,[9] an action that the social media giant took in 2017 against accounts attributable to the Russian trolls. "Many times," Google informed a Senate investigating committee, "the misleading content looks identical to content uploaded by genuine activists."[10]

Flooding the Communication Climate of Battleground States

As I noted in chapter 2, by amplifying anti-Clinton and pro-Trump messages in swing states, the trolls helped shift the communication climate in favor of anti-Clinton messaging by and among like-minded Trump supporters. Support for this idea comes from researchers at Oxford's Computation Propaganda Project, who examined 1.2 million tweets from both the last ten days of the campaign and the period around the debates. Selected for study were those 140-character messages that included location information, a link, and an election-related hashtag. Of those that fell into this category, around 20 percent could be characterized as "polarizing and conspiracy content," and included links to junk news, WikiLeaks, or Russian sources, like Sputnik and RT.[11] Of particular note is their finding that levels of misinformation were higher in swing states than in noncontested ones. It is possible, they conclude that in the closing days of the 2016 campaign, Twitter users in key states got more fake news than real news and more polarizing content than substantive information about consequential differences between the major contenders. Of course, not all of this originated with the Russians. But the evidence marshaled in this book suggests that they were part of the process of upping the weight of the anti-Clinton content in the media mix in the final phase of the election.

Liking and Sharing Increased Impact

The persuasive advantage of social media posts over traditional ads is obvious. Among the many things that are off-putting about political ads on radio and TV is their transparent intent to persuade, a characteristic cued by the required disclaimer indicating sponsorship. When social media posts are relayed by a friend rather than a campaign, they sidestep that hurdle. To increase the chances that those receiving the messages would identify with the messenger, the Russian trolls created accounts supposedly from personable swing-voters. Former FBI agent Clint Watts told the Senate Intelligence Committee that "you see somebody and they look exactly like you, even down to the pictures."[12] Among the imposters was the persona Melvin Redick of Harrisburg, Pennsylvania, described by the *New York Times* as "a friendly-looking American with a backward baseball cap and a young daughter" who "turned out to be a remarkably elusive character. No Melvin Redick appears in Pennsylvania records, and his photos seem to be borrowed from an unsuspecting Brazilian."[13] Redick's profile "lists Central High School in Philadelphia and Indiana University of Pennsylvania as his alma maters; neither has any record of his attendance. In one of his photos, this purported Pennsylvania lifer is sitting in a restaurant in Brazil—and in another, his daughter's bedroom appears to have a Brazilian-style electrical outlet."[14]

Even if the original source hides behind a benign pseudonym, likes, shares, and comments telegraph that our peers accept the shared ideas. We are disposed to embrace content certified by others who share our values.[15] Additionally, belief that one's own community endorses the content increases both uncritical acceptance of it and one's disposition to share it with friends. This is the process of interpersonal influence known as "two-step flow" that I discussed in chapter 2. At the same time, by liking, sharing, and commenting we increase our own commitment to the expressed sentiment. High levels of perceived communal agreement also prompt more sharing. In a corollary effect known as the spiral of silence, also explored in chapter 2, the sense that one's own views are outliers increases the likelihood that, instead of dissenting, we will disengage.

In the Russian posts, some of the appeals to endorse content were explicit. So, for example, the Kremlin-tied Facebook page "Being Patriotic" posted a close-up of a supposed homeless veteran overlaid with the appeal "Like and Share If You Think Our Veterans Must Get Benefits Before Refugees." In a fear-based appeal of the sort discussed in chapter 2, another troll message asked "Who is behind this mask? A man? A woman? A terrorist?" Also superimposed on that post's picture of women in burqas[16] was the plea "Like and share if you want Burqa banned in America. Stop all invaders." That appeal elicited 1,100 comments and 55,000 shares.

The virality of that instance is not unique. Facebook's data indicate that the 29 million Americans who directly received the Facebook troll posts transformed them into signals of communal identity as they diffused them to the newsfeeds of about 97 million others for a total reach of Russian Facebook content (including ads) of 126 million.[17] That figure translates to nearly one out of four in the total US population, or roughly half of the adults.

Securing viewer likes for specific types of content also is a means of identifying individuals susceptible to subsequent messaging, a topic that I will treat at greater length in chapter 7. Indeed, one important study confirmed that Facebook "likes" predict political attitudes better than do human assessments.[18] That scholarly finding is important because the more than 3,500 Russian Facebook ads now in public view were targeted by generic interests, a method that by one account exhibits "a lower level of sophistication than targeting a voter"[19] but that may nonetheless be effective.

Notably some forms of generic issue interest such as concerns about immigration may have carried high predictive power in 2016. Moreover, the groups that were the object of efforts to mobilize and demobilize—including

Figure 6.1 "Down With Hillary!" Facebook event from the "Being Patriotic" account.

young liberals, blacks, those tied to the military, and evangelicals—were not difficult to target demographically. And the revelation that "Russian-linked Facebook ads specifically targeted Michigan and Wisconsin,"[20] the two most closely decided states in the nation, suggests that the trolls were more sophisticated than some accounts suggest.

The troll content was designed to be engaging, even lighthearted. Early-stage messages crafted to elicit likes included fanciful boxing matches. One of these portraying Satan wrestling Jesus bore the caption "Press 'like' to help Jesus win!" In it the dialogue reads:

SATAN: IF I WIN CLINTON WINS!
JESUS: NOT IF I CAN HELP IT!

PRESS 'LIKE' TO HELP JESUS WIN!

Figure 6.2 "Army of Jesus" Facebook post featuring Satan and Jesus arm-wrestling while wearing boxing gloves.

SATAN: If I win Clinton wins!
JESUS: Not if I can help it!

The accompanying appeal of this sponsored content casts Trump as a candidate with "godly moral principles" who is not only "honest" but "cares deeply for this country." By contrast, Clinton is "evil," has committed crimes, and lies.

Another iteration cast Clinton as Satan about to punch Jesus. Viewers could cheer Jesus on by "liking" the message. The act of registering approval of such posts made it possible for trolls to recontact susceptible

Figure 6.3 "Army of Jesus" Facebook post featuring a satanic Clinton and Jesus arm-wrestling while wearing boxing gloves.

constituencies with later appeals. So too the arm-wrestling contest between Satan and Christ.

Importantly, the Russians both created original messaging and amplified the impact of already existing US-generated content. "YouTube videos of police beatings on American streets. A widely circulated internet hoax about Muslim men in Michigan collecting welfare for multiple wives. A local news story about two veterans brutally mugged on a freezing winter night. All of these were recorded, posted or written by Americans," observed an article in the *New York Times* in October 2017.[21] "Yet all ended up becoming grist for a network of

Facebook pages linked to a shadowy Russian company that has carried out propaganda campaigns for the Kremlin, and which is now believed to be at the center of a far-reaching Russian program to influence the 2016 presidential election."

Visual Telegraphy Increases Virality and Memorability

From the 1988 mug shot of "Willie Horton" to the image of 2004 Democratic nominee John Kerry windsurfing, the history of political persuasion is filled with evidence that visuals can be powerfully telegraphic and evocative. The likelihood that the Russian-bred content would spread and be quickly and uncritically processed was enhanced by its use of such visuals[22] and by the emotionally charged nature of their messages.[23] So, for example, American flags and a bald eagle appeared in a "Being Patriotic" ad whose message ("welcome every patriot we can reach") generated 530,000 impressions and 72,000 ad clicks, at a cost of 330,000 Rubles ($5,700).[24] In similar fashion, a "Heart of Texas" ad picturing a line of Texas Rangers on horseback, a bolt of lightning breaking through the clouds in the background, condemned the Clinton-Obama policy of "amnesty" for "illegals" and warned "DON'T MESS WITH TX BORDER PATROL. ALWAYS GUIDED BY GOD." Another shows Clinton's face obscured by a dramatic black X. As I discussed in an earlier chapter, magnifying an attack used in independent expenditure US-generated anti-Clinton ads, an Instagram image from the IRA-backed "american.veterans" featured a grieving widow embracing a flag-draped coffin, as the text recalled a Clinton statement taken out of context from the Benghazi hearings: "Hillary Asks 'What Difference Does it Make?' Follow Veterans_US If You Know The Difference."

Visual and verbal memes were mutually reinforcing. Where hashtags called for incarcerating Clinton (e.g., "#Hillary4Prison"), so too did posts showing her in prison garb. The Russians personified that meme by hiring a person to impersonate Clinton wearing prison stripes at a troll-created Florida rally. Fake Facebook accounts such as "Clinton FRAUDation" telegraphed why the former Secretary of State should be jailed. A troll ad declared "Ohio Wants Hillary for Prison."[25]

Artful Deception

In rallies and online, the Russians increased the amount of anti-Clinton deception circulating in 2016. Accordingly, a placard at a supposedly "pro-Clinton" July 2016 rally proclaimed "Support Hillary. Save American Muslims."[26] The same poster falsely quoted the Democratic Party's nominee declaring "I think Sharia Law will be a powerful new direction of freedom." The Russian trolls also upped the amount of viral deception circulating against the Democrat by diffusing such false claims as 50,000 homeless veterans are starving and dying, Clinton Foundation donations went to the Clintons themselves, and the double-barreled whopper that as a young lawyer Clinton was fired by the Watergate Committee for lying.

Deceptive uses of the hacked content were on vivid display when the Russian poseurs cropped content to distort an article Clinton had forwarded to Podesta. The refashioning made it seem as if the former Secretary of State had used a racial slur to describe a person who was a Muslim. In an op-ed in an Israeli outlet, the author of the forwarded piece had observed that the police investigating a case in which a man who was Muslim was left to die may have thought of him as a "sand n-----." As an NBC analysis discovered, the trolls' dirty work created the illusion that "Clinton was referring to Muslims using the epithet." The final Kremlin-tied product took the form of posts such as one October 15, 2016, tweet saying, "RT @ObamaBash: Never #HillaryBecause While calling Trump a racist in a leaked email she referred to a Muslim man as a 'SAND N-----,' " from user @hyddrox.[27]

In a like vein, NBC found that when his brother asked John Podesta in an email that was later hacked whether he planned to attend a "Spirit Cooking" dinner party by performance artist Marina Abramović, the Russians turned that overture into a confession that the family was involved in satanic rituals funded by the Clinton Foundation:

- "BREAKING: Clinton Foundation Paid Occult 'Spirit Cooking' Priestess 10K For 'Operational Support' "—@WorldnewsPoli (November 5, 2016)

- "RT @_Makada_: WikiLeaks: Clinton Campaign Chair John Podesta Attended Satanic 'Spirit Cooking' Ritual #SpiritCooking"—@_NickLuna_ (November 4, 2016)

- "RT @KevinAnth: I liked a @YouTube video from @markdice https://t.co/jPvIB1pNTr Hillary Clinton 'Spirit Cooking' Satanic Ritual"—@JohnLarsen

Here too conservative sites amplified the deceptive messaging. The radio host and Fox News personality Sean Hannity tweeted "LEAKED EMAIL appears to link Clinton Campaign Chairman to bizarre occult ritual."[28] The *Drudge Report* tweeted out a similar message.

It is tempting to dismiss as beyond belief allegations such as those that accused Clinton of "heading a secret pedophilia ring in the United States," said that she funded or was being funded by ISIS supporters, photoshopped her image to show her shaking hands with the mastermind of the 9/11 attacks, or insinuated that her aide, Huma Abedin, had "ties to radical Islam."[29] Yet some found such nonsense plausible. An *Economist/ YouGov* poll revealed that "[o]ne of the most notorious internet rumors of the 2016 presidential campaign, that there was a pedophile ring in the Clinton campaign, with code words embedded in the hacked emails of Clinton campaign manager John Podesta, is seen as 'probably' or 'definitely' true by more than a third of American adults."[30] Importantly, the poll "was conducted after an armed North Carolina man tried to 'self-investigate' the claim by going to the District of Columbia pizza restaurant that was alleged to be the center of the ring earlier this month [December 2016] and found nothing. But even afterwards only 29% are sure the allegation is 'definitely' not true."[31]

While accepting false allegations is problematic in its own right, so too is expanding the audience's tolerance for extreme rhetoric.[32] Under some circumstances, discourse norms can change quickly. An experiment conducted before and immediately after the 2016 election identified such a norm shift in the form of a causal relationship between Donald Trump's political popularity and "individuals' willingness to publicly express xenophobic views."[33]

In short the evidence that the trolls manufactured content that was liked and shared is cogent. Their use of visual telegraphy is noteworthy. At least some of their deceptions gained traction. Their messaging affected the communication climate by increasing the amount of anti-Clinton content circulating in it. Where many of their posts contained disfluencies and odd grammar, others were indistinguishable from US-generated ones. And notably, much of what they did simply amplified existing US content. But persuasive messaging means little if it fails to reach a susceptible audience capable of voting in a decisive state. In the next chapter I will explore how the trolls targeted needed voters.

7

The Fifth Troll Prerequisite
Well-Targeted Content

The Russian trolls had access to a ready-to-read playbook on how to reach voters susceptible to mobilizing or demobilizing appeals. This "how-to" manual took the form of punditry and reporting in mainstream news, the easy-to-use targeting capacities of the platforms, and hacked Democratic voter data. But before assessing its utility, let's first ask whether the troll messaging was drowned out by other campaign stimuli and if their energies were dissipated on activities unrelated to the election of Clinton or Trump.

Unsurprisingly, the platforms' most common argument against Russian influence suggests that if the total amount of their social media activity is the numerator, and the denominator is the sum of all campaign-related content, there is relatively little Kremlin-tied communication in the 2016 media stream. Facebook made a version of this argument in April 2017 when it declared that "while we acknowledge the ongoing challenge of monitoring and guarding against information operations, the reach of known operations during the US election of 2016 was statistically very small compared to overall engagement on political issues."[1] In a similar vein, a January 2018 update from Twitter noted that "automated election-related content associated with Russian signals represented a very small fraction of the overall activity on Twitter in the ten-week period preceding the 2016 election." Specifically, Twitter claimed that "we have identified 13,512 additional accounts, for a total of 50,258 automated accounts that we identified as Russian-linked and Tweeting election-related content during the election period, representing approximately two one-hundredths of a percent (0.016%) of the total accounts on Twitter at the time."[2] The same argument was advanced by Russian president Putin, who alleged that "[t]he information coming from media outlets like Russia Today . . . turned out to be one hundredth of a percent of the overall information flow in the United States, just one hundredth of a percent. Do you think that this fraction had any impact on the election? This is just nonsense, don't you see?"[3]

The flaw in these exculpatory assertions is that the messaging that matters is not the total in the numerator but the amount that reaches the right voters. This is the case because political targeting works by delivering tailored messages to susceptible voters in locations that matter. Efficient means of audience identification reduce the amount of communication needed to influence an election.

Alternative arguments against troll influence suggest that the Russian operatives were lousy at targeting and focused on ends not tied to electoral outcome. Making the first point, on September 6, 2017, Facebook reported that "[a]bout one-quarter of the Russian ads were geographically targeted, and of those, more ran in 2015 than 2016."[4] Advancing the same underlying point, Senator Richard Burr (R-NC) stressed that "almost five times more ads were targeted at the state of Maryland than of Wisconsin."[5] "In particular," he noted, "where voters in Maryland, a state firmly in the Democratic column, were the intended viewers of 262 ads, those in the contested state of Wisconsin were the audience for 55. More ads targeted Washington, D.C., than the battleground commonwealth of Pennsylvania."[6] Of course, a focus on ads ignores the far greater reach of the trolls' organic content.

Skeptics of Russian influence on the election's outcome have also pointed[7] to posts and ads focusing on Texas.[8] A number of Russian accounts, such as "Heart of Texas" and @TEN_GOP (which falsely identified itself as a

Tennessee Republican group) did indeed bear names tied to nonbattleground states. And, Senator Burr has pointed out that, since most of the fifty-five ads run in Wisconsin appeared before that state's primary, they could not have been a "surgically executed" attempt to elect Trump. However, pre-primary efforts in Wisconsin could have helped identify susceptible voters in what turned out to be a decisive Electoral College state and reinforce antagonism to Obama and, hence, his heir apparent, or done both. At the same time, by emphasizing issues central to his candidacy, Heart of Texas's focus on gun rights, illegal immigration, border security, and neglected veterans may have been attempting to drive up Trump's popular vote.

There is an election-related explanation for a focus on other nonbattleground locales as well. What the Maryland tack and D.C. focus suggest to me is that the Russians were trying to stir intergroup hostilities in the backyard of a major media market. After all, virtually every widely read and viewed news outlet in the country has a D.C. staff. Recall that, since Baltimore, Maryland, and Ferguson, Missouri, were the sites of violent protests against the police shooting of black men, both locales attracted sustained national media attention. Capitalizing on this reality, the Russians bought a Facebook ad geo-targeting those two cities.[9] "All of those protesters in Ferguson, your hand [sic] are covered with blood! #CopsWillBeCops #FergusonShooting," tweeted a Russian troll styling herself @EvaGreen69.[10]

According to Burr, the three most heavily targeted states were Maryland, Missouri, and New York. The Big Apple, a home base of the broadcast networks as well as the *Wall Street Journal* and the *New York Times*, was the focus of efforts by the Russian Facebook page "Being Patriotic." Using a photo of Clinton obscured by a large black X, and claiming "Hillary Clinton is the co-author of Obama's anti-police and anti-Constitutional propaganda," the Russian operatives publicized a "Down With Hillary" protest in July of 2016 outside her New York campaign headquarters. In response, 180 individuals indicated interest and 45 reported that they would attend. The same page also called for a pro-Trump demonstration on September 11, 2016, in Manhattan.[11]

The Russian trolls did create one confrontation that drew national attention, not during the campaign but as a result of discussion at the 2017

Figure 7.1 Image from a "Stop A.I. (Stop All Invaders)" Facebook post with the text "Who is behind this mask? A man? A woman? Burqa is a security risk and it should be banned on U.S. soil!".

congressional hearings where, Burr pointed out, two Russian-created Facebook groups identifying themselves as the anti-immigrant "Heart of Texas," with 250,000 followers, and the pro-Muslim "United Muslims of America," with 320,000 followers, each posted notification of an event at a Houston Islamic Center on May 21, 2016, the first as a protest, the second as a counter-protest.[12] The resulting clash led a local news outlet to observe that

> [a] group calling themselves Heart of Texas called for the rally to protest what they consider "Islamization" of Texas—sparked in part by the recent opening of a privately funded library inside the downtown center. *The group had also encouraged followers to bring legal firearms* [emphasis added]. Although the Heart of Texas group never showed, about 10 people bearing flags of the United States, Texas and the Confederacy were there. "This is America. We have the right to speak out and protest," said Ken Reed, who wore a T-shirt emblazoned with

the phrase "White Lives Matter." "We feel Texas, our great state and the United States is being threatened by the influx of Islam."[13]

Had the dueling protests turned violent, they could have generated national news and with it heightened voter awareness of the cultural tensions the Trump campaign was attempting to magnify. If that was the trolls' goal, in this case, they failed.

However, a focus on nonbattleground activities should not obscure those that homed in on key states. So, for example, the 200,000 followers of the "Being Patriotic" Facebook page saw appeals to join "Miners for Trump" rallies in Philadelphia and Pittsburgh in October 2016.[14] A troll ad promoting one of these rallies gained 7,282 impressions.[15] Unsurprisingly, since Philadelphia is far from a coal mine, no agitators in miner's garb showed up in South Philadelphia's Marconi Plaza. But seeing miners as a natural constituency for Trump made sense. He had after all promised that ending Obama's "war on coal" would revive that sector of the economy. And the troll content served as a reminder that Trump championed miners.

As we anticipate future troll actions, it is important to recognize that their skills increased with practice, a reality evident in the fact that in fall 2016 their ads addressing miners sought out "increasingly specific demographics: from people within 50 miles of New York, to people in Allentown, Erie, and Scranton, whose job title was 'Coal miner.'"[16] Across 2016, the Russian operatives also learned new tricks by experimenting with ways to use Facebook's "lookalike custom audiences" and to improve the reach of their messages through testing.

Troll efforts to draw supporters to rallies made more headway in some locales than others. Recall that late in the campaign, the Republican nominee jetted to the Twin Cities, an adept move since that state's 46.4 percent to 45 percent victory for Hillary was much narrower than history would have forecast. So the Russians were electorally on point when in July 2016 they helped organize a protest "near Minneapolis, [where] nearly 300 people rallied in support of Philando Castile, a man fatally shot by a police officer during a traffic stop."[17] So effective were the trolls at camouflaging their identity that some locals who supported the effort continue to deny Russian involvement.[18] The Russian factotums had other successes as well. After Internet

Research Agency (IRA) operatives managed to instigate an August 20, 2016, "patriotic state-wide flash mob" in Fort Lauderdale and Coral Springs, two of the seventeen cities in the battleground Sunshine State to which appeals were made, "videos and photos" from those locations were "reposted to a Facebook page run by a local Trump campaign chair."[19] In May 2018, when House Democrats released more than 3,500 Russian ads placed on Facebook from 2015 to late 2017, they reported that in that period the trolls created 129 events, viewed by more than 300,000 people. Approximately 62,000 signaled plans to attend.[20]

In addition to being told to target "purple states like Colorado, Virginia & Florida," an unsurprising insight gleaned by undercover Russian operatives visiting the United States,[21] the trolls had access to at least three sources of information about how to identify and reach voters needed to affect the outcome: hacked voter models from battleground states, including Pennsylvania and Florida, access to punditry identifying the electoral needs of the candidates, and toolkits designed to help advertisers reach prospective customers on the platforms.

Publicly Accessible Analysis of the Candidates' Objectives and Tactics

For an operative able to make sense of English, the web is a storehouse of knowledge about the electoral needs and strategic choices facing US presidential contenders. Note the cascade of tips contained in an August 2016 CNN online article bearing the title "Florida: The Swingiest Swing State."[22] "With 29 electoral votes," it began, "Florida is the biggest prize of the battleground states. But the difference between winning and losing the Sunshine State is often very small. 'In 2012, Obama just won Florida over Romney by just over .9%,' said Susan MacManus, a distinguished professor at the University of South Florida. 'This is a fiercely fought for state.' There are currently about 4.4 million registered Republicans and nearly 4.6 million Democrats. But the voters both campaigns want are the nearly 3 million independents who give this swing state its swing." The article goes on to identify and specify their interests. "Who are they [the independents]?" it asks. "Data shows they're young, part of the influx of new residents drawn to work rather than retire.

Gone are the days a candidate could only talk about Social Security. Younger voters have other concerns including jobs and the environment."

The young aren't the only citizens coveted by both parties. "These swing voters include Hispanics," says the online post. "In a state long known for the influence of the Cuban population, the number of Puerto Ricans with less traditional right-leaning politics is growing quickly." Which party is courting them? "Republican organizers say they are paying close attention to these new arrivals. 'We're focused on the economy and really how we can help them really achieve that American dream that most Puerto Ricans are looking for,' said Sofia Boza, the deputy Hispanic media press secretary at the Republican National Committee." Where can one find these prized citizens? "The I-4 corridor between Tampa and Daytona Beach is the hottest battle ground in this battleground state."

How could a troll know that this is the area on which the Republicans are focusing? "Trump was there last week." How could a Russian in St. Petersburg know that Florida should take priority over other battleground states? "Since early June, more money has been spent on television ads in Florida than any other state, with Clinton forces outspending Trump and his allies $20 million versus $1.6 million." However, the candidates don't need more TV spending. "But Republicans say the key to Florida isn't going big with TV. It's going small. Identifying what they call 'turfs'—pockets of 6,000 to 7,000 voters where they focus hundreds of local volunteers. It's grassroots politics 101, straight out of the Obama Florida playbook." What is the Clinton strategy? "The Clinton campaign is trying to rewrite the playbook, going after Republican voters. 'We have a lot of Republicans particularly in south Florida that aren't happy with their nominee who we're having conversation with,' said Scott Arcenneaux, a senior adviser for Hillary Clinton for America."

Where else should Kremlin-tied efforts to elect a candidate place resources? "When most people think of battleground America, they think of Florida and Ohio, two of only three states (along with Nevada) that have voted for the winner of every presidential election since 1996," noted an essay in *FiveThirtyEight* titled "Why Pennsylvania Could Decide the 2016 Election."[23] "They tend *not* to think of Pennsylvania as a classic 'swing state.' . . . But in 2016, Pennsylvania could be the keystone of the Electoral College and the ultimate arbiter of whether Donald Trump or Hillary Clinton resides at

1600 Pennsylvania Avenue." How would an outsider know where to concentrate? "Western Pennsylvania is driving the state's rightward drift—its voting patterns now resemble greater Appalachia's more than those of the Philadelphia suburbs. Once dominated by steel towns and union Democrats, the region has reveled in a fracking/natural gas boom that has more recently experienced a downturn and has revolted against EPA [Environmental Protection Agency] regulations."

The preoccupation of pundits and reporters with polling and the horse race, a phenomenon documented in 2016 in Thomas E. Patterson's Kennedy School study,[24] could have increased the precision of Russian targeting as well. Published polls also revealed constituencies that needed shoring up by each major party aspirant. At the same time, reporting on the candidates' travel schedules provided cues about which states kept them awake at night.

Whatever the source of the Russian insight that Florida was a crucial state, the trolls got the message. Information released as part of the Mueller indictment revealed that the state that decided the 2000 election was an object of special Kremlin attention in 2016. "If we lose Florida, we lose America. We can't let it happen, right? What about organizing a YUGE pro-Trump flash mob in every Florida town?" noted an impersonator cloaked in the pseudonym Matt Skiber.[25] The Hillary prison cage on the truck bed that I mentioned earlier was built in Florida and inspired imitators there. The trolls also focused their efforts on creating "Florida Goes Trump" rallies across the state. The February 2018 Mueller indictment revealed as well that "Defendants and their co-conspirators also used false U.S. personas to contact multiple grassroots groups supporting then-candidate Trump in an unofficial capacity. Many of these groups agreed to participate in the 'Florida Goes Trump' rallies and serve as local coordinators."[26] Presumably anticipating a close outcome there, the St. Petersburg saboteurs alleged in early November that "tens of thousands of ineligible mail in Hillary voters are being reported in Broward County, Florida."[27] The county is, of course, a Democratic stronghold.

Also on the trolls' radar screen, by one account, were Wisconsin and Michigan. According to a media report of remarks by Senate Intelligence Committee member Mark Warner (D-VA), those two decisive states were a focus of special Russian attention. "The Russians appear to have targeted women and African-Americans in two of the three decisive states, Wisconsin and Michigan, 'where the Democrats were too brain dead to realize those states were even in play,'" Warner reportedly noted. "Twitter's and Facebook's search engines in those states were overwhelmed, he [Warner] said, meaning they couldn't discern fake news from real news. 'On your news feed, you suddenly got ... 'Hillary Clinton's sick' or 'Hillary Clinton's stealing money from the State Department,' said Warner."[28] This evidence is important because, as I suggested in chapter 2, imbalances in messaging tend to shift votes.

Stolen Voter Models

As part of the release of hacked data, Democratic Congressional Campaign Committee (DCCC) turnout models for Florida and Pennsylvania, among other states, were posted online.[29] The Mueller indictments revealed that the hackers also had the Democrat's presidential turnout model. Such access could have helped the trolls identify susceptible voters. A portion of the hacked content was delivered to a Florida operative. A week and a half after Aaron Nevins, a Florida GOP lobbyist who is also a campaign consultant and blogger, solicited material from Guccifer 2.0, he received 2.5 gigabytes of Democratic Congressional Campaign Committee (DCCC) documents in his Dropbox account. Of the hacked Florida voter files that he posted on his blog, Nevins said, "Basically, if this was a war, this is the map to where all the troops are deployed."[30]

The purloined trove included what Nevins described as "the targeting spreadsheets," which "contain the Democrats targeting plans in several battleground states, including the Early Voting Targeting plans in Florida, Kentucky, Pennsylvania, Texas, West Virginia, and Virginia, broken down by city/district/county/media market."[31] Of particular interest to an operative, whether foreign or domestic, focused on the Sunshine State was a "pivot table that allows you to easily sort the Democrat's targeting priorities throughout Florida by district and city!" For example, the Democrats in Florida had "a target base of 50469 in St. Petersburg and 1190 in St. Pete Beach. Of those in St. Pete Beach, 633 will be getting persuasion pieces and 376 are hardcore Democrats identified for turnout."

Another form of theft is noteworthy for what it portends about future foreign interventions. In Illinois, Russian hacking of the election system "gained access to the state's voter database, which contained information such as names, dates of birth, genders, driver's licenses and partial Social Security numbers on 15 million people, half of whom were active voters. As many as 90,000 records were ultimately compromised."[32] Bloomberg also reports that "[a]ccording to [a] leaked NSA [National Security Agency] document, hackers working for Russian military intelligence were trying to take over the computers of 122 local election officials just days before the Nov. 8 election."

Targeting Structures in Social Media

Since the tech giants' platforms were designed to efficiently reach the customers coveted by advertisers, it is unsurprising that they have unique capacities and user-friendly means to home in on desired audience members. Among other ways, Facebook permits messengers to single out users by ideology (i.e., very liberal, moderate, conservative, very conservative), political affiliation, political activity, a sensitivity issue (e.g., gun control), news consumption, county, ZIP code, location within a five-mile radius, personal profile, demographics, and interests.

The Russians exploited these capacities. So, for example, the Facebook ad showing Jesus arm-wrestling Satan was targeted to reach "People age 18 to 65+ interested in Christianity, Jesus, God, Ron Paul and media personalities such as Laura Ingraham, Rush Limbaugh, Bill O'Reilly and Mike Savage."[33] By contrast, "People ages 18 to 65+ interested in military veterans, including those from the Iraq, Afghanistan and Vietnam wars" were the audience for the Instagram ad featuring the widow sobbing over the casket of her slain husband. Ads featuring Muslims who supported Clinton's candidacy "were targeted at Facebook users who might fear Muslims."[34] "American tech companies have set up the infrastructure needed to 'hack an election,'" argues data journalist and scholar Jonathan Albright. "Russian groups simply purchased the ability to target specific groups of Americans before, during, and *after* the election through Facebook's self-service psychographic advertising services."[35]

The structures in place to facilitate "following" and "sharing" provide other targeting cues. Facebook's business model, notes University of North Carolina information and library science professor Zeynep Tufekci, "involves having people go to the site for social interaction, only to be quietly subjected to an enormous level of surveillance. The results of that surveillance are used to fuel a sophisticated and opaque system for narrowly targeting advertisements and other wares to Facebook's users."[36] Accordingly, the trolls focused material on those "users in cities that had had episodes of racial unrest, including Ferguson, Missouri, Baltmore and Cleveland," who also had liked the Russian-backed "Black Matters" page.[37] In like fashion, "People ages 18 to 65+ who like the [troll] group 'Being Patriotic' or have friends connected to the group" were the intended audience for a March 2016 ad amplifying a news account in which the mother of one of those killed in the attack on the compound in Benghazi said there was a "special place in Hell" for individuals like Clinton.[38]

We know from the Mueller troll indictment that the Russian operatives "tracked the performance of the content they posted over social media [and] . . . tracked the size of the online U.S. audiences reached through posts, different types of engagement with the posts (such as likes, comments, and reposts), changes in audience size, and other metrics."[39] In this process, bots can serve as sophisticated stalkers. "[B]ots can be programmed to search for certain keywords and particular users," notes Sue Halpern, a scholar-in-residence at Middlebury. "That could account for why Russian bots were propagating anti-Clinton messages in places like Wisconsin: they might have simply been following the lead of other pro-Trump Twitter users. Moreover, once the bots' Russian handlers saw attention being focused on the Rust Belt near the end of the campaign by Trump's team, they would not have needed insider information to direct their fake accounts to spread false information in those precincts."[40]

Identifying those who "like" a certain message carries with it additional information useful in addressing others of similar disposition. Indeed, in an interview with the *Guardian*, Andy Wigmore, the communication director of the Brexit group Leave.EU, characterized a "like" on Facebook as their campaign's most "potent weapon."[41] "[U]sing artificial intelligence, as we did, tells you all sorts of things about that individual and how to convince them with what sort of advert," he notes. "And you knew there would also be other people in their network who liked what they liked, so you could spread. And then you follow them. The computer never stops learning and it never stops monitoring." In one large-scale study, "likes" were used not only to accurately differentiate Republicans from Democrats and African Americans from Caucasians but also to predict such "sensitive personal attributes" as "sexual orientation, ethnicity, religious and political views, personality traits, intelligence, happiness, use of addictive substances, parental separation, age, and gender."[42]

One reason to want to know the extent to which, if at all, the Russian targeting was similar to that of the Trump campaign is that, in addition to Facebook's online tools, to which both the Republican and Russian campaigns had access, the Trump consultants benefited from direct help from employees of that platform. In the words of campaign aides Corey Lewandowski and David Bossie, Facebook sent "someone over to give the campaign a hand setting up and teaching them the platforms."[43] Moreover, "[w]henever the [Trump] team needed help with Facebook, they would call—who else?—Facebook, and the company would give him [digital director Brad Parscale] all the help he needed." The Republican's staff may have benefited as well if its digital ad firm, Cambridge Analytica, made use of Facebook data now known to have been gotten under false pretenses and without the consent of millions of users whose personal data were mined.[44] A convergent Russian-Trump targeting strategy could occur under a number of different conditions. Someone in the Trump orbit could have shared the expertise gotten from Facebook or from this unauthorized mining. Or Facebook's online tools coupled with sophisticated stalking by bots could have helped the Russian operatives achieve the goals they and the Trump campaign shared.

Whereas in November 2017, Facebook General Counsel Colin Stretch told an investigating committee, "*We have not seen overlap* in the targeting [emphasis added]," in January 2018, the tech giant reported that it had found "only what appears to be *be insignificant overlap* [emphasis added]" between the ad targeting of the Kremlin group and the Trump presidential campaign.[45] At the same time the platform noted that it had not located evidence that the Russian IRA based its ad buys on US voter registration data and characterized that Kremlin-backed entity's activities as "relatively rudimentary, targeting broad locations and interests." Importantly Facebook also stated that it "does not believe it is in a position to substantiate or disprove allegations of possible collusion" between the Russian efforts and the Trump campaign.[46] In sum, we do not know at this time whether the Russians had Trump campaign help in figuring out how to magnify turnout for Trump and minimize it for Clinton.

Neither the existence of troll activities outside the battleground states nor their amount of messaging establishes that key voters in consequential states were or were not reached by the Russians. Three sources of targeting knowledge increased the likelihood that they could find such voters: platforms built to facilitate locating and addressing subpopulations of buyers and hence voters; public analyses of candidate needs, plans, and priorities in the press; and voter plans hacked from Democratic files.

For the trolls to have affected the outcome, a number of conditions would have had to have been met. They include: the content would have to be: extensive enough to make a difference in an environment surfeited with other campaign messaging; consistent with Trump's electoral interests; focused on constituencies whose mobilization or demobilization was critical to a Trump victory; consistent with what we know about persuasive communication; and have reached and affected needed voters in key states. Although knowable, the extent to which trolls reached such voters is an open question. More readily confirmed are the ways in which they helped shape the legacy media flow. In particular, their bots contributed to spikes in trending that in turn helped drive anti-Clinton content into news.

By contrast, for the hackers and their abettors to have influenced the outcome, in the campaign's final month they would have had to shape the news and debate agendas and shift the messaging balance against Clinton. Because news coverage injected the Russian-hacked content into the electoral dialogue at key points in the closing month of the election, the case for the impact of the theft and release of Democratic content is stronger than that for the impact of the trolls. It is that case which the chapters in Part III address.

Let me conclude Part II by situating it in the overall structure of the book. The task of Part I was setting in place two crucial premises. Accordingly chapter 1 justified the conclusion that the Russians masterminded the hacking and social media machinations of interest. To establish that it is plausible that their spies and saboteurs affected votes and voters through interpersonal and mass-mediated means, chapter 2 reprised the kinds of changes produced in past campaigns by priming, agenda setting, framing, contagion, and reweighting the communication environment.

With these predicates in place, Part II focused on five preconditions of troll influence. In turn the chapters asked whether their messaging was sufficiently widespread, well aligned with Trump's interests, addressed to constituencies he needed to influence, followed established principles of persuasion, and was well targeted. The answer to four of these questions is yes. In the case of the fifth, there is suggestive but inconclusive evidence of effective targeting.

Before turning to Part III of the book, let me pause to set the impact of the Russian-hacked content in sharp relief. Doing so will take the form of thought experiments designed to answer two questions: If the private conversations and documents of winning campaigns of elections past had been burgled, could the release of the unearthed information have changed their electoral equations? And if Podesta's counterparts in the Trump campaign had been hacked and the contents WikiLeak'd at the same rate and volume as the purloined Democratic content, how would that more symmetrical state of affairs have affected the media mix?

So frequently did stolen Democratic content punctuate the media agenda and so recurrent was its use that its presence now seems both inevitable and unobjectionable. After all, the Democrats did not contest its accuracy and it is possible that at least some of it could have been uncovered by the reporters themselves. At the same time, its origins seem irrelevant. After all, the private conversations of advisors seep into news through back channels all the time. The conclusion that its publication was unproblematic seems obvious. After all, didn't it reveal things about Hillary Clinton that the public was entitled to know and the press had surmised all along? Indeed, its release even seems laudable. Why shouldn't the public know what Hillary said in her speeches and what an aide wrote to a friend about conservative Catholics?

Lost in these "after alls" are three key differences between press "discoveries" and ones phished by foreign nationals. The Democratic content was stolen by foreign agents, deployed to rescue one candidacy and under-mine another, and was strategically released at key points in the election cycle to those ends.

**

A Brief Interlude of What-Ifs

Although he won the Electoral College 303–219, in 1960 John Kennedy bested Richard Nixon in the popular vote by just over 112,000 votes. Had the Massachusetts Democrat failed to carry Illinois, which he won by 9,000 votes, and had he also come up short in Texas, which he took by 46,000, Nixon would have won the Electoral College. Suppose that just before the 1960 Democratic Convention was about to begin in Los Angeles, an enterprising burglar unearthed and released private documentation that Kennedy required serious ongoing treatment for Addison's Disease, a diagnosis that his campaign had vigorously denied but which was confirmed when autopsy results were released years after his death. Or, speculate that just before the first general election debate, a sleuth passed evidence to an enterprising journalist confirming that the book *Profiles in Courage*, for which the rising Democratic star had been awarded the Pulitzer Prize in 1957, was largely ghostwritten. And to compound the hypothetical, imagine that just before the final Kennedy-Nixon debate, evidence emerged that the Democratic nominee's father had pulled strings to ensure that his son would be awarded the Navy and Marine Corp medal and Purple Heart for supposed heroism involving the rescue of his crew after the sinking of PT 109. Each would subject JFK to the claim that he had dissembled about a consequential matter. Each undercuts a key element in his carefully crafted biography.

And just for good measure, let me posit that as voters were about to trudge to the polls, they learned that instead of using it to blunt anti-Catholic bigotry, the Kennedy campaign was deploying an ad edited from his speech to the Protestant ministers of the Greater Houston Ministerial Association to boost Catholic turnout. As time buy data later confirmed, that ad was airing intensively in Catholic strongholds to draw what Kennedy termed his "co-religionists" from the Republican fold into which roughly half had flocked in 1956. (Those seeking evidence for these four revelations can find it in *Packaging the Presidency*.) With such supposed "strategies," "secrets," and "scandals" in the headlines, Kennedy would probably not have won that close election. But note that I could change the equation markedly by uncovering comparable details about Nixon and his campaign.

To level the gym floor in 2016, imagine that interlopers uncovered and released all of the 2015–2016 emails found in the accounts of Michael Flynn, Donald Trump Jr., Kellyanne Conway, and Trump's lawyer Michael Cohen. Under these circumstances, in the final debate, Hillary would have reminded voters of confirmed Russian and WikiLeaks overtures to Trump's oldest son and namesake. Voters would have learned that an "executive at Vkontakte, or VK, Russia's equivalent to Facebook, emailed Donald Trump Jr. and social media director Dan Scavino in January [2016] and again in November [2016] . . . , offering to help promote Trump's campaign to its nearly 100 million users."[47] Russian ties would have become a dominant narrative, with the revelation that Trump's son-in-law Jared Kushner, Donald Trump Jr., and then–Trump-campaign-chair Paul Manafort met with a Russian government-tied lawyer at Trump Tower in June 2016 after being promised information hostile to Clinton, a promise that elicited an emailed response from Donald Trump Jr. that enthused, "If it's what you say I love it." And for those more interested in the salacious than the subversive, the *Access Hollywood* storyline would have been revived with the revelation of an alleged payment and nondisclosure agreement that supposedly suppressed an account of a 2006 consensual sexual encounter between Trump and an adult film star.[48]

Awash in raw material, reporters would have reveled in publicizing the clashes and candid back-and-forth of Republican campaign insiders discussing tactical maneuvers to deal with the Trump University lawsuit, the *Access Hollywood* tape, the *Wall Street Journal* account of the role of the *National Enquirer* in silencing a former Playboy Playmate who was allegedly a Trump mistress,[49] and press revelations of questionable dealings by the Trump Foundation. Then imagine as well that something that Trump had refused to disclose, a revelation akin to Clinton's "Wall Street speeches," was opened to public view. Perhaps his complete medical records or tax returns or both. The stream of hacked content about Clinton that gushed out in October and early November would now be matched by a flood of Trump "secrets."

As I suggested in chapter 2, one of the reasons that, in the past, ads aired in contested races rarely shifted votes is that the effects of one side's messaging blunted those of the other and vice versa. When the amount of messaging is roughly balanced on each side, and the content is comparably damaging or advantageous and deployed with equal skill, the effects tend to cancel each other out.[50] In October and early November, the hacked Democratic content reweighted the news environment in Trump's favor.

Not so in my thought experiment where messages hostile to Clinton would be counterbalanced by those inimical to Trump. This change would increase the likelihood that voters who disliked both would split between the two contenders or alternatively vote for Hillary in greater numbers than they in fact did. In either scenario, Clinton would be more likely to carry the states needed to win the Electoral College.

The reason for playing through these hypotheticals is to suggest that Russian hacking of Democratic email and the press coverage that responded to its release unfairly altered the news message balance against Clinton. In social media, Trump and the Russians then gained the advantage that comes from fashioning attacks legitimized by mainstream press coverage of the stolen, strategically released content. With that as a backdrop, we now turn to examining the nature and extent of hacked content in news as well as in the final debates and its possible influence on the decision of FBI director James Comey to make public his decision to reopen the Clinton server investigation on October 28.

Part Three

How the Russians Affected the News and Debate Agendas in the Last Month of the Campaign

I n presidential campaigns, some days matter more than others. So, for example, the market crash made September 15, 2008, an instance of note. In 2016, the days that mattered most occurred between October 7 and November 8. In the first seventeen hours of that first date, Hurricane Nate was poised to strike the Gulf Coast states, a DHS-ODNI intelligence report confirmed that the Russians were behind the hacking of the DNC, the *Access Hollywood* tape was posted online, and a first tranche of Russian-hacked Podesta materials was WikiLeak'd. On the second of the two dates, Donald Trump was elected the 45th president of the United States.

Three major events punctuated the period in-between. Two were presidential debates, the first on October 9 and the second on the 19. The third event of note was the nine-day drama that dominated news from October 28 through November 6 as FBI agents struggled to determine whether emails found on a seized laptop would incriminate the Democratic nominee. While all of this was transpiring, an unprecedented number of early ballots—more than forty-five and a half million—were being cast for president of the United States.[1] The question of interest in this part of the book is, "By altering the media and debate agendas and the amount of negative content about Clinton in the media stream, did Russian-hacked content affect enough of those votes to change the outcome of the 2016 election?"

The case that I will make in the chapters in Part III is that the WikiLeak'd material added arguments to Trump's rhetorical arsenal, created a counter-vailing narrative to the one emanating from the release of the *Access Hollywood* tape, changed the contour of two presidential debates, and, throughout critical weeks of the general election campaign, fostered an anti-Clinton agenda and frame in news. The Democratic content accessed and leaked by the Russians also increased the amount of attack and in some cases also the level of deception actively circulating about the former First Lady. And, by possibly influencing the behavior of FBI Director James Comey, Russian activities also may have affected voters in the final week and a half of the campaign.

Before continuing, let me take a minute to note some of the interactions between the Trump campaign and WikiLeaks.

***

A Sidebar on the Trump Campaign and WikiLeaks

As I noted in an earlier chapter, the January 2017 report of the FBI, CIA, and National Security Agency confirmed that Russian trolls "amplified stories on scandals about Secretary Clinton and the role of WikiLeaks in the election campaign."[2] So too did candidate Trump. After searching transcripts from the last month of the campaign for the words "WikiLeaks" and "Trump," *PolitiFact* found that "Trump said the word 'WikiLeaks' about 137 times in campaign rallies, interviews, speeches, his tweets and other social media presence, and debates."[3]

Not only did the Republican nominee regularly invoke WikiLeak'd content in tweets and on the stump, but contacts between that entity and the

Trump campaign have been confirmed. On July 27, the real estate mogul made the plea, "Russia, if you're listening, I hope you're able to find the 30,000 emails that are missing." (The July 2018 indictments show that the Russians tried to breach Clinton's personal office servers for the first time that evening.) Responding to Trump's October 10 claim that he loved WikiLeaks,[4] emails released by Donald Trump Jr. confirm that the site reached out to the nominee's namesake to say, "Strongly suggest your dad tweets this link [wlsearch.tk] if he mentions us." Why? "There's many great stories the press are missing and we're sure some of your follows [sic] will find it." Minutes later the candidate tweeted "Very little pick-up by the dishonest media of incredible information provided by WikiLeaks. So dishonest! Rigged system!"

Additionally, on October 14, 2016, Trump's oldest son tweeted: "For those who have the time to read about all the corruption and hypocrisy all the @wikileaks emails are right here: http://wlsearch.tk/."[5] On the stump on October 31, candidate Trump observed, "This WikiLeaks is like a treasure trove," and on November 4, "Boy, I love reading those WikiLeaks."

In complementary fashion, the trolls drove the hacked content into news by amplifying strategically leaked Democratic emails and documents. Through reverse-engineering, Facebook uncovered five steps the Russians took in service of maximizing the impact of the stolen materials:

- Private and/or proprietary information was accessed and stolen from systems and services (outside of Facebook);

- Dedicated sites hosting this [sic] data were registered;

- Fake personas were created on Facebook and elsewhere to point to and amplify awareness of this [sic] data;

- Social media accounts and pages were created to amplify news accounts of and direct people to the stolen data.

- From there, organic proliferation of the messaging and data through authentic peer groups and networks was inevitable.[6]

8

The Effect of Russian Hacking
on Press Coverage

Evidence that the trolls were attuned to Trump's need for a hospitable news environment comes from an investigation by the Associated Press of "36,210 tweets from Aug. 31, 2015, to Nov. 10, 2016, posted by 382 of the Russian accounts" shared with congressional committees by Twitter.[1] "Disguised Russian agents on Twitter rushed to deflect scandalous news about Donald Trump just before last year's presidential election," concluded the study, "while straining to refocus criticism on the mainstream media and Hillary Clinton's campaign."[2] In other words, they worked feverishly to focus the media agenda on Clinton's vulnerabilities and away from Trump's. As I noted in an earlier chapter, their success was pronounced in the period surrounding the Democratic National Convention. As the following chapters will argue, it was as well in the last four and a half weeks of the campaign.

Three revelations make October 7 an especially consequential date in the history of the 2016 contest. First, at 3 p.m. on that Friday, two days before the second general election presidential debate, a joint statement from the

Department of Homeland Security (DHS) and the Office of the Director of National Intelligence (ODNI), from which I quoted at greater length earlier, declared that the Russian government had directed the "recent compromises of e-mails from U.S. persons and institutions." The same report revealed that disclosure of the email on sites such as DCLeaks.com and WikiLeaks and by Guccifer 2.0 was "consistent with the methods and motivations of Russian-directed efforts."[3]

Of that first bombshell of the day, Secretary of Homeland Security Jeh Johnson recalled, "This was the United States government accusing the Russian government of interfering in our election through cyber-hacking activity. That's a big deal, and I expected it to be above the fold, and I expected it to be something that would have a lot of currency over the following days."[4] It wasn't and didn't.

As Ned Price, a former spokesperson for the National Security Council, told the 2017 Aspen Security Forum, the media ran with that story "from 3:30 to 4:00 P.M."[5] The changeover occurred at about 4:05 p.m., when the *Washington Post* posted both the story of the so-called *Access Hollywood* tape and the hot mic recording itself.[6] That explosive revelation quickly overshadowed the DHS-ODNI document. "We had so much traffic that the system to track web traffic broke," recalled the *Washington Post's* David Fahrenthold, who posted the story and recording that catapulted the phrase "grab 'em by the pussy" into the media lexicon and the history books.[7]

On that 2005 tape, Donald Trump could be heard bragging to *Access Hollywood's* Billy Bush not only that he kissed women without their consent but that, because of his status as a star, he could do whatever else he wanted, including grabbing them "by the pussy." On the same tape, whose contents were variously described by reporters as "lewd" or "vulgar," the self-aggrandizing star of *The Apprentice* asserted that he tried but failed to "fuck" a specific married woman whose subsequent cosmetic surgery rendered her less appealing to him.

But the day wasn't yet over. As breathless cable commentary and replays of Trump's claims of celebrity entitlement were displacing the intelligence assessment, a third seismic shift then produced the most long-lived effect on press coverage of the three. In an apparent attempt to deflect attention from Trump's salacious remarks, at 4:32 p.m.[8] WikiLeaks released a first cache of emails stolen by Russian operatives from the account of Clinton campaign director John Podesta. Other material purloined from that account would be dispatched into the media stream on a regular basis for the remainder of the campaign. Lost in the news' focus on what Trump would cast as "locker-room banter," and his opponents would characterize as a confession of "sexual assault," was Podesta's Friday evening tweeted response to the invasion of his email account: "I'm not happy about being hacked by the Russians in their quest to throw the election to Donald Trump. Don't have time to figure out which docs are real and which are faked."[9]

The question "with what intent" had the Russians hacked the Democrats and mounted an anti-Clinton social media campaign was answered in the January 6, 2017, US intelligence report titled "Assessing Russian Activities and Intentions in Recent U.S. Elections." Issued by the ODNI and drafted by the CIA, FBI, and National Security Agency, that document confirmed that "Russia used trolls as well as RT [Russia Today] as part of its influence efforts to denigrate Secretary Clinton. This effort amplified stories on scandals about Secretary Clinton and the role of WikiLeaks in the election campaign."[10] Their efforts sought to "undermine public faith in the U.S. democratic process, denigrate Secretary Clinton, and harm her electability and potential presidency."

The trolls worked hard to deflect attention from the Trump *Access Hollywood* scandal. An Associated Press investigation revealed that "Tweets by Russia-backed accounts such as 'America_1st_' and 'BatonRougeVoice' on October 7, 2016, actively pivoted away from news of an audio recording in which Trump made crude comments about groping women, and instead touted damaging emails hacked from Clinton's campaign chairman John Podesta."[11] The Russian efforts also redirected attention to a discredited characterization of Hillary Clinton's activities as a young trial lawyer. " 'MSM (the mainstream media) is at it again with Billy Bush recording. . . . What about telling Americans how Hillary defended a rapist and later laughed at his victim?' tweeted the America_1st— account, which had 25,045 followers at its peak, according to metadata in the archive." That message was posted "just hours after The Washington Post broke the story about Trump's comments to Bush."[12]

Evidence of the Impact of Hacked Content on the News

Columbia University social media researcher Jonathan Albright's analysis of more than 36,000 Russian tweets found a concerted effort to affect the news agenda in thirty major cities by amplifying such actual news stories as Trump's improved standing in the polls or details about the FBI investigation into Hillary's use of a private server while Secretary of State.[13] "Someone reading all of the [tweets by the troll who styled himself or herself] Amelie Baldwin . . . would have seen Clinton portrayed as a sickly, dishonest criminal under investigation by the FBI and eager to open America's borders to dangerous immigrants," noted a *Washington Post* write-up of Albright's work. "Trump, by contrast, appeared in the [trolls'] tweets as a bold, widely respected leader gaining in the polls with the support of gay voters and African Americans, despite being unfairly maligned by journalists."

From the first release just before the Democratic convention in the summer to the dumps of the Podesta tranches in October and November, the Russian-hacked Democratic emails infected press coverage. "Although Trump received more overall media attention," concluded a study from the Berkman Klein Center for Internet & Society at Harvard University, "the email-inflected scandal-oriented coverage (the private server, Democratic National Committee [DNC] emails, and the Podesta emails) garnered the most attention from mass media during the campaign, followed by the coverage of issues that defined the Trump campaign."[14] Contributing to that pattern was a Russian Facebook group calling itself "DC Leaks" that used fake personae to "seed" hacked information from Podesta and DNC emails to journalists,[15] an activity confirmed by Facebook General Counsel Colin Stretch. "Americans extensively engaged with our publications," bragged WikiLeaks founder Julian Assange after the election. "According to Facebook statistics," he alleged, "WikiLeaks was the most referenced political topic during October."[16] To encourage use of the hacked materials, WikiLeaks issued 118 tweets touting its finds.[17]

In order to chronicle the impact that the availability of the ill-gotten Democratic content had on what the public was told by media reporters and reports in the crucial final month of the 2016 election, I will divide that period into four sometimes-overlapping blocks: the Sunday, October 9 interview shows, the two and a half weeks between the first debate and the resumption of the Comey investigation, the two last debates, and the nine of the last eleven days of the campaign in which the resurrected FBI investigation was in the headlines.

Before taking on that task, it is important to make note of the case advanced in an article in *FiveThirtyEight*, contending that "you might have expected a decline in the percentage of Americans who trusted Clinton after WikiLeaks began its releases. . . . But the percentage of Americans who found Clinton to be honest or trustworthy stayed at around 30 percent in polling throughout October and into November."[18] Over the part of this period that we tracked, Annenberg Public Policy Center national polling data agree. Perceptions of the trustworthiness of the Democratic nominee did not change (see appendix 1). One explanation may be that since evaluations of Clinton on that trait were already low, they may have reached their floor.

But one other perception did shift downward. Before exploring it, a bit of background is in order. As you may recall, Clinton aide Huma Abedin's husband, Anthony Weiner, resigned from Congress in 2011 after being caught sending sexually suggestive pictures of himself to a number of adult women. In fall 2016, Clinton emails were discovered on a laptop of his that was seized as part of a criminal investigation into his sexting with a fifteen-year-old girl. This discovery raised the possibility that some of these emails may not have been reviewed as part of the investigation into Clinton's reliance on a private server during her time as Secretary of State. On October 28, FBI Director James Comey notified Congress that he had reopened the probe that he had closed in July.

The Annenberg survey in question assessed public opinion before the date on which the public learned of the new probe. Whereas in our three Annenberg Public Policy Center national random samples of the US adult population, 59 percent considered Clinton qualified to be president in the first period (September 27–October 2), by the third (October 20–25) that percentage figure had plummeted by 11 points to 48 percent (see the tables, wordings, and methods in appendix 1). In the same period, perception of Trump's temperament, trustworthiness, and that he shared voters' values improved, in the first case from 26 to 31 percent, in the second from 28 to 34 percent, and in the third from 27 to 35 percent. All three changes are significant.

Of particular note is the fact that the two most damaging unforced errors of the Clinton campaign occurred in early September and so were already baked into public opinion well before the period in which these surveys registered a significant drop in the public's belief that she was qualified to be president. Her observation that "you could put half of Trump's supporters into what I call the basket of deplorables" was made on September 10. The next day, she abruptly left a 9/11 memorial ceremony in New York City and seemingly collapsed as she was helped to her car. This chain of early-September events fueled both Trump's claims that Clinton lacked the stamina to be president and the troll conspiracy theories that alleged that she was fatally ill. Both moments also increased her susceptibility to the charge that she said one thing in public and another in private. In the first instance, by casting a quarter of the electorate as deplorable, she called her slogan "Stronger Together" into question. In the second, a cough that she had attributed to allergies was instead already-diagnosed pneumonia.

Although a strong performance in the first debate on September 26 did a great deal to quiet concerns about her health, the effects of the deplorables remark were more long-lived. They included a jump in sales of T-shirts branding individual wearers as an "Adorable Deplorable," or proclaiming "I Am a Deplorable.[19] Her disdainful aside also refocused troll attention and led to creation of the "clinger . . . deplorable" meme that the trolls successfully amplified.

After Hillary's two self-inflicted wounds in early September, the only new publicly available information about her in the period between our first and third surveys came from her performance in the second and third debates and from the strategic leak of content hacked by the Russians. In short, from October 3rd to the twentieth, a period *after* Trump's poor and Clinton's strong performance in the first debate and *before* Comey's investigation of the contents of the Weiner laptop, there was a significant increase in positive evaluations of Trump's temperament, trustworthiness, and alliance with voters' values and a significant drop in perceptions that Clinton is qualified to be president. What makes this finding particularly intriguing is the fact that the *Access Hollywood* story appeared during this time. Although the Clinton campaign was hammering Trump's temperament in ads during these weeks, there was comparatively little paid Trump messaging on cable or TV.

One explanation for the Clinton drop is that the scandal-framed, Trump-primed, troll-amplified press coverage of the WikiLeak'd content depressed the assessments of Clinton's qualifications. After all, the staff rivalries and intrigue burbling through the stolen emails and memoranda seemed to call into question either her choice of aides or her managerial aptitude. Indeed, the emails revealed that her own staff occasionally questioned her judgment, a finding that those of us in management will find unsurprising. In one case, they did so as they groused about the need to derail a trip that could be construed as a quid pro quo for a contribution to the Clinton Global Initiative. As I noted earlier, Trump drew on the hacked disclosures to cite John Podesta's seeming questioning of Hillary's judgment as well.

On the Republican side, the improved perceptions suggest that something blunted the expected effects of the *Access Hollywood* revelations on assessments of Trump. These changes in evaluations of the two candidates are consistent with evidence that a focus on the hacked Democratic emails persisted in news where the *Access Hollywood* scandal all but disappeared. They suggest as well that the dominant themes of the Clinton ads had played themselves out and were no longer producing additional effects.

Importantly, as I will show in greater detail in a moment, the impressions of the candidates reported by those who had viewed the second or third presidential debates differed from non-viewers on a key hack-related dimension. Both of these encounters featured out-of-context questions drawn from the stolen Democratic emails. After each of these two debates, viewers were more likely than non-viewers to report that Clinton's public and private statements differed. More on that in the next chapter.

How Leaked Segments from Clinton's Speeches Changed the Sunday, October 9, News Agenda and Framing

Confronted with a smorgasbord too bountiful for the serving table, on October 9, the day of the second presidential debate, the broadcast and cable networks had an agenda challenge. How should they apportion the interview time in their hour-long Sunday morning shows among three competing stories that had broken on October 7—the report that the Russians were behind the DNC hacking, the lewd Trump-Bush exchange, and the WikiLeak'd Podesta emails containing segments of the Clinton speeches that her staff had flagged as problematic? The lineup of guests reveals which was shunted aside. Neither DHS Director Jeh Johnson nor Director of National Intelligence General James Clapper appeared on *Meet the Press* (NBC), *Face the Nation* (CBS), *This Week* (ABC), *State of the Union* (CNN), or *Fox News Sunday with Chris Wallace* (Fox News).

By sidetracking the declaration that the Russians were behind the hacking and counterbalancing the *Access Hollywood* disclosures with supposed revelations from the leaked Clinton speeches, the press coverage of the stolen Podesta content threw Trump not one but two lifelines. In the subsequent news coverage and in the final two debates, the illegal Russian provenance of the stolen content was all but ignored by journalists. The efforts by Clinton and her surrogates to focus the hacked content through a Russian-tinted lens failed. Henceforth its origin would be WikiLeaks.

Had the Podesta content not been injected into the news agenda that weekend, the Sunday shows would have featured both the DHS-ODNI conclusion that the Russians were behind the hacking and the *Access Hollywood* tape. Neither advantaged Trump. Instead the tape and the leaked speech segments dominated the Sunday shows. The frame through which the press processed both asked what voters should make of the contrast between the private and public remarks of the two contenders. Where Clinton's defenders tried to reconcile her closed-door and on-the-record remarks, Trump's argued that the 2005 comments on the *Access Hollywood* tape were outdated and not a reflection of who candidate Trump was. The boasts of sexual conquest were simply locker-room banter, the candidate's defenders contended, and not indicative of either his real attitudes or actual behavior.

At the same time, the Republican's defenders contended that Clinton's private comments betrayed her true beliefs. Spotting the irony in that position, *Meet the Press* moderator Chuck Todd asked Trump champion Rudy Giuliani, "What does that say if you believe that Hillary Clinton says one thing in private and that means what she really is is what she is in private, should we assume what Donald Trump did in that *Access Hollywood* bus is really what

Donald Trump is like in private?"[20] At the same time, Todd noted about one of Clinton's leaked speech segments, "It sounds like what she's saying is, 'Well, I'm going to tell you one thing here in this private speech and I am going to have a public position another way.'"

As I argued in chapter 2, framing matters. The Sunday-morning shows created an equivalence frame between the *Access Hollywood* remarks and the Clinton speech segments, a balancing act abetted by political reporters' preternatural preoccupation with the strategic implications of campaign events,[21] a predilection that increased viewer cynicism in field experiments that Joe Cappella and I summarized in *Spiral of Cynicism: The Press and the Public Good*.[22] Instead of asking whether either the Trump or Clinton disclosure had implications for governance, moderator John Dickerson previewed the lineup for *Face the Nation* by saying, "[K]ey Republicans are fleeing the campaign and saying he should step aside. We will assess the damage with Trump adviser Rudy Giuliani. And as some of Hillary Clinton's speeches to Wall Street banks are leaked, we will talk to campaign manager Robby Mook about how she will handle the fallout."[23]

Despite the assumption that the damage was evenly distributed, the penalty exacted by the newly available content was ultimately more sustained for the Democratic contender than for her counterpart. Not only did most of the Republican leaders who fled Trump in the wake of the release of the lewd tape return to his side, but a survey by *Politico/Morning Consult* taken just after the release of the *Access Hollywood* recording found support for his candidacy dropping by only a single point.[24] Meanwhile, ongoing WikiLeak'd content ensured that the supposed disjuncture between the public and private statements of Democrats punctuated the news for the remainder of the campaign. And, in the short run, consistent with Trump's interests, the strategically timed release of Russian-hacked Podesta emails on October 7 created a counterbalanced press narrative. On one side of that scale was the story of the media celebrity's crude remarks about women; on the other, contrasts between the public and private statements of Hillary Clinton.

Meanwhile, as he moved from Sunday show to Sunday show, Trump gladiator and former mayor of New York Rudy Giuliani parlayed his interpretation of the leaked Democratic speech segments into the contention that the *Access Hollywood* tape should not disqualify Trump. Instead, he offered a balancing argument of his own: the country faced a choice between two flawed candidates. "So, we have two Hillary Clintons, which says we have a person who's a liar," he told Fox's Chris Wallace.[25] "[W]e've got two candidates that have flaws." "Maybe people should step back and take a look at the fact that we have flawed candidates on both sides," he said on CBS's *Face the Nation*. "I know the WikiLeaks revelations kind of got dwarfed by this, but that shows *a person who is one person in private and another person in public*, a person who fought very, very hard to keep those private when she was running against Bernie Sanders because they make apparent every[thing] Bernie Sanders was saying about her and she was lying about while she was running [emphasis added]."[26]

On the October 9 Sunday interview programs, the Republican nominee was advantaged by the shows' downplaying of the intelligence report as well as by the ways in which the moderators and guests cast that document. The prospect that the October 7 intelligence community's revelations would matter to voters was dimmed as well by counterproductive language chosen by Clinton's own defenders. Attributing a report to the ODNI and the DHS secretary should be expected to elicit more positive appraisals than crediting it to the government or the administration. Not only do the words "Homeland Security" and "national intelligence" have positive resonance and a specificity that "government" and "the administration" lack, but government is less well regarded than the positive functions it performs. At the same time, "the administration" implies that the report's conclusions may reflect the self-interest of the political party in power.

In key instances in which the report was discussed, it was attributed not to the agency and department that generated it but to the "administration" or the "government," in other words, to generally disapproved faceless bureaucrats or to those in the employ of the incumbent Democratic president. "[T]he *administration* came out and said definitively that Russia was behind that DNC hack [emphasis added]," said *This Week*'s moderator, George Stephanopoulos.[27] On *Fox News Sunday*, John Podesta, who served as chair of the Clinton campaign, adopted a related linguistic frame by attributing the report to "U.S. senior members of the *U.S. government* [emphasis added]."

The ways in which the hosts cast their questions also circumscribe audience interpretations. When Fox's Wallace asked Podesta, "So, John, what's her real view? Crack down on big money or kiss up to them?" the host was not only assuming the existence of a real and a feigned stance but also adopting language that approved of one ("crack down") and disapproved of the other ("kiss up"). At the same time, the Fox moderator was posing those two choices not only as antithetical but also as the only ones available to Clinton. He also was positing that "kissing up" was a "view" when instead "crack down" implied a position on a range of issues and "kiss up" signaled an attitude. Neither formulation invited the policy discussion that might have ensued had he instead asked, "So will she tighten, maintain, or loosen the regulations known as Dodd Frank?"

Before selecting "crack down" rather than "kiss up," Podesta tried to situate his answer in the context of DHS-ODNI confirmation that Russian hacking had made the supposed speech segments available:

Well, Chris, I think we should take a step back and say how we got here, which is that the Russians, as U.S. senior members of the U.S. government confirmed, have been hacking into Democratic accounts, and now they've hacked into my account. They've put out documents purported to be from my account.

But I think if you look at what she said in this campaign, to get to your question—I would just say, you know, this should be of concern to everyone that the Russians are trying to influence our election.

But I'll answer your question directly, which is as she said all throughout this campaign, she'll crack down on Wall Street. She said it, too, there's nothing that she hasn't said in private that she doesn't say in public. She's put forward the most aggressive Wall Street plan of any candidate, really.

Had the WikiLeak'd Clinton speech segments not appeared, Johnson and Clapper would have been central figures in the news agenda that weekend, including as headliners on the Sunday shows. In those encounters, reporters would have challenged their motives and fielded alternative hypotheses. The responses would have elicited additional news attention. In this more extended inquiry, the public's awareness both of the report's findings and of arguments questioning them would have increased. In the process, the agenda-setting power of journalism would have made the report more salient to voters.

Among the attacks that Johnson and Clapper anticipated before deciding to release the document was the concern that it would be viewed as an attempt by the incumbent Democratic administration to influence the election. A second worry, later exploited by Trump, was that, since it was gathered by the same players who made the discredited claim that there were weapons of mass destruction in Saddam Hussein's Iraq, the intelligence about Russian hacking and trolling would be cast as unreliable. Alternatively, of course, one could hypothesize that an agency chastened by that earlier disaster would try to avoid a rerun at all costs by increasing its scrutiny of evidence, heightening its diligence in testing alternative explanations, and erring on the side of understating its conclusions.

Before proceeding, a word about the underlying structure of interview shows. For practical purposes, in them, the Democrat being interviewed offers one view of events or of a policy and the Republican an alternative, often contrary, one. The moderator ordinarily maintains psychological distance by being antagonistic to both. Although conventional, that pattern is not universal. By adopting as their own the premises of one side, moderators can create a dominant frame.[28] On October 9, they did just that when they presupposed not only that the leaked speech content had not been fabricated or altered by the hackers or WikiLeaks but instead represented what Clinton actually said and also that what she said in private contradicted what she said in public. Despite their refusal to confirm its accuracy, in the process of answering questions about the leaked content, the Democrats tacitly conceded that what one read in the disclosures was what her audiences had actually heard. However, they did not grant that her public and private remarks diverged.

It is not difficult to document that the Sunday show hosts sided with the Republicans in assuming that what they had in hand from WikiLeaks were the words Clinton actually spoke. On CBS John Dickerson said "some of Hillary Clinton's speeches to Wall Street banks are leaked,"[29] on NBC Chuck Todd talked about "some speech excerpts,"[30] ABC's George Stephanopoulos characterized them as "emails talking about those speeches she gave to private groups back before she started to run for president,"[31] and on Fox, Chris Wallace noted "Clinton was saying something very different from what she said on the campaign trail when she was talking in those big money, closed door speeches to Wall Street bankers."[32] By contrast, on *Fox News Sunday*, Podesta characterized the speech segments as "documents purported to be from my account." Likewise, on CNN, Democratic vice presidential nominee Tim Kaine asserted that "I don't think we can dignify documents dumped by WikiLeaks and just assume that they're all accurate and true."[33] And importantly, the toxic Wall Street speech frame, burnished by Bernie Sanders in the primaries to attack Clinton for her closed-door remarks to the likes of Goldman Sachs, was being applied here to speeches delivered to a group of Brazilian bankers and a housing coalition!

Also problematic for Clinton was the fact that three of the Sunday hosts truncated a key sentence of a speech to those bankers in a way that opened her to a broader attack than was warranted by the original text. On CNN's *State of the Union*, Jake Tapper said, "Take a look—quote—'My dream is a hemispheric common market with open borders some time in the future.'" Fox's Wallace said, "She says her dream is open trade and open borders across the western hemisphere." In these two cases, the print on screen showed ellipses at the end of that sentence. Not so on *Face the Nation*, which introduced a period at the end of "some time in the future."

Specifically, the screen prints on the Sunday shows read:

- *Face the Nation* (CBS):

   "My dream is a hemispheric common market with open trade and open borders, some time in the future."

- *State of the Union* (CNN):

   WikiLeaks: Clinton on "open borders": "... in a 2013 speech, Clinton told an audience that her 'dream is a hemispheric common market, with open trade and open borders ...'"
   "WikiLeaks posts apparent excerpts of Clinton Wall Street speeches" Saturday.

Figure 8.1 *Face the Nation* (CBS) still from October 9, 2016. A representation of Clinton's "open borders" quote on the October 9, 2016, Sunday-morning interview show.

Figure 8.2 *State of the Union* (CNN) still from October 9, 2016. A representation of Clinton's "open borders" quote on the October 9, 2016, Sunday-morning interview show.

Figure 8.3 *Fox News Sunday* still from October 9, 2016, part 1. A representation of Clinton's "open borders" quote on the October 9, 2016, Sunday-morning interview show.

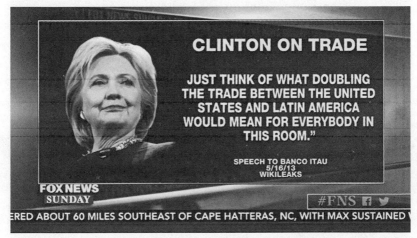

Figure 8.4 *Fox News Sunday* still from October 9, 2016, part 2. A representation of Clinton's "open borders" quote on the October 9, 2016, Sunday-morning interview show.

- *Fox News Sunday* (Fox):

  [Screen one] CLINTON ON TRADE "My dream is a hemispheric common market, with open trade and open borders . . ." [lower screen: Speech to Banco Itau 5/16/13 WIKILEAKS]

  [Screen two] CLINTON ON TRADE "Just think of what doubling the trade between the United States and Latin America would mean for everybody in this room." [lower screen: Speech to Banco Itau 5/16/13 WIKILEAKS].

- *This Week* (ABC):

  "My dream is a hemispheric common market, with open trade and open borders, some time in the future with energy that is as green and sustainable as we can get it, powering growth and opportunity for every person in the hemisphere." WIKILEAKS.

On two of the shows, a Clinton representative objected to the truncation. Because their exchanges bear importantly on an answer the Democratic standard-bearer would give in the final debate, let me quote their defenses

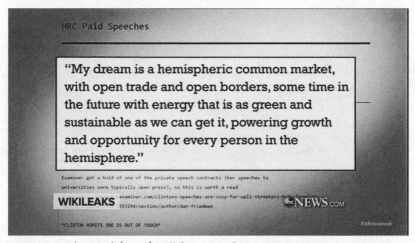

Figure 8.5 *This Week* (ABC) still from October 9, 2016. A representation of Clinton's "open borders" quote on the October 9, 2016, Sunday-morning interview show.

at length. The first comes from CBS's *Face the Nation* and involves host John Dickerson and Clinton campaign manager Robby Mook:

DICKERSON: Well, the final thing I will ask you about is, Donald Trump has said Hillary Clinton supports open borders. She has said absolutely wrong. Fact-checkers have said wrong. But there's a quote in here: "My dream is a hemispheric common market with open trade and open borders." So, she did say it.

MOOK: Well, first of all, I can't verify these documents. But, second of all, you clipped off the last part of the sentence, where she was referring to green energy. She said . . .

DICKERSON: Well, she said sometime in the future.

MOOK: She said that she wants a market where green energy can flow. She was talking about integrating green energy between North and South America. But, again, I don't know that these are actually true. But if the question is, does Hillary Clinton support throwing open our borders, absolutely not. And she is going to do everything she can to fight to protect the interests of workers in this country. That is actually why she voted against the Central American Free Trade Agreement when she was a senator.

The second happened on Fox, where Wallace not only abbreviated the quote to eliminate the clause about energy (with ellipses added on the first screen) but on a second screen without introductory ellipses he added a sentence from a part of the speech that, according to the WikiLeaks attribution of pagination, actually occurred earlier on page 14 in the address (that addition reads: "Just think of what doubling the trade between the United States and Latin America would mean for everybody in this room"). Wallace also implies that in the quoted segment, Clinton is speaking about both trade and immigration. Not only does the word "immigration" not appear in the three excerpts to the Brazilian bank released by WikiLeaks but, as I will show later, it is not a topic Clinton ties to the phrase "open borders" elsewhere either.

Here too Clinton representative John Podesta tried, although more confusedly than Mook, to put the sentence back in context. In the process, however, he seemed to concede that Clinton could have been talking about immigration as well as energy, an assumption he may have adopted from Wallace's question:

WALLACE: During the campaign, Clinton has taken a tough line on both trade and on immigration. But here's what she said in a big money speech to a Brazilian bank, "My dream is a hemispheric common market with open trade and open borders. Just think of what doubling the trade between the United States and Latin America would mean for everybody in this room." John, open trade, open borders?

PODESTA: Look, you could pluck a few words if that's what she did say out of context. I think, again, she's put forward and has been for and has constantly, you know, championed and voted for comprehensive immigration reform that modernizes our border security. She—when she was secretary of state, she talked about creating a hemispheric effort to bring clean energy across the continent from the tip of South America to Canada, to invest in clean and renewable energy, to invest in the transmission that would clean up our energy system.

Only on ABC's *This Week* was Clinton's full sentence quoted by the moderator: "My dream is a hemispheric common market with open trade and open borders some time in the future, with energy that is as green and sustainable as we can get it, powering growth and opportunity for every person in the homeland." (The document released by WikiLeaks and ABC's print on screen say "in the hemisphere" not "in the homeland."[34]) But Stephanopoulos then goes on to digest the statement by saying, "Open trade and open borders" before adding this tactical coda, "This is the kind of thing that, had this come out, as he pointed out, Mr. Giuliani pointed out, is to have this come out during the primaries with Bernie Sanders, this would have been devastating to Hillary."

Throughout, the dominant frame in which the moderators cast the Clinton speech segments was hypocritical contradiction between private and public stances, a characterization consistent with the one being pushed by both Trump and the trolls. On October 7, 2016, Donald Trump Jr. retweeted multiple tweets from WikiLeaks' account regarding the release of the Podesta emails, including: "RT @wikileaks: Secret paid Clinton speech: 'You need to have a public position and a private position on policy' #PodestaEmails https://t.c…"[35]

Employing the same frame, on *Fox News Sunday*, one of Wallace's teases for the Podesta segment said "hacked e-mails show Clinton was telling bankers something very different from what she was telling voters. We'll ask John Podesta, Clinton's campaign chairman, about the stark contradictions between what she was saying in public and private. It's a *Fox News Sunday* exclusive." On NBC's *Meet the Press*, Chuck Todd noted, "Trade, for instance, seems to be one topic where she seems to say one thing behind the scenes and one thing publicly. How do we trust her trade position, for instance?"

A number of the shows also featured a speech passage that would figure in that evening's presidential debate. *Meet the Press*'s Todd capsulized it this way:

> There was one speech excerpt from Hillary Clinton that implied, and let's take a look at it, it implied the idea that she says one thing. "But if everybody's watching, you know, all of the back room discussions and the deals you know, then people get a little nervous, to say the least. So you need both a public and a private position." It sounds like what she's saying is, "Well, I'm going to tell you one thing here in this private speech and I am going to have a public position another way."

On CBS, Dickerson made the same point. "We have had this week some leaks about these speeches that Hillary Clinton gave to Wall Street banks. In one of the speeches, she said this—quote—'But, if everybody is watching, you know, all of the backroom discussions and the deals, you know, then people get a little nervous, to say the least, so you need both a public and a private position.' Isn't that idea that there is a public and a private position what worries voters about Hillary Clinton?" Contrary to the Wall Street frame introduced by the moderator, the speech in question was an April 2013 address to the National Multi-Housing Council. Both of these shows abbreviated it in a way that fed the narrative of public/private contradiction. That framing was unsupported by the disclosed text, which read:

> CLINTON: You just have to sort of figure out how to—getting back to that word, "balance"—how to balance the public and the private efforts that are necessary to be successful, politically, and that's not just a comment about today. That, I think, has probably been true for all of our history,

and if you saw the Spielberg movie, *Lincoln*, and how he was maneuvering and working to get the 13th Amendment passed, and he called one of my favorite predecessors, Secretary Seward, who had been the governor and senator from New York, ran against Lincoln for president, and he told Seward, I need your help to get this done. And Seward called some of his lobbyist friends who knew how to make a deal, and they just kept going at it. I mean, politics is like sausage being made. It is unsavory, and it always has been that way, but we usually end up where we need to be. *But if everybody's watching, you know, all of the back room discussions and the deals, you know, then people get a little nervous, to say the least. So, you need both a public and a private position. And finally, I think—I believe in evidence-based decision making.* I want to know what the facts are. I mean, it's like when you guys go into some kind of a deal, you know, are you going to do that development or not, are you going to do that renovation or not, you know, you look at the numbers. You try to figure out what's going to work and what's not going to work. (Clinton Speech For National Multi-Housing Council, 4/24/2013) [emphasis added][36]

In the debate that evening, when Clinton says that she was speaking in the context of the popular *Lincoln* film, an audience unfamiliar with the original passage might reasonably conclude that she was being disingenuous. In fact, she was not.

The underlying structure of the Sunday shows' account of the Clinton speech excerpts was capsulized concisely near the close of *Face the Nation*. "[T]hese excerpts of her speeches, the ones they have been trying to keep under lock and key, finally got out," said moderator John Dickerson. "There is a difference between Hillary Clinton in public and private. Isn't that her underlying challenge?" Providing clear evidence that the contradiction between the public and private is a dominant frame, *USA Today*'s Susan Page responds, "It is."

What I have argued here is that, by facilitating a release of segments privately flagged as problematic by Clinton's staff, the Russians elicited a press narrative that offset the one about Trump generated by the *Access Hollywood* tape. That same Russian move magnified a press frame asserting that Clinton says one thing in public and another in private. And, as I will demonstrate in a moment, that perspective was insinuated into the last two debates, where the WikiLeak'd segments served as justification for that inference.

Hacked Content Altered the Press Agenda in the Final Weeks of the Election

Before launching the argument that Russian subterfuge affected the press agenda in the final debates as well as in the final month of the election, recall that earlier I showed that, between October 3 and 20, perceptions that Clinton was qualified to be president dropped as perceptions of Trump's temperament, trustworthiness, and sharing of voters' values rose. The intervening two and a half weeks included not only the controversy over Trump's *Access Hollywood* boasts but also the postings of Podesta content by WikiLeaks, the release of the DHS-ODNI report attributing the hacking to Russia, and the last two presidential debates. That period is important because it begins after the effects of her "deplorables" comment, health cover-up, and first debate performance had marinated into the public opinion mix. And it ends before the reopening of the Comey investigation on October 28. Since the only new information forthcoming about Clinton during this period came from the WikiLeaks-disclosed hacked content and the second and third presidential debates, it is plausible to assume that public exposure to the hacked content and to the debates accounts for part of that change. In a moment, I will parse out the effects of including WikiLeak'd content in the two debates. But before doing so, we need to determine the extent to which the stolen emails pervaded the press stream.

From October 7 through Election Day, the hacked content and the reopened Comey investigation played a substantial role in shaping the press agenda. A study by social science researcher Duncan Watts and economist David Rothschild of 65,000 sentences written not "by Russian hackers" but "overwhelmingly by professional journalists employed at mainstream news organizations, such as *the New York Times, the Washington Post*, and *the Wall Street Journal*,"[37] found that "the various Clinton-related email scandals—her use of a private email server while secretary of state, *as well as the DNC and John Podesta hacks*—accounted for more sentences than all of Trump's scandals combined (65,000 vs. 40,000) and more than twice as many as were devoted to all of her policy positions [emphasis added]."³⁸ Their essay, titled "Don't Blame the Election on Fake News. Blame It on the Media," concludes that "to the extent that voters mistrusted Hillary Clinton, or considered her conduct as secretary of state to have been negligent or even potentially criminal, or were generally unaware of what her policies contained or how they may have differed from Donald Trump's, these numbers suggest their views were influenced more by mainstream news sources than by fake news."

What Watts and Rothschild's analysis of news underplays is the fact that the DNC and Podesta hacks on whose contents the legacy outlets were reporting existed only because of illegal Kremlin-backed actions. Without that stimulus, the media could not have covered the disclosures. So if the question is not "did content written by Russians" affect the outcome but "did the strategic release of hacked content coupled with a complementary social media stream" accomplish that end, then the nature and extent of the press coverage that existed only because of the release of the hacked Democratic content become critical.

On key points of comparison, coverage of WikiLeaks content in October displaced a focus on the vulnerabilities of both candidates with one on Clinton alone. The featured content centered not on a comparative or contrastive frame focused on both the Clinton and Trump foundations, or on suspect dealings at Trump's foundation alone but on ethical concerns about the Clintons' philanthropy. Not on the cozy relationship between Trump and such conservative commentators and alt-right outlets as *Breitbart, Drudge*, Fox, Rush Limbaugh, and Sean Hannity, but on the supposedly incestuous relationship between the Democrat and the mainstream media. Not on the corporate ties of both, or on Trump's employment practices and business dealings, but on Clinton's speaking fees, refusal to release the texts of addresses to various interest groups, and public versus private sentiments. Not on the allegations of the more than a dozen women who said that the real estate mogul–turned–TV star had sexually propositioned or assaulted them, or on the ways and reasons that the Russians were attempting to sabotage the election, but on the intrigue involved in Democratic efforts to undermine Sanders's prospects and on explorations of supposed Clinton hypocrisy.

In the process, anti-Clinton effects may have been magnified by the public's conflation of different email "scandals." One surrounded the FBI investigation into the possibility that classified content existed on her private server. Another involved indiscrete emailed content obtained by a Freedom of Information Act request made of the State Department. A third was tied to the release of material gotten by Russian hacking of Democratic email accounts. Because the press telegraphed the investigation into Clinton's problematic use of an unauthorized private server while Secretary of State as the "Clinton email investigation," and the WikiLeaks disclosures were of emails, voter conflation of the two would be unsurprising. "We knew voters were making no distinction between the WikiLeaks emails and the political emails and John Podesta's emails and Hillary Clinton's emails from secretary of state," Clinton pollster Joel Benenson told Yahoo![39] "That was something we couldn't overcome unless we were gonna have to try to proactively, like, do a tutorial in Hillary's emails, which would've been politically ludicrous."

Evidence that hacked content punctuated news coverage throughout October comes from a search of the *New York Times*, which reveals these headlines:

- "Leaked Speech Excerpts Show a Hillary Clinton at Ease with Wall Street" (Oct. 7, 2016)

- "Highlights from the Clinton Campaign Emails: How to Deal with Sanders and Biden" (Oct. 10, 2016)

- "Hillary Clinton Aides Kept de Blasio at Arm's Length, WikiLeaks Emails Show" (Oct. 10, 2016)

- "Donald Trump Finds Improbable Ally in WikiLeaks" (Oct. 12, 2016)

- "Hacked Transcripts Reveal a Genial Hillary Clinton at Goldman Sachs Events" (Oct. 15, 2016)

- "Email about Qatari Offer Shows Thorny Ethical Issues Clinton Foundation Faced" (Oct. 15, 2016)

- "A WikiLeaks Lesson for Mrs. Clinton" (Oct. 21, 2016)

- " 'We Need to Clean this Up': Clinton Aide's Newly Public Email Shows Concern" (Oct. 25, 2016)

- "Donations to Foundation Vexed Hillary Clinton's Aides, Emails Show" (Oct. 26, 2016)

- "Chelsea Clinton's Frustrations and Devotion Shown in Hacked Emails" (Oct. 27, 2016)

- "WikiLeaks Lays Bare a Clinton Insider's Emphatic Cheers and Jeers" (Oct. 29, 2016)

- "CNN Parts Ways with Donna Brazile, a Hillary Clinton Supporter" (Oct. 31, 2016) ["CNN has severed ties with the Democratic strategist Donna Brazile after hacked emails from WikiLeaks showed that she shared questions for CNN-sponsored candidate events in advance with friends"]

Press uptake continued to Election Day, when a *New York Times* headline read, "Julian Assange Releases More Emails and Defends WikiLeaks' Mission."

Not only did the dump of the first bundle of Podesta emails within an hour of the October 7 release of the *Access Hollywood* tape benefit the Republican by helping dilute the news focus on the hot mic recording, but the regular release of fresh Podesta content created an ongoing persistent WikiLeaks story line (see Figure 8.6).

Here too *Breitbart* and Trump reinforced each other's uses of the stolen communication. On October 13, 2016, for example, topping that site's list of the "biggest bombshells dropped by WikiLeaks" was the disclosure that "Clinton dreams of a world with 'open trade and open borders.' "[40] The reach of the *Breitbart* site was considerable. In July 2016, its traffic was reported to be at "9 percent of the market, with 18 millions [*sic*] visitors" and its growth had also "outpaced that of other sites in the politics category during 12 out of the past 14 months, according to comScore data."[41] An examination of media sources whose content generated the highest number of links about the debate over immigration found that *Breitbart* was surpassed only by the *Washington Post*, the *New York Times*, and the Pew Research Center.[42] In October 2016, the alt-right site claimed more than 250 million page views.[43]

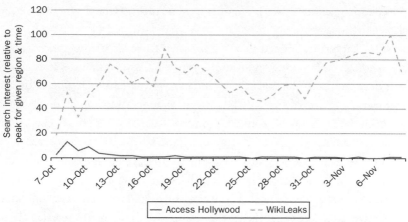

Figure 8.6 Google Trends for "WikiLeaks" and "Access Hollywood" from October 7 to November 8, 2016 (United States). Search interest over time is "relative to the highest point on the chart for the given region and term." Google Trends (2017, November 15) Compare: Access Hollywood, WikiLeaks. Retrieved from https://trends.google.com/trends/explore/ TIMESERIES?date=2016-10-07%202016-11-08&geo=U.S.&q=Access%20 Hollywood,WikiLeaks&hl=en-U.S.&sni=5.

By February 2017, as noted in a story in Axios, the site had "moved ahead of The Washington Post, Fox News, Walmart and Yelp on the Alexa top sites ranking that combines measures of visitors and pageviews [sic]."[44]

Run by Trump supporter and later short-term White House advisor Steve Bannon, *Breitbart* also drew on Russian-hacked Democratic content to amplify Trump's ongoing attacks on supposed media–Clinton complicity. "WikiLeaks Reveals Long List Of Media Canoodling With Hillary Clinton," read one headline.[45] Another said: "WikiLeaks: Journalists Dined At Top Clinton Staffers' Homes Days Before Hillary's Campaign Launch."[46]

The impact of the stolen emails was most pronounced in the final month of the campaign, a time when late deciders were breaking for Trump.[47] Over 72 percent of people who searched for WikiLeaks from June onward did so during October or the first week of November.[48] As I noted earlier, a study by scholars at Oxford University found that eleven of sixteen swing states were exposed to higher levels of "content from Russian, WikiLeaks and junk news sources" than the average across the nation in the final ten days of the presidential election.[49] And, of course, imbalances in messaging have been shown to move votes.

This chapter has argued that the release of hacked Democratic content put media agenda setting and framing into play against Clinton in the final month of the 2016 election. The agenda reset created on October 9 by the October 7 release of the Russian-stolen Democratic content displaced a focus on the DHS-ODNI confirmation that Russians were the hackers with a counterbalanced equivalence frame, balancing the *Access Hollywood* tape against the leaked Clinton speech segments. Instead of asking how we could know that the Russians were behind the hacking, the October 9 Sunday-show moderators asked what effect the disclosures would have on the candidates' respective campaigns and what the tape and speech segments revealed about the private versus public selves of the contenders. In subsequent weeks, news accounts of hacked content focused on Clinton's vulnerabilities. Throughout the final month of the campaign, as early voting was ramping up, WikiLeaks elicited high levels of searches. And as all of this was taking place, in the period between October 3 and 20, perceptions that Clinton was qualified to be president dropped and perceptions of Trump's temperament, trustworthiness, and alliance with voters' values improved.

The Effect of Hacked Content on the Last Two Presidential Debates

Throughout the primaries, Senator Bernie Sanders called for the release of the texts of speeches that Hillary Clinton had given to Wall Street firms. By failing to produce them, his former Senate colleague from New York not only fueled the assumptions that her private and public stands diverged but also invited suspicions that her commitment to regulation produced in response to the Great Recession was not what it appeared to be. The ongoing Clinton-Sanders to-and-fro over those addresses primed the salience of the issue both with Sanders's voters and with reporters. As a result, when WikiLeaks released partial texts of some of them two days before the second debate,[1] it didn't take much for Trump, Trump-aligned media, and Russian operatives to assert that Clinton had had good reasons to conceal them.[2]

In the second general election presidential debate, on October 9, the moderator, Martha Raddatz, mentioned WikiLeaks but neither the Russian hacking that put the heretofore hidden speech segments in that site's possession nor the fact that the content was ill-gotten. At the same time, she reminded viewers that Clinton had refused to release the material. Unlike the hosts of the Sunday-morning shows, however, Raddatz did repeatedly cast them as "purported excerpts" when she said,

> This next question comes from the public through the bipartisan Open Debate Coalition's online forum where Americans submitted questions that generated millions of votes. This question involves WikiLeaks' release of purported excerpts of Secretary Clinton's paid speeches, which she has refused to release. And one line in particular, in which you, Secretary Clinton, purportedly say you need both a public and a private position on certain issues. So, Tu from Virginia asks, "Is it okay for a politician to be two-faced?" Is it acceptable for a politician to have a private stance on issues?

Contrary to the inference invited by Raddatz's evocation of millions of votes, the question she chose had generated little online enthusiasm. Ignoring the nominations that had elicited mass support, Raddatz opted instead for one that garnered only thirteen votes but fit the frame set by the Sunday shows earlier that day: "Is it okay for politicians to be two-faced?" To that question, the veteran journalist added, "Is it acceptable for a politician to have a private stance on isssues?"[3] Unmentioned was the discussion of Steven Spielberg's film *Lincoln*, which had contextualized Clinton's original remarks about public and private positions.

Nor was the WikiLeaks-based question in the third debate context-rich. There, moderator Chris Wallace truncated a key sentence without benefit of ellipses by saying, "[W]e've learned from WikiLeaks, that you said this. And I want to quote, '*My dream is a hemispheric common market with open trade and open borders*' [emphasis added]."

A Debate Question about "Two-Faced" Clinton

Access to hacked email containing supposed excerpts from the Clinton closed-door speeches changed the content of the final two 2016 debates.[4] At issue in the second, with its audience of 66.5 million viewers,[5] were rambling thoughts Clinton expressed in a talk (for which she was reportedly paid

$225,000) delivered not to a Wall Street bank but to the National Multi-Housing Council. In the last chapter, my discussion of uses to which this speech fragment was put in the Sunday-morning interview shows included the entire passage posted by WikiLeaks. In it, the former Secretary of State cited Lincoln's actions as an illustration of the need "to balance the public and private efforts that are necessary to be successful politically," and noted that the Spielberg film had shown Lincoln doing this:

> You just have to sort of figure out how to—getting back to that word, "balance"—how to balance the public and the private efforts that are necessary to be successful, politically, and that's not just a comment about today .... [and then 120 words about Lincoln]. But if everybody's watching, you know, all of the back room discussions and the deals, you know, then people get a little nervous, to say the least. So, you need both a public and a private position.

In the second debate, moderator Martha Raddatz cited but did not quote that statement while asking the question submitted by a "voter": is it acceptable for a politician to be "two-faced"? Before attacking the disclosure of the speech content as Russian-based, saying that Putin's minions wanted Trump elected and demanding that the Republican nominee release his tax returns, Clinton responded by setting the hacked statement in the context of Steven Spielberg's popular film about Lincoln, to which she also had alluded in the original speech to the housing council: "And you have to keep working at it and yes, President Lincoln was trying to convince some people, he used some arguments, convincing other people, he used other arguments." Since neither the Sunday shows nor Raddatz featured the *Lincoln* reference, some undoubtedly heard Clinton's response as a dodge. Trump's rejoinder attacked Clinton's honesty and implied inaccurately that the original speech had been to Goldman Sachs and had not referenced the *Lincoln* film:

> Look, now she is blaming—she got caught in a total lie. Her papers went out to all her friends at the banks, Goldman Sachs and everybody else. And she said things, WikiLeaks, that just came out. And she lied. Now she's blaming the lie on the late great Abraham Lincoln. That's

when—okay, Honest Abe never lied. That's the good thing. That's the big difference between Abraham Lincoln and you. That's a big, big difference. We're talking about some difference.

The impact of the Russian grab and dump of private emails didn't end there. Instead, in the third and final debate, it took a particularly insidious form.

A Debate Question Presupposing Support for "Open Borders"

In the final debate, which reached more than 71.6 million,[6] the moderator Chris Wallace drew on hacked content to ask whether the Democratic nominee dreamt of open borders. As I noted earlier, that query was based on a WikiLeaks-disclosed speech to a Brazilian bank, which Wallace reduced both on his Sunday interview show and in the final debate to the claim that Clinton had said that her dream was "a hemispheric common market with open trade and open borders." Omitted from Wallace's question was the rest of the sentence, which in its entirety read: "My dream is a hemispheric common market, with open trade and open borders, some time in the future with energy that is as green and sustainable as we can get it, powering growth and opportunity for every person in the hemisphere."[7]

If a single expression soldered Trump's central appeals into one resonant phrase, "open borders" was it. For the businessman-turned-candidate, those two words translated into immigrants crossing the border to rape, murder, drive down wages, and steal jobs; trade policies that transformed working-class dreams into a nightmare; and terrorists threading their way toward a next 9/11. Accordingly, in tweets Trump indicted Ohio governor John Kasich for voting "for NAFTA open borders," castigated Hillary for "open borders immigration policies [that] will drive down wages for all Americans—and make everyone less safe," alleged that "If our border is not secure we can expect another attack," and asked "When is the media going to talk about Hillary's policies that have gotten people killed like Libya open borders . . . ?" In short, here was a central point of contrast stressed by the Republican throughout the campaign. As such, the appearance of a speech segment that employed the phrase was a gift to his campaign.

Tweets were not the only venue in which Trump indicted "open borders." An ad aired by his campaign in Ohio, Pennsylvania, North Carolina, and Florida also stressed the difference between Clinton's supposed support for them and Trump's protection of the nation's identity and safety. Under the Democrat, the ad contended that "[t]he system stays rigged against Americans. Syrian refugees flood in. Illegal immigrants convicted of committing crimes get to stay. Collecting Social Security benefits, skipping the line. Our border open. It's more of the same, but worse."[8] Under Trump, America is "secure. Terrorists and dangerous criminals: kept out. The border: secured. Our families: safe. Change that makes America safe again."

The attack was a mainstay of the Trump stump speeches as well. In an October 10 rally in Pennsylvania, it took the form of a charge that

Hillary Clinton's radical call for open borders, meaning anyone in the world can enter the United States without any limit at all, would end the United States as we know it today. . . . By the way, weeks ago, I called out Hillary Clinton for supporting open borders and the media said I was wrong. Now, I've been proven right. Where is the media rushing to correct these false stories? Because in the WikiLeaks, it was all about open borders, free trade for everybody.[9]

Importantly, in their final debate, what the Republican contended was: "Very unfair that somebody runs across the border, becomes a citizen. Under her plan you have open borders. You would have a disaster on trade and you will have a disaster with your open borders." Hillary contested Trump's claim that she supported open borders. "We will not have open borders," she declared in response to Trump. "That is a rank mischaracterization. We will have secure borders. But we will also have reform."

Following that exchange, Wallace introduced the controversial WikiLeak'd speech content without a Russian frame: "Secretary Clinton, I want to clear up your position on this issue because in a speech you gave to a Brazilian bank for which you were paid $225,000, we've learned from WikiLeaks, that you said this. And I want to quote, 'My dream is a hemispheric common market with open trade and open borders.'" As Wallace was completing the question, Trump interjected: "Thank you." His interruption led Wallace to reiterate "That's the question. Please, quiet, everybody. Is that your dream? Open borders?"

The Democrat responded by arguing that Wallace had taken the statement out of context. The cited passage was talking about energy, she argued: "If you went on to read the rest of the sentence, I was talking about energy. We trade more energy with our neighbors than we trade with the rest of the world combined. And I do want us to have an electric grid, an energy system that crosses borders." She then proceeded to attack WikiLeaks, note the intelligence agencies' confirmation of Russian interference, and call on Trump to acknowledge Russian interference and reject Putin's help in the election.

Trump responded instead:

TRUMP: That was a great pivot off the fact that she wants open borders. Okay? How did we get on to Putin?

WALLACE: Hold on, folks. Because this is going to end up getting out of control. Let's try to keep it quiet. For the candidates and for the American people.

TRUMP: Just to finish on the borders, she wants open borders. People are going to pour into our country. People are going to come in from Syria. She wants 550% more people than Barack Obama. And he has thousands and thousands of people. They have no idea where they come from. And you see, we are going to stop radical Islamic terrorism in this country. She won't even mention the words and neither will President Obama. So I just want to tell you. She wants open borders.

In its evaluation of that attack, FactCheck.org (which I co-founded with Brooks Jackson) wrote,

Trump repeatedly claimed Clinton "wants to have open borders," which Clinton called "a rank mischaracterization." Wallace asked Clinton to explain comments she made to a Brazilian bank—revealed via WikiLeaks—that "My dream is a hemispheric common market with open trade and open borders." But as Clinton noted, that wasn't the whole quote. It continues: "... some time in the future with energy that is as green and sustainable as we can get it, powering growth and opportunity for every person in the hemisphere." Clinton said she was "talking about energy. . . . And I do want us to have an electric grid, an energy system that crosses borders." In fact, Clinton said at the debate, "I have been for border security for years. I voted for border security in the United States Senate. And my comprehensive immigration reform plan of course includes border security." We have found all of that to be true.[10]

To that, let me add a note. Trump is incorrect in assuming in the last debate that the speech segment Wallace cited was about immigration. In full, the WikiLeak'd paragraph alluded to trade and energy but not immigration or immigrants. Nonetheless, the Republican nominee alleged that the passage was an admission about her immigration plans ("she wants open borders. People are going to pour into our country").

One of the things I confirmed when writing *Eloquence in an Electronic Age* and co-authoring *Presidents Creating the Presidency: Deeds Done in Words* with Karlyn Kohrs Campbell is that, when speaking extemporaneously or answering questions, candidates and presidents often beckon stock, well-rehearsed arguments from memory. The rhetorical repertoire of most is highly predictable. They reflexively repeat themselves. As a result, reporters don't need a crystal ball to predict what most candidates will say next in a stump speech.

Clinton is no exception. In public and, it turns out, in private, as well, she links the words "open borders" to trade, energy, and disease prevention but not to her position on immigration. The hacked speech segments released by WikiLeaks demonstrate that this is the case even when she is speaking behind closed doors to the bank CIBC about Mexico, the country that was a central focus of Trump's controversial immigration positions. In a WikiLeak'd paragraph attributed to that speech, she said,

> The North American future that I imagine is one that would give us energy connectivity, give us a much more open border where goods and services more easily flowed, would give us the chance to put our heads together about what else we can do together, bringing Mexico in to continue the work we have started on health care like early warning

systems for epidemic diseases. We saw that in 2009 with the spread of a particularly virulent form of the flu that first came to our part of the world and Mexico, and because of the cooperation, because of the investments we made, were able to stop it in its tracks.[11]

In the weeks that followed, the Republican standard-bearer kept his focus on "open borders" on the stump and in tweets, among them this one from October 20: "Moderator: Hillary paid $225000 by a Brazilian bank for a speech that called for 'open borders.' That's a quote! #Debate #BigLeagueTruth."[12]

In short, Russian-hacked content was used in the crucial third debate to create an extended discussion of a topic magnifying the sense that a ballot for Clinton meant increased cultural dislocation and economic anxiety. Because in Pennsylvania, Michigan, and Wisconsin jobs that once sustained communities have been outsourced, the Trump attack on "open borders" had special resonance for key constituencies there. Also reinforced by the moderator's eliding of the sentence and by Trump's rejoinder was the assumption that Hillary's statements in private diverged from those she made in public. Because this is a common frame in US elections, priming it is easy.

Resonant in Western culture at least since Plato's well-known discussion of shadows in the cave, the appearance-versus-reality lens, in US politics, takes the form of questions about a candidate's actual rather than presented self, real versus publicly expressed beliefs, diagnosed rather than self-proclaimed health, audited rather than feigned financial circumstances, and lived rather than conjured biography. In a system in which a person rather than a platform is on the ballot, it makes sense for the citizenry to ask: Will the policies on which the candidates campaigned be the ones they try to implement? Does the projected image faithfully forecast the dispositions and aptitudes that will shape the victor's conduct in office or is it a disguise? At key times in the nation's history, failures to raise these questions have led to voter disappointment. So, for example, months after he was reelected based on the illusion that he was still up to the job, FDR died in office. And, although he promised that "Asian boys" would prosecute the Vietnam War, LBJ escalated US involvement.

Unsurprisingly, controversies expressed in the public-versus-private schema had been percolating for much of 2016. Had Clinton given private assurances to Wall Street insiders that contradicted her campaign promises to hold them accountable for abuses? wondered Sanders. If not, why not release the texts? At the same time, a commonplace attack on Trump alleged that his tax returns contained proof that he had exaggerated his business prowess and wealth, paid less than his fair share in taxes, and was indebted to foreign partners.

What this means is that late deciders were likely to see the back-and-forth of the campaign through a well-worn cognitive schema questioning the perceived fidelity of appearance to reality, and the public persona to the private person. This accessibility increased voters' susceptibility to media frames asking whether what they could see was what they would get. Consistent with this supposition, an Annenberg Public Policy Center survey comparing the views of debate watchers to those of non-viewers in the presence of controls found that those who viewed debate 2 or debate 3 were significantly more likely than non-viewers to subscribe to the belief that Clinton says one thing in public and another in private. By the same measure, the third debate reduced perceptions that that description applied to Trump (see appendix 2, and for additional analysis of debate effects, see appendix 3). An increase in perception that Clinton "says one thing in public and another in private" predicts a small but significant drop in reported intention to vote for her (see appendix 4).

Debate viewing did not create but rather reinforced the impression that the private and public Clinton were sometimes at odds with each other. After all, as I noted earlier, the candidate who campaigned on the slogan "Stronger Together" had said to a private gathering on September 9 that "to just be grossly generalistic, you could put half of Trump's supporters into what I call the basket of deplorables." But our survey data suggest an additional effect on Clinton's prospects as a result of debate exchanges that occurred because of Russian hacking.

In short, the Russians can claim credit for one question damaging to Clinton in each of the last two October general election debates. Because these face-offs attract the largest audiences of the campaign, as I noted in chapter 2, debate viewing has the capacity to alter perceptions of the candidates. Our research suggests that watching either of the last two of 2016 did just that. Importantly, the effect that we find is consistent with the assumption embedded in the WikiLeaks-based questions. In each case, the Clinton texts were attributed not to Russian hacking but to WikiLeaks. In each, the moderator framed the issue in a fashion that disadvantaged Clinton. And in both instances, the statement attributed to the Democrat was sundered from context. In other words, the moderators turned hacked content into questions damaging to the Clinton candidacy. And the stolen goods lent credibility to the predicate of those moderator queries.

Our exploration doesn't end with the effects of the WikiLeak'd hacked content on news coverage and debates. In the next chapter we turn to another form of possible Russian intervention: Russian-held content that may have shaped the media agenda in the final week and a half of the campaign.

10

The Russian Effect on the Media Agenda in the Last Days of the Election

n presidential contests within living memory, two "October surprises" stand out. Although in the long term neither ultimately signified anything, in the short run, the sound and fury that they evoked changed each campaign in noteworthy ways. The first was National Security Advisor Henry Kissinger's October 26, 1972, disclosure that "peace [in Vietnam] is at hand." In the second, FBI Director James Comey stated on October 28, 2016, that his agency was scrutinizing newly found Clinton emails. Both announcements altered the electoral dynamic in the final days of a presidential election. Not only did Kissinger's revelation displace Watergate in the news but it also eroded the central rationale for Democratic nominee George McGovern's anti-war candidacy.[1] Yet, from 1972 to the April 1975 fall of Saigon and the surrender of South Vietnam, peace proved elusive. Meanwhile, the Watergate cover-up ended Nixon's presidency. Nor were new revelations forthcoming from the Clinton emails lurking on the Weiner laptop. A week and a half after reviving the investigation, on Sunday, November 6, the FBI director declared that, after an "extraordinary amount of high quality work in a short period of time," his July recommendation that she not be charged remained unchanged.[2]

Because the news narrative about the FBI probe was consistent with the Sanders-Trump media theme alleging that Clinton was hiding something, the suspense-filled Comey enterprise carried particular persuasive potential. "The FBI would not have reopened this case at this time unless it were a most egregious offense," declared the Republican nominee.[3] Since influence is greatest as voters are making up their minds, factors that underscore one contender's vulnerabilities late in the campaign are especially likely to affect the votes of conflicted citizens. Although 2016 voters knew the outcome of the Comey scramble more than a full day before the polls opened, as his agents were working through the nights, absentee ballots were flooding in and late deciders mulling their options.

Confirmation that the FBI investigation affected the news agenda comes from observation as well as expert analysis. "The story dominated news coverage for the better part of a week, drowning out other headlines," recalled political analyst Nate Silver.[4] "In just six days [between the reopening and closing of Comey's probe], the *New York Times* ran as many cover stories about Hillary Clinton's emails as they did about all policy issues combined in the 69 days leading up to the election," concluded Microsoft researchers Duncan Watts and David Rothschild. "The Comey incident and its subsequent impact on Clinton's approval rating among undecided voters could very well have tipped the election."[5]

Their evidence is consistent with political communication theorist Thomas Patterson's more encompassing content analysis of the mainstream news. From the beginning to the end of the week of October 23–30, his Kennedy School study found that the percentage of Clinton's mainstream press coverage that focused on scandal spiked from 14 percent to 23 percent.[6] The rise didn't end there. In the following week, from October 30 through November 7, it increased again from under a quarter (23 percent) to over a third (37 percent). In those final two weeks of the campaign, negative reporting on Clinton exceeded that about Trump by 7 percent. Patterson confirms that the increase was driven by the Comey coverage,[7] which accounted for one hundred stories, forty-six of them on the front page. This finding is important because it suggests that in this critical period, the news messaging environment was weighted against Clinton. As the evidence in chapter 2 suggested, weighting can affect vote intentions.

The case that it shifted preferences is compelling. "She'd led Trump by 5.9 percentage points in FiveThirtyEight's popular vote projection at 12:01 a.m. on Oct. 28," notes Silver.[8] "A week later—after polls had time to fully reflect the [Comey] letter—her lead had declined to 2.9 percentage points. That is to say, there was a shift of about 3 percentage points against Clinton." "At a maximum," argues Silver, "it might have shifted the race by 3 or 4 percentage points toward Donald Trump, swinging Michigan, Pennsylvania, Wisconsin and Florida to him, perhaps along with North Carolina and Arizona. At a minimum, its impact might have been only a percentage point or so. Still, because Clinton lost Michigan, Pennsylvania and Wisconsin by less than 1 point, the letter was probably enough to change the outcome of the Electoral College." Sam Wang of the Princeton Election Consortium finds the same effect. "Opinion swung toward Trump by 4 percentage points, and about half of this was a lasting change," he writes.[9] "This was larger than the victory margin in Michigan, Pennsylvania, Florida, and Wisconsin. Many factors went into this year's Presidential race, but . . . Comey's letter appears to have been a critical factor in the home stretch."

What has any of this to do with Russia? To this point, the case that the Russians helped elect Trump hinges on the trolls' reweighting of the communication in social media streams against Clinton, their amplification of anti-Clinton content through manipulation of trending, the WikiLeaks blunting of the negative effects of the *Access Hollywood* disclosures with the release of the Clinton speech segments, WikiLeak'd Podesta content displacing the revelation from Homeland Security and national intelligence sources that the Russians were the hackers and infecting the news and debate agendas with stolen content.

If information gotten by Russian hackers or disinformation confected by Russian operators played a role in triggering Comey's decision to reveal to Congress and hence the public the existence of the Weiner laptop investigation, then the agenda-setting and weighting effects elicited by the FBI probe of its contents are theirs. If so, they slashed Clinton's prospects in the final week and a half of the campaign.

Here is the backstory. In early July 2016 the FBI director publicly characterized Clinton's use of a personal server while Secretary of State as "extremely careless" but recommended against charging her. In his May 2017 testimony before the Senate Judiciary Committee, he attributed the fact that he had made his unprecedented July 2016 public statement to "a number [of] things [that] had gone on, some of which I can't talk about." One of the *disclosed* factors was the unscheduled meeting between Bill Clinton and Attorney General Loretta Lynch on her plane on a tarmac in Phoenix, Arizona, in June 2016.[10] Specifically, Comey recalled:

> The normal way to do it [conclude the server investigation] would be to [have] the Department of Justice announce it. And I struggled as we got closer to the end of it with the—*a number of things had gone on, some of which I can't talk about yet* [emphasis added], that made me worry that the department leadership could not credibly complete the investigation and declined prosecution without grievous damage to the American people's confidence in the—in the justice system.
>
> And then the capper was—and I'm not picking on the—the Attorney General Loretta Lynch, who I like very much—but her meeting with President Clinton on that airplane was the capper for me. And I then said, you know what, the department cannot by itself credibly end this. The best chance we have as a justice system is if I do something I never imagined before, step away from them and tell the American people, look, here's what the FBI did, here's what we found, here's what we think. And that that offered us the best chance of the American people believing in the system, that it was done in a credible way.

In *A Higher Loyalty*, the former FBI director reveals that when he first learned of the "impromptu" meeting between Bill Clinton and Lynch on the tarmac on June 27, "I didn't pay much attention to it. . . .[T]o my eye, the notion that this conversation would impact the investigation was ridiculous."[11] But he goes on to document the power that media agenda setting and framing exerted on his perceptions, "As the firestorm grew in the media, I paid more attention, watching it become another corrosive talking point about how the Obama Justice Department couldn't be trusted to complete the Clinton email investigation."

In the former FBI director's telling, his July 5, 2016, statement was made because both "a number of things had gone on, some of which I can't talk about yet, that made me worry" and the "capper"—the Clinton-Lynch meeting. The undisclosed reason was probed at a May 2017 hearing of the Senate Judiciary Committee and focused on who sent and received "a troubling email. . . the Russians hacked from Democrat operatives" allegedly providing "assurances that Attorney General Lynch would protect Secretary Clinton by making sure the FBI investigation 'didn't go too far.'" After refusing to answer questions about it on the grounds that doing so would call for a classified response, the FBI director revealed that he had "briefed leadership of the intelligence committees on that particular issue."[12] He also promised classified answers behind closed doors to the questions "What steps did the FBI take to determine whether Attorney General Lynch had actually given assurances that the political fix was in no matter what? Did the FBI interview the person who wrote the email? If not, why not?"

Because in his testimony to the Senate Intelligence Committee in June 2017 Comey labeled some "public accounts" of the classified matter "nonsense," I am going to rely on them only to the extent that they are consistent with what we otherwise know from Comey.[13] The conclusion that Russian content was the undisclosed factor in Comey's July decision can be drawn from accounts in the *New York Times*, the *Washington Post*, and CNN. "During Russia's hacking campaign against the United States," reported the *New York Times* in April 2017, "intelligence agencies could peer, at times, into Russian networks and see what had been taken. Early last year, F.B.I. agents received a batch of hacked documents, and one caught their attention. The document, which has been described as both a memo and an email, was written by a Democratic operative who expressed confidence that Ms. Lynch would keep the Clinton investigation from going too far, according to several former officials familiar with the document."[14] The May 2017 account in the *Washington Post* differs in what it reports the FBI obtained: "[i]n the midst of the 2016 presidential primary season, the FBI received what was described as a Russian intelligence document claiming a tacit understanding between the Clinton campaign and the Justice Department over the inquiry into whether she intentionally revealed classified information through her use of a private email server."[15]

At issue in the *Post*'s account was a Russian intelligence document referring to a "supposed email describing how then-Attorney General Loretta E. Lynch had privately assured someone in the Clinton campaign that the email investigation would not push too deeply into the matter." The *Post* also reported, "If true, the revelation of such an understanding would have undermined the integrity of the FBI's investigation." The result? "Current and former officials have," according to the *Post*, "said that Comey relied on the document in making his July decision to announce on his own, without Justice Department involvement, that the investigation was over."

In *A Higher Loyalty*, Comey calls the "material" at issue a "development still unknown to the American public to this day," describes it as coming "from a classified source,"[16] and treats it as "unverified."[17] Reporting by CNN suggests that he knew that the material was fraudulent.[18] Here the shifting referent for "information" or "material" may be causing confusion. After piecing Comey's testimony, writing, and interviews together, it seems likely that the FBI confirmed the existence of a document in the hands of the same Russians who were responsible for releasing hacked content through Guccifer 2.0 and DCLeaks.

In it, according to the *Post*, a Democratic operative, identified as "then-chair of the Democratic National Committee, Rep. Debbie Wasserman Schultz (D-Fla.)," reportedly "sent an email to Leonard Benardo, an official with the Open Society Foundations, an organization founded by billionaire George Soros and dedicated to promoting democracy" alleging that "Lynch had been in private communication with a senior Clinton campaign staffer named Amanda Renteria" and "told Renteria that she would not let the FBI investigation into Clinton go too far."[19] But contrary to the representation in that supposed document, Wasserman Schultz and Benardo told the *Post* they did not know each other and Lynch told the FBI she did not know Renteria.

However, Comey's rejoinder to the assumption by *PBS NewsHour*'s Judy Woodruff that the information was known to be false suggests the possibility that either the Russian document or the email to which it referred was real but the information about Lynch was mistaken or fabricated. "The information was legitimate," he stated. "Now, whether what it said was true about Loretta was a very different question." He then added that, "people have said, you know, it was forgeries or bogus. Not true. But whether the substance of the information was accurate or not, I saw no reason to believe that."[20]

Statements by Senator Lindsey Graham (R-SC) on CBS's *Face the Nation* in June 2017 indicate that in closed-door testimony Comey "never mentioned it was a fake."[21] Graham then said, "I don't know if it's a fake or not." In that same interview, the South Carolina Republican confirmed that Comey "told members of the House and the Senate that the main reason he jumped into the election last year and took over the job of attorney general is because he believed there were emails between the Democratic National Committee and the Department of Justice that compromised the Department of Justice, and he thought the Russians were going to release these emails. That's why he jumped in and took over Loretta Lynch's job." Apart from press reporting and Graham's comments, my reason for thinking that the content in question consisted of a *Russian*-hacked email or *Russian* memorandum alluding to one is Comey's remark that the stolen emails posted by DCLeaks and Guccifer 2.0 "made very real the prospect that the classified material relating to Loretta Lynch might drop at any moment, not decades from now."

Consistent with the notion that the FBI director did not believe that Lynch had promised the Clinton campaign special treatment, he neither sought her recusal nor raised the issue with her or her deputy attorney general, Sally Q. Yates.[22] "If he had any concerns regarding the email investigation, classified or not, he had ample opportunities to raise them with me both privately and in meetings. He never did," Lynch recalled.[23]

Evidence of even a wink and a nod from the attorney general to the Clinton campaign would have prompted congressional investigation by the Republican-controlled House and Senate as well as attendant headlines. "[I]f the intel wasn't fake, where are the subpoenas and obstruction-of-justice indictments that naturally follow?" asks *Wall Street Journal* columnist Holman W. Jenkins, Jr.[24] Neither headlines nor subpoenas have materialized. No one has uncovered and reported evidence that the alleged Lynch exchange happened.

In Comey's view, the potential existence of such content—whether fraudulent or not—in Russian hands put him in a no-win situation. "[T]he release of that material, the truth of which we had not verified, would allow partisans to argue, powerfully, that the Clinton campaign, through Lynch, had been controlling the FBI's investigation," he writes.[25] In short, if Comey did not publicly distance the Clinton server investigation from Lynch by holding the July press conference on his own, he believed that hacked or forged content being held in reserve by the Russians could be released to discredit the FBI and Justice Department and to suggest that the system was indeed rigged.

Protecting the identity of the FBI's methods is a possible reason for the classified status of the controversial content. Another is cover-up. After characterizing it as "an intercepted Russian document," and also as "a Democratic Party email that, in turn, referred to a private conversation in which Attorney General Loretta Lynch assured a Clinton aide that Ms. Lynch would sit on the email investigation," the *Wall Street Journal*'s Jenkins forecasts that "this matter will remain classified for 'decades' because it is embarrassing to Mr. Comey and the FBI. It's also embarrassing, perhaps fatally so, to the intelligence agency that presented the intercept to Mr. Comey. The implication ought to set your hair on fire. Mr. Comey's first intervention led to his second intervention, reopening the Hillary investigation 11 days before the election, which he now concedes he might have resisted if he had not been sure Mrs. Clinton was going to win anyway."[26]

Insinuating forged documents into the media stream would not have been a new troll trick. When the Russian "steal-and-leak strategy" was deployed against the liberal Open Society Foundation, run by George Soros, the *New York Times* reported that some of the private documents "turned out to have been altered to make it appear as if the foundation was financing Russian opposition members."[27] The fact that the supposed hacked email of concern to Comey implicates a Soros associate fits the Russian playbook. Whether the material was hacked from a Democratic account by the Russians, or forged and made to appear to have been hacked, or was an inaccurate or accurate Democratic message that was simply referenced in intercepted Russian communications, it was, by the FBI director's own admission, a factor driving his decision to make the July 5 public statement.

Comey's July public pronouncements could have increased the likelihood that he would decide that he had to notify key members of Congress
(and hence the public) that the investigation had been revived in late
October. In that earlier event, he had gone out of his way to explain how
exhaustive the FBI's process had been. Moreover, he had justified including
"more detail about our process than I ordinarily would, because I think the
American people deserve those details in a case of intense public interest."
Public interest in the FBI's workings had not waned by late October. Had he
not made those public July declarations and had the case instead been closed
with a simple recommendation against referral, the pressure Comey felt to
notify Congress might have been reduced. By contrast, the direct route
from Russian threat to October disclosure assumes that Comey anticipated
release of Russian content after Clinton was elected and moved to protect
or alternatively ensure the legitimacy of her presidency by demonstrating
to Congress and, as a result, the public that the FBI had done its job.

We can't conclusively know the extent to which the "unverified" content
in Russian hands factored into Comey's decision to disclose the reopened
Clinton email investigation on October 28th. Human motivations are complex
and human memory both inexact and subject to self-protective distortion. In
the unlikely event that Comey kept a daily diary, it remains out of public view.
In his 2017 testimony he said that his July 2016 press conference was attributable to the classified material and the Clinton-Lynch tarmac meeting. Senator
Graham reported that, in closed session, Comey claimed that the former was
"the main reason he jumped into the election and took over the job of attorney
general." That revelation justifies the conclusion that Comey would not have
made his expansive public statement in July 2016 were he not concerned about
the release of the Russian-held material. The alternative to holding the press
conference presumably was simply issuing a statement reporting that the FBI
had closed the investigation after finding no basis for filing criminal charges.
Comey told a Senate committee in May 2017, that in the spring of 2016 he
"struggled" with the question, "how do we credibly complete the investigation
of Hillary Clinton's e-mails if we conclude there's no case there? The normal
way to do it would be to the Department of Justice announce it."[28]

One reason that the Russian material may have mattered in October is that
it factored in Comey's decision to go public in July and that going public in

July played some role in deciding to make the October investigation known. The testimony by Comey that introduces that possibility states in full:

> That was a hard call for me to make to call the attorney general that morning and say I'm about to do a press conference and I'm not going to tell you what I'm going to say. And I said to her, hope someday you'll understand why I think I have to do this. But look, I wasn't loving this.
>
> I knew this [presumably the press conference] would be disastrous for me personally, but I thought this is the best way to protect these institutions that we care so much about. *And having done that* [I assume the referent here is the press conference], *and then having testified repeatedly under oath we're done*, this was done in a credible way, *there's no there there*.
>
> That when the Anthony Weiner thing landed on me on October 27 and there was a huge—this is what people forget—new step to be taken, we may be finding the golden missing e-mails that would change this case. *If I were not to speak about that* [the Weiner laptop investigation], *it would be a disastrous, catastrophic concealment* [emphasis added].[29]

As the sections that I have italicized suggest, what I hear Comey saying is that his press conference and repeated testimony under oath (that there was no "there there") led him to conclude that failure to speak about the reopened investigation would constitute "disastrous, catastrophic concealment." In other words, in the absence of the July event and follow-up testimony under oath, he may not have felt compelled to alert Congress to the existence of the new probe. After all, notifying Congress of investigations is neither inevitable nor routine. The FBI, for example, was investigating contacts between those in the Trump campaign and Russians without letting Congress know.

Moreover, despite the existence of the press conference and his previous testimony, there is reason to believe that had Comey thought that the outcome of the election was uncertain, he might not have notified Congress. Here another media effect enters the stage. "I had assumed from media polling that Hillary Clinton was going to win," writes the former FBI director in his memoir.[30] "I have asked myself many times since if I was influenced by that assumption.... Certainly not consciously, but I would be a fool to say it couldn't have had an impact on me. *It is entirely possible that*, because I was making decisions in an environment where Hillary Clinton was sure to be the next president, *my concern about making her an illegitimate president by concealing the restarted investigation bore greater weight than it would have if the election appeared closer* or if Donald Trump were ahead in the polls [emphasis added]." In short, he could have been silent about the restarted probe. We don't know whether Comey's decision to disclose the reopened investigation was affected by "unverified" material in Russian hands, including content that, according to the Office of the Inspector General, alleged that Comey "was attempting to influence the [midyear] investigation by extending it to help Republicans win the election" (June 2018, pg. 171). We know that Comey worried that the Lynch allegation could be used to discredit the FBI's work. But its disclosure could also have been used to argue that Clinton's was an illegitimate presidency secured by a cover-up of the laptop investigation. If Comey foresaw that circumstance, then the Russian-held content may have affected his decision to notify Congress.

The October 28 decision and its attendant press coverage altered the electoral dynamic in a period in which large numbers of absentee ballots were being cast and those who disliked both Clinton and Trump were disproportionately deciding that they would cast a vote for the Republican or (perhaps more accurately) against the Democrat.

As I noted a moment ago, on November 6—two days before the polls officially opened on Election Day—Comey informed congressional leaders that the new investigation had not altered his July conclusion. Just as asserting that a person is not guilty associates them with the notion of guilt, the headlines reporting that outcome were problematic for Clinton. "FBI Director to Congress: Still No Charges Recommended after Latest Clinton Emails Reviewed," declared the write-up on the CBS News website.[31] "FBI Declares It Is Finally Done Investigating Hillary Clinton's Email," noted *USA Today*.[32] Absentee ballots had been cast during the period encompassing the news coverage of the Comey probe. Voting decisions had been made.

With the vigor of a '60s rock classic, a backbeat of FBI disclosures pulsed into the news media in the closing days of October. On October 28: the Comey notification. On October 30: a confirmation that the Clinton Foundation probe was justified. On October 30: seeming dismissal of a Trump-Russia link. In the second case, when a reporter inquired about "reports saying that the FBI's deputy director, Andrew McCabe, had given a 'stand down' order regarding an investigation of the Clinton Foundation," an editorial in the *Wall Street Journal* noted, he "authorized a leak of a phone conversation in which Mr. McCabe plays the hero by pushing back when a high-ranking Justice Department official complained that New York FBI agents were still looking into the Clinton Foundation." In the resulting October 30, 2016, *Journal* article, McCabe is quoted asking, "Are you telling me that I need to shut down a validly predicated investigation?"[33] The response was "Of course not." Based on a report from the Justice Department's inspector general, McCabe was fired for lying about his role in leaking the information.[34] But in the period of interest here, reporting of that FBI leak confirmed that the FBI deputy director considered the investigation of the Clinton Foundation warranted, a revelation whose suasory power was bolstered by its unexpected nature. After all, McCabe's wife had run for the Senate as a Democrat in a campaign financed in part by Virginia Governor Terry McAuliffe, a Clinton loyalist.

The next day, an October 31 *New York Times* headline and frame effectively sabotaged the Clinton campaign's arguments about Russian intrigue and intent. "Investigating Donald Trump, F.B.I. Sees No Clear Link to Russia," it read.[35] In the article itself the notion that no "clear" link has been found was qualified to refer instead to no "conclusive or direct link."

For the Clinton cause, the revelations in the piece were devastating. They not only undercut the October 7 confirmation that the Russians were behind the hacking, but also subverted the Democratic assertions that the Russians were trying to help Trump and that Trump was Putin's puppet. Throughout, the article also dismissed a "clear," "conclusive," or "direct" link between *Trump himself* and the "*Russian government.*" "Law enforcement officials say that none of the investigations so far have found any conclusive or direct link between Mr. Trump and the Russian government," the piece noted. "And even the hacking into Democratic emails, F.B.I. and intelligence officials now believe, was aimed at disrupting the presidential election rather than electing Mr. Trump." A later paragraph added that "Mr. Comey would not even confirm the existence of any investigation of Mr. Trump's aides when asked during an appearance in September before Congress. In the Obama administration's internal deliberations over identifying the Russians as the source of the hacks, Mr. Comey also argued against doing so and succeeded in keeping the F.B.I.'s imprimatur off the formal findings, a law enforcement official said." By saying that Comey kept the FBI's "imprimatur" off the October 7 attribution of the hacking to the Russians, the article invited the possibility that the FBI and its director disputed that conclusion. Instead, in his book Comey explains his abstention as adherence to a "powerful norm" that "we should try to avoid, if possible, any action in the run up to an election that could have an impact on the election result. In October 2016, there was no good reason for the FBI to speak about the Russians and the election. Americans already knew what was happening, so the FBI could reasonably avoid action."[36] As the Comey October notification as well as the revelations in these *New York Times* and *Wall Street Journal* articles attest, in matters concerning Hillary Clinton but not Donald Trump, that norm was more honored in the breach than in the observance.

Buried in the tenth paragraph of that *Times* article was a sentence that should have been its lede. "Intelligence officials have said in interviews over the last six weeks that apparent connections between some of Mr. Trump's aides and Moscow originally compelled them to open a broad investigation into possible links between the Russian government and the Republican presidential candidate."[37] And even here, the word "originally" obscures the ongoing nature of the investigation.

When Comey closed the email investigation on November 6, the Russian troll account @TEN_GOP urged that its followers retweet a demand from "The American People" that Comey resign or be impeached. Juxtaposed with a scowling image of him were the words: "FBI DIRECTOR COMEY RESIGN NOW—The American People." "RT if you think that FBI Director Comey should be impeached for blocking the investigation & abetting a criminal," said the tweet. In January 2018 Twitter confirmed that this appeal was among those that "received significant engagement."[38]

A substantial body of research confirms that once individuals make a decision, they dismiss or downplay information that runs counter to it.[39] Moreover, scholarship on the correction of misinformation suggests that a single announcement is unlikely to undo the attitudinal effects of even short-term exposure to the presumption of wrongdoing.[40] In the case of

Figure 10.1 @TEN_GOP tweet asserting that FBI Director James Comey should resign.

the revived email probe, new suspicions clouded the Clinton candidacy for nine days. During that period, her efforts to demonstrate that the Russians were trying to defeat her and elect Trump were undercut by leaks presumably from members of Congress and individuals in the intelligence community, and a resulting *New York Times* framing that does not withstand the test of time. Nor does the McCabe leak to the *Wall Street Journal* hold up well. The probe of the Clinton Foundation has yielded no referrals. Importantly, most of the early ballots in 2016 were cast during the peak coverage of the hacked content, the two debates featuring it, and the nine days in which the FBI's reopened investigation cast a shadow over the Clinton campaign.[41]

To this point I have shown that a sufficiently large group of susceptible voters existed to change the outcome of the 2016 election. In order to affect their decision about whether and, if so, for whom to vote, the Russians needed their troll content to accomplish five objectives or their hacked content to accomplish one: For the trolls to matter, they had to: (1) engage in sufficiently widespread messaging; (2) focus on issues compatible with Trump's strategic needs; (3) address constituencies he had to mobilize and demobilize, (4) employ persuasive content that was amplified in swing states, was visually evocative, and whose power was magnified by sharing, liking, and commenting; and (5) target their appeals well. For the hackers to change the outcome, they had to affect the news and debate agendas and anti-Clinton message weighting as late deciders were mulling their decisions. Although the case for adept troll targeting remains tentative, the reach of the hacked content is clear. If a Russian hacked or forged document played a role in the Comey-prompted anti-Clinton news coverage of the final week and a half of the campaign, the case for Russian influence becomes even more conclusive. With that summary as a preface, in the next chapter I will indicate what we don't, can't, and do know about the relationship between the Russian interventions and the 2016 electoral outcome.

What We Don't, Can't, and Do Know About How Russian Hackers and Trolls Helped Elect Donald J. Trump

M y subtitle forecast answers to the questions "What don't, can't, and do we know?" Let me now turn to answering them. In doing so, I do not wish to underplay the extent to which Clinton's actions and rhetoric made the contest close enough for her to lose. Factors in the "might have been" or "if one could do it over" column for Democrats include, among others, her missteps as a candidate (e.g., "deplorables" and the initial failure to disclose that she had been diagnosed with pneumonia), the poor strategic choices of the Clinton campaign (e.g., not focusing on key states or offering a compelling vision of a Clinton presidency), her decision to use a personal server as Secretary of State, and her private and public messaging about the attack on the US compound and deaths of four Americans in Benghazi (e.g., an email to her daughter that appeared to attribute the attack to a terrorist group and her statement "What difference does it make?" in the Benghazi hearings were ripe for reinterpretation by the trolls, conservative media, and the Trump campaign).

Also in the mix were the stark stylistic differences between the two major party nominees. Unlike Trump, whose freewheeling rhetoric was consistent with the assumption that "what you see is what you get," Clinton's wariness of the press, caution when speaking extemporaneously, and discomfort with personal narrative all invited audiences to read between the lines while also asking, what wasn't she saying? At the same time, the notion that her public and private positions might diverge on issues such as trade was reinforced by reports that as First Lady she privately opposed the North Atlantic Free Trade Agreement (NAFTA) while publicly championing it.[1]

Nor should we ignore the fact that the Democratic incumbent president had access to but chose not to use a bully pulpit capable of focusing the nation on the Russian treachery. Rather than waiting to do so until after the election, President Obama could have punctuated the October 7 Homeland Security and national intelligence revelations by visibly seizing the Russian compounds near New York City and on Maryland's Eastern Shore and immediately expelling the thirty-five "intelligence operatives" who instead would be ousted in December. Of course, we can't know whether taking those actions during the campaign rather than after the election would have worked in Clinton's favor or, as the incumbent may have feared, against her.

My analysis here assumes that all of these Clinton and Obama factors are givens and everything that happened in 2016 is baked in *other than those changes and actions precipitated by the Russian interventions*. In that scenario, what difference would adding the Russian-held and hacked content and troll messaging make?

What We Don't Know

Among the things that we don't currently know is the extent to which candidate-controlled messaging reached the electorate in the campaign's final month. Specifically, was Trump out-advertising Clinton? When one candidate outspends the other on ads in some periods and media but not others, the overall effects become more difficult to assess. In a move that may have protected her lead in the popular vote, from October 18 to October

30 Clinton dramatically outspent Trump on televised and cable ads.[2] During this period, her national spots aired almost two and a half times as often as his.[3] Not so in the closing days when Trump delivered a televised closing argument in the form of a $7-million two-minute ad. In it, he proclaimed, "Our movement is about replacing the failed and corrupt political establishment with a new government controlled by you, the American people."[4] Although Clinton outspent him significantly on television ads overall, Trump's campaign invested nearly $39 million in last-minute TV buys.[5] Since ad effects decay quickly[6] but are most pronounced among those still making up their minds, this spending pattern may have helped Trump hold down Clinton's advantage in the popular vote and given him a boost with late deciders.

To know whether that is the case we would also have to factor in the relative amounts or effects of the ad spending and related messaging in other venues, including radio and online, by each campaign and by the independent groups backing them. (Available evidence suggests that, in the final month, Trump outspent Clinton on digital advertising while her campaign bought more time on air than his.)

Historically, disparities in ad spending have shifted votes except in cases in which the messaging of one candidate was poorly targeted or less resonant than that of the other.[7] At this point, we can't readily document the content of the web or radio ads or determine how well targeted they were. Federal Election Commission reports do reveal that the Trump campaign and Republican Party deployed about $5 million of digital ads to get out the vote in Michigan, Wisconsin, Pennsylvania, and Florida.[8] It is also possible that one candidate or the other had the more savvy appeals.

Moreover, because the Russian messages complemented those being burnished by the Trump campaign and its legitimate allies and were appearing in some of the same channels, we can't readily separate the impact of one from the other. At this point, we also don't have access to the data that would permit us to model the troll social media stream and identify its likely recipients. A rigorous study would require examining the content produced by all of the players, including the Russians, determining the targeting of each message, and then finding a way to assess effects. The reason gaps in evidence matter is that one can only ascertain the effects of a supplementary messaging stream after first accounting for or controlling the impact of the other communication in the environment. What we can know, however, is that an increase in volume that alters the message weighting can in turn influence voters and votes.

What We Can't Know

Even if all of the needed data mysteriously appeared, after the fact we have no good way to isolate the effects of troll-generated and hacked content from the impact of multiple other sources and forms of electoral communication. And, because we lack real-time, rolling cross-sectional polling data tied to media messaging and exposure in each of the three decisive states, conclusions about the synergy between the Russian-generated social media messages and press reporting on the hacked content will inevitably remain less than conclusive.

Other hurdles stand between probable exposure to troll messaging and air-tight inferences about its electoral impact. It is easier to divine why people voted the way they did than why they opted out. Although a sample of voters can be interviewed as they leave their polling stations, there are no comparable polls of nonvoters.

Large-scale representative panels that track the views of the same individuals over time can serve as an alternative. But those who run them have had trouble recruiting the kinds of voters that swung the election to Trump. And even if the national panels had overcome these limitations, they can't generate reliable inferences about a small shift in voting or nonvoting in three states because none had a large representative sample empaneled in each of the decisive jurisdictions. In short, if Trump won because Russians motivated some potential voters to stay home, we have no ready way to confirm that that is what happened. Importantly, because after-the-fact recollections are untrustworthy, to be truly reliable, evidence about whether and for whom an individual voted should be gathered in real time. A large panel does exist that overcomes some of these concerns as best one can. In chapter 3, I cited its analysis of 2012 Obama voters who did not vote in 2016.

Because we lack a large swath of the potential electorate exposed neither to the trolls' social media amplifications nor to the media's reporting on the

Russian-hacked material, we cannot use a tested means of assessing the extent to which these stimuli affected voters' perceptions of Clinton or Trump and, with them, the election. In past contests, scholars have isolated ad effects by comparing the attitudes of comparable individuals in battleground and nonbattleground states. To do that in the 2000 election, my co-authors and I analyzed the content of the ads; factored in the data on ad buys; linked the content to the amount of exposure in media markets; matched markets to voting precincts; recorded national news; and linked all of that to daily tracking of changes in attitudes and vote preferences in a large, nationally representative sample of the public. By comparing the attitudes of survey respondents in ad-clogged battleground markets to those of voters in ad-free zones, we were able to capture the effects of exposure to these messages. Because we lack a reliable way to locate either internet advertising and messaging or those exposed to it, and, in the case of media coverage of the hacked content, the entire nation was exposed to the resulting reporting, our 2000 model no longer works.

Even if we managed to surmount those barriers, other confounding factors remain difficult to untangle. It is easier to figure out what people did than why they did it. And multiple factors, some of them beyond conscious awareness, may influence a decision. Rain may have depressed or sunshine motivated turnout in some locales. In the absence of the option to support a candidate other than Trump and Clinton, some of those balloting for Stein might have simply decided to stay home. Black voters may have opted out because they were less enthusiastic about Clinton than Obama. Veterans and white evangelicals, traditionally Republican constituencies, may have simply "come home" to their preferred party. However, all of these effects would have been more likely if pro-Trump or anti-Clinton issues, candidate traits, or emotions were made to seem more important to target voters, a probable effect of exposure to the Trump-aligned Russian messaging and hacked content.

Finally, we can't know how, if at all, the "unverified" content in Russian hands factored into Comey's decision to disclose the re-opened Clinton email investigation on October 28. From the available evidence, we can only know that it may have. As I noted in chapter 10, the indirect hypothesis posits that the prospect of a Russian leak combined with the Clinton-Lynch tarmac talk to lead Comey to hold the July press conference, which in turn prompted the late-October disclosure. The direct route from Russian threat to October notification assumes that his anticipation that the Russians would release the document after Clinton's election led him to demonstrate to Congress and the public that the FBI had not protected her candidacy by choosing to be silent about the revived investigation. However, in the absence of contemporaneous evidence of intent, we can't know whether the Russian-held content led to a decision whose effect on the press and campaign agenda was great enough to have cost Clinton the election.

What all of this means is that efforts to make an ironclad case that Russian machinations altered the election's outcome will be thwarted by unknowns that include the absence of daily survey tracking of relevant questions in the last five weeks in three key states, an inability to separate the effects of similar content streams, the absence of the wherewithal to discern why individuals in specific states and demographics decided not to vote, the nonexistence of an electoral cohort unexposed to the stolen Democratic content, and our inability to know how Russian-held or fabricated content factored into the FBI director's decision to go public with word of the reopened Clinton investigation.

What We Do Know

Still, we do make most of life's decisions based on less-than-rock-solid, incontrovertible evidence. My case that the uses of Russian-hacked Democratic materials influenced voters is built on scholars' understanding of the effects of linguistic priming, media agenda setting and framing, the susceptibilities of late deciders, the dispositions of those who view both candidates unfavorably, the effects of imbalances in the amount of negative information available about alternative candidates, and scholarship on how debates affect voter attitudes. It is scaffolded on evidence that the hacked content not only altered the media and debate agendas but also increased the level of negative press about Clinton. And it is bolstered by the possibility that Russian access and anticipated use of illegally gotten or fabricated Democratic content shaped a key decision by FBI Director Comey.

If the same sorts of effects that scholars have documented in past elections occurred in 2016, particularly those produced by agenda setting, framing, two-step flow, weighting and peer influence, then the trolls' messaging helped Trump and hurt Clinton as well. We do not know whether it was well enough targeted to change the outcome. But the likelihood exists. The notion that they contributed to his win is fortified by the fact that their theory of his electoral needs was sound, their messaging was sufficiently adept and extensive enough to matter, and their themes aligned with those of his campaign.

Like Trump's message, the trolls' appeals tapped into the economic frustrations as well as the related threat their target audience attributed to the multiracial, multinational, ecumenical culture championed by the Clinton campaign and the Obama White House. Unease about cultural change not only predicted a Republican vote but also played a more significant role in a Trump ballot in 2016 than a Romney one in 2012. As I noted earlier, negative attitudes toward immigration, black Americans, and Muslims were more central to support for Trump than for the Republican standard-bearer in 2012.[9]

At the same time, evidence that the trolls' messaging was not simply cacophonous[10] comes from the fact that they tried to mobilize, demobilize, and shift the sorts of voters that Trump needed to win. Consistent with Russian-created appeals, the percentages of white evangelicals and those in military households who supported Trump increased after the summer, and a combination of Sanders's supporters and blacks avoided the ballot box in numbers that would have been great enough to put Clinton over the top had they instead cast ballots for her in key states. Moreover, had the 2016-over-2012 increase in the Green Party vote gone instead to Clinton, the Democrat would have carried Michigan and Wisconsin. Additionally, black turnout was down from years past and white turnout was up. With all of these pro-Trump elements at play simultaneously, and being reinforced by troll and hacked content, the number of combinations that produce the votes he needed to win multiplies and with it the likelihood that Russian interventions designed to affect those factors altered the election's outcome.

Scholarly research predicts that increasing the salience of anti-Clinton topics, frames, and language will increase the likelihood that they will figure in the candidate evaluations of late deciders, a group that is more susceptible to media effects to begin with. At the same time, upping the amount of content hostile to Clinton should change the communication climate in ways inimical to her interests. In this scenario her supporters would be more likely to fall silent. And, importantly, negative information is more quickly and deeply processed than the positive kind and is also more readily retrieved from memory.[11] With all of these factors at play, late deciders—who disapproved of both candidates—voted disproportionately for Trump.[12]

The conclusion that Russian trolls and hackers helped elect a US president draws support from decades of scholarly work probing the effects of agenda setting, framing, priming, message weighting, debates, negative information, contagion, peer influence, and the spiral of silence. As earlier chapters have argued, the Kremlin-tied interventions functioned in each of these areas in ways that in past elections have produced discernible effects, many of them larger than the one required to alter the 2016 outcome.

The case that Russian machinations affected the news and debate agendas in ways hostile to the Clinton candidacy is particularly cogent. Not only did reporters' framing of the hacked Democratic content disadvantage Clinton but it magnified news, debate, Trump, and troll themes of corruption and disingenuousness that are especially lethal when attached to a female candidate. In 2016, the Russian-hacked private emails also altered the news agenda at key points in the election cycle, including the Democratic convention, the weekend of the disclosure of the Access Hollywood tape, and the final four weeks of the campaign.

This occurred with the complicity of the news media which concluded that the content was reliable and worthy of dissemination. In the final month of the campaign, coverage of the hacked content not only reshaped the media agenda but increased the relative amount of anti-Clinton content in the communication stream. Exposure to that messaging is a plausible explanation for the erosion in public confidence that Clinton was qualified to be president that occurred after the first debate but before the reopening of the Comey investigation. Additionally, viewers of either of the two intervening debates were more likely than non-viewers to report a difference between Clinton's public and private sentiments, an assessment consistent with the one presupposed in the moderators' and Trump's use of the hacked content. These negative post-debate perceptions predict a reduced likelihood that a respondent will project voting for the Democratic nominee.

Finally, with speculation about this latest Clinton "scandal" dominating the headlines, the numbers preferring Clinton over Trump dropped during the last-minute Comey investigation. If Russian intrigue led to the nine days of publicized suspicion that eroded Clinton's support in the election's final week and a half, the case that Russian activities swung the election to Trump becomes even more conclusive.

Afterword
Where Does This Leave Us?

Some awaken each morning knowing down to their DNA that any discussion of Russian influence is "fake news," advanced to undercut the legitimacy of the president they elected. Others believe just as viscerally that the only way the star of *The Apprentice* could have been elected was through subterfuge, whatever its source. Because the Russian cyberpiracy, espionage, and assaults of 2016 were not a one-off, we cannot afford to let partisan impulses or public apathy stand in the way of hardening our defenses.

"At a minimum, we expect Russia to continue using propaganda, social media, false-flag personas, sympathetic spokespeople, and other means of influence to try to exacerbate social and political fissures in the United States," Director of National Intelligence Dan Coats told the Senate Intelligence Committee on February 13, 2018.[1] "We have seen Russian activity and intentions to have an impact on the next election cycle," reported CIA Director Mike Pompeo. "There should be no doubt that Russia perceives its past efforts as successful and views the 2018 U.S. midterm elections as a potential target," added Coats,[2] who argued as well that "[w]e need to inform the American public that this is real. We aren't going to allow some Russian to tell us how to vote, how we ought to run our country. I think there needs to be a national cry for that."[3]

That cry should be heard and acted on by those who unwittingly helped the Russians achieve their ends in 2016. Of this congregation, five are of particular note. The press. The platforms. The citizenry. Past and prospective candidates. And the polarizers who have created a climate conducive to distrust and discord.

The Press

The success of the Russian "steal and release" strategy depended on reporters and editors. Would they invest the stolen content with significance unmerited by its substance? Would they obscure its Russian origins? The answer to both was "yes." "The overhyped coverage of the hacked emails was the media's worst mistake in 2016," observed *New York Times* columnist and associate editorial page editor David Leonhardt in May 2017, "one sure to be repeated if not properly understood. Television was the biggest offender, but print media was hardly blameless."[4]

With few exceptions, journalists have failed to publicly engage the question "what should reporters and editors have done differently?" Some, notably individuals at the *New York Times*, including Leonhardt, Amy Chozick, and the Pulitzer Prize–winning team of Eric Lipton, David E. Sanger, and Scott Shane, have acknowledged the ways in which US journalists did Russia's bidding. Chozick, for example, recalls about the *Times'* decision to "confirm" and "contextualize" the hacked Podesta emails on October 7, 2016, "I didn't argue that it appeared the emails were stolen by a hostile foreign government that had staged an attack on our electoral system. I didn't push to hold off on publishing them until we could have a less harried discussion. I didn't raise the possibility that we'd become puppets in Putin's shadowy campaign. I chose the byline."[5] She was not alone. "Every major publication, including the *Times*, published multiple stories citing the D.N.C. and Podesta emails posted by WikiLeaks, becoming a de facto instrument of Russian intelligence," concluded Lipton and his colleagues, whose assessment I share.

"Mr. Putin, a student of martial arts, had turned two institutions at the core of American democracy—political campaigns and independent media—to his own ends."[6]

The opportunity costs were high. Imagine that half of the time devoted to reading and writing about the hacked emails had instead been dedicated to exploring the implications of the October 7 national intelligence assessment. The superficial, unsustained coverage of its process and conclusions is a failure worthy of study in journalism classes. In significance, press neglect of that document rivals the 1988 failure to explore the impending savings-and-loan crisis and the foreseeable demise of the Soviet Union. If "what might have been" is the test, the underplayed Russia story is eclipsed only by press neglect of the Hart Rudman report's warnings about attacks of the kind that occurred on 9/11.

Compounding this journalistic lapse is the October 31 *New York Times* story whose lede alleged that there was no clear Trump-Russia link. As I noted earlier, submerged in the piece was confirmation that the FBI had been investigating contacts between those allied with the Trump campaign and high-level Russians. Had that revelation topped the story and the piece generated the pick-up that the *Times* has historically elicited, the resulting news reports might have counterbalanced the breathless ones that wasted space speculating on what Comey would find in the FBI's ultimately fruitless scouring of the emails on the Weiner laptop.

When the Clinton speech excerpts were WikiLeak'd, the performance of the otherwise admirable journalists who host the Sunday-morning interview shows was wanting as well. By ignoring the second clause in Clinton's sentence about "open borders," they, with a single exception, sucker-punched her candidacy. A second regrettable moment occurred in the final debate, where the moderator, Chris Wallace, truncated the same statement in the same way. As the co-author of a book on presidential debates who also has served on two commissions seeking to reform them, I can recall no other instance in which a statement by a candidate has been as egregiously sundered from its context in a presidential debate. As I noted in the relevant chapter, the Annenberg polling data suggest that Clinton's prospects were damaged by that Russian-generated debate exchange as well as by a similar use of negatively framed hacked content in the second debate. Throughout the general election campaign season, the press also normalized the hacked content by referring to its origins as "WikiLeaks" and its substance as "emails." By conventionalizing the notion that the Russians merely "meddled," reporters are doing the same in the run-up to the 2018 contests.

My critique assumes that the mainstream press still matters. It does. But for how much longer is an open question. Although it is not a topic I have treated in the book, it is worth noting that the Russian operatives both exploited and magnified distrust of the press. In troll world, the mainstream media were covering up such supposed "scandals" as Clinton's terminal illness and the Democrats' complicity in the death of a young Democratic National Committee (DNC) staffer. This blurring of the lines between credible and bogus sources further erodes the ability of the press to serve as a credible watchdog.

The Social Media Platforms

Although there was not a Russian behind every tree in 2016, there was one behind some high-volume social media accounts and sites. Facebook, Instagram, Twitter, YouTube, and Tumblr were among the tech giants that unwittingly became conduits for Russian propaganda. Those in charge of them not only didn't anticipate the malign uses to which their systems could be put, but also failed to identify and thwart the illegal troll efforts to influence voters. The glacial pace with which the platforms uncovered and disclosed election-related abuse does not invite confidence in their readiness to prevent a sequel. Since it took them more than a year to figure out what went wrong in 2016, how can we expect them to prevent a recurrence in 2018 and 2020? Nor is faith inspired by revelations that the Trump campaign's digital firm secured unauthorized access to data on millions of Facebook users.

Nonetheless, both regulatory and voluntary changes are afoot that fall into five broad and somewhat overlapping categories. To provide a sense of the range of the platforms' responses, let me briefly highlight a few reforms that fall into each. The first involves blocking and notification. The second, disclosure. The third, supplementary information. The fourth, preventing foreign nationals from buying candidate ads. The fifth, removing some of the capacity of advertisers to pander to the baser emotions of a platform's audience.

Not only have the platforms removed past troll content, but they have also developed "improvements in machine learning and artificial intelligence, which can proactively identify suspicious behavior at a scale that was not possible before—without needing to look at the content itself."[7] As a result, Facebook, for example, reports that it "now block[s] millions of fake accounts each day as people try to create them—and before they've done any harm." And a number of the platforms have notified those who interacted with a troll account. "When we uncovered these accounts," Tumblr informed these users, "we notified law enforcement, terminated the accounts, and deleted their original posts. While investigating their activity on Tumblr, we discovered that you either followed one of these accounts linked to the IRA, or liked or reblogged one of their posts." Twitter "notified all 1.4 million affected users that they saw election disinformation."[8]

On the disclosure front, in late 2017 the Federal Election Commission required that political ads containing images or videos on Facebook include disclaimers indicating who paid for them.[9] Google reports that it will reveal funders as well. Meanwhile, YouTube is including a marker on all government-funded content. So, for example, videos uploaded by the Russian state-sponsored RT (formerly Russia Today) now carry the notice that "RT is funded in whole or in part by the Russian government."

Efforts that offer contextualizing information have been rolled out as well. Facebook has promised to show all of the ads that a specific page buys and Twitter is forecasting a dashboard with information about the buyer, run time, and target of ads. Additionally, Facebook now algorithmically surfaces fact-checks alongside popular content that has been debunked by one of its partnering organizations, among them FactCheck.org, which I co-founded and which is staffed by reporters in the policy center that I direct.

Additionally, to prevent foreign nationals from funding some types of political ads on the platform, going forward Facebook will require that advertisers mentioning a candidate for federal office provide a verification code transmitted to them by a postcard sent through the US postal service to a US address. Google will ask the same kinds of prospective advertisers to submit their IRS employer identification numbers, in the case of political action committees, and, in the case of individuals, to provide government-issued identification and a Social Security number. However, neither tech giant is including ads focused on issues in its plans. Since most of the trolls' paid messaging fell into that category, the omission is concerning.

As I argued in my discussion of targeting, the trolls located their desired audiences by harnessing the capacities built into the platforms. Although Facebook has not disclosed which terms have been removed from its targeting system, in addition to shutting down known IRA troll accounts (a move that Twitter made as well), it also has sunset one-third of the targeting categories exploited by the trolls to sow discord in the populace.[10] Facebook also has disabled "a form of advertising targeting called Partner Categories, which allowed prominent third-party data aggregators like Experian and Acxiom to provide clients with offline data like purchasing activity to inform ad targeting."[11]

The Citizenry

Those who retweeted troll content or unwittingly assisted St. Petersburg operatives in populating rallies are testaments to the blinders that ideology can place on one's critical faculties. So too are those who shared bogus stories that did not originate with the trolls. Among them were ones bearing headlines such as "Pope Francis Shocks World, Endorses Donald Trump for President" and "FBI Agent Suspected in Hillary Email Leaks Found Dead in Apparent Murder-Suicide."

Although I prefer to characterize it as viral deception (VD), with the homage to venereal disease a deliberate ploy to convey that it should not be transmitted, by one estimate, roughly one in four Americans visited a fake news website in the period between October 7 and November 14, 2016.[12] Despite the fact that much of this content was not troll-created, its popularity remains problematic. Worrisomely, the most popular fake news stories were more widely shared on Facebook than the most popular mainstream news ones.[13] Although recall of the heavily circulated deceptive stories may have been too small to have affected the election's outcome, the phenomenon is still troubling.[14] And, of course, influence can exist even when recall does not.

Empowering users with information and motivating its use may minimize both the platforms' past vulnerabilities and those susceptibilities that the trolls exploited in their users. If viewers can be incentivized to take advantage of them, structures such as YouTube's unmasking of the creators of content (e.g., RT) should help prospective voters assess whether or not to trust the messengers. Because the assessment of messages is affected by the credibility of their source, knowing that a site mimicking the design and logo of a legitimate news outlet is an imposter also should make a difference. If Facebook users can be lured into reading corrective information before digesting a disconfirmed story, the effects of the misleading content should prove less powerful, as well. Guides to spotting disinformation are also being integrated into the curricula of some schools. But because humans uncritically process congenial content and tend to reject the uncongenial kind, the power of informational solutions is limited. By preventing access to start with, efforts to identify and block imposter accounts hold promise while also posing challenges beyond the scope of my inquiry here.

The Candidates

The two major party nominees increased our collective vulnerability to Russian machinations in very different ways. Trump did so by what he said and did, and Clinton by what she failed to do. In the former case, imagine that the mercurial tycoon had responded to the intelligence report about Russian hacking by not only castigating the Russian spies as LOSERS but also by promising that his campaign would make no use of the stolen content. Before telling his supporters that the Russian cybersoldiers' actions constituted an undeclared cyberwar on our electoral system, in my hypothetical he also might have tweeted a demand for prompt retaliation. Minus the tweeting and the LOSER label, I will wager that past Republican nominees John McCain and Mitt Romney would have chosen that course of action. Trump, of course, did not. Instead, he cited the WikiLeak'd content with relish and earlier in the campaign publicly urged Russia to find "the 30,000 [Clinton] emails that are missing"; said, "They probably have them. I'd like to have them released"; and forecast that "I think you will probably be rewarded mightily by our press." (Unfortunately, that last assertion is probably accurate.)

On the Democratic side, had Clinton released the misnamed "Wall Street" speech texts when Sanders first called on her to do so, the notion that she was hiding something would not have become a commonplace assumption driving the press narrative. With time to scrutinize and argue over what she actually said and meant, Sanders, reporters, and the interested public would have exhausted the issue long before the hacked Podesta emails were WikiLeak'd.

The Polarizers

Also blameworthy are those trafficking in toxic forms of polarization. This was an election rife with enmity and "enemies." Gone in 2016 was the assumption that those in the leadership of the other political party were persons of goodwill and integrity. Instead of being philosophical, disagreements were personal. Motives were routinely impugned. Distrust was the norm. Were the climate not so polarized and were there still some modicum of trust on both sides, the Republican congressional leadership, and Senate Majority Leader Mitch McConnell in particular, might have joined the Democrats in condemning the Russian hacking. At the national party level, the Republican National Committee chair, Reince Preibus, might have done the same with his DNC counterpart, Donna Brazile. Neither happened.

Partisan distrust isn't limited to elites. Increasingly, Republicans and Democrats "dislike, even loathe" those on the other side.[15] In 1958, "33 percent of Democrats wanted their daughters to marry a Democrat, and 25 percent of Republicans wanted their daughters to marry a Republican," notes political communication scholar Lynn Vavreck. "But... by 2016, 60 percent of Democrats and 63 percent of Republicans felt that way."[16] Importantly, "hostility towards the opposite party is at its highest when conservative subjects are exposed to negative ads and can customize their news environment."[17] The trolls did not create but instead exploited existing fissures in the country.

Increasingly, the public does not trust those of the other party to fairly manage government either.[18] Had a discernible swath of the electorate not been disposed to distrust the integrity and fairness of the leadership of those on the other side of the aisle, neither the idea that the October 2016 intelligence report was partisan nor the notion that the balloting process might be rigged by the Democrats would have seemed plausible. And FBI Director Comey would have had no cause to fear that, if disclosed, untrustworthy Russian-held material would prove persuasive.

Moreover, anticipating polarized responses may have circumscribed the behaviors of those charged with leading. If President Obama chose not to publicly condemn and penalize the Russian interventions in real time because doing so could be perceived as trying to influence the election, then our toxic political culture tied the hands of an incumbent in a potentially consequential way. One can draw a like conclusion about the actions Comey took out of fear that the possible Russian release of suspect claims about Lynch could be parlayed by partisans against the FBI. Also fueled by cross-aisle distrust were worries that partisans could turn public confirmations that the Russians had hacked some states' election computer networks into assertions that electoral outcomes were suspect.

Fathoming what happened in 2016 is important in part because the Russian cyberattacks represented a phase change in US electoral politics. When in 2000, a low-level employee of George W. Bush's media adviser pseudonymously relayed Republican debate prep to the Gore campaign, the Democrats turned it over to the FBI. Because the materials had been sent through the post office, the culprit was eventually convicted of mail fraud. By contrast, when the 2016 Russian hacking of the Democratic Congressional Campaign Committee yielded Democratic plans, they were posted by Guccifer 2.0 and digested in media. Where Osama bin Laden tried to influence the 2004 presidential election with an October 29, 2004, statement on the Arab-language network Al Jazeera, in 2016, Russian trolls, their true identity disguised, dispatched disinformation directly to US voters on social media sites. Whereas in 2008 the Chinese hacked the Obama and McCain campaigns to secure intelligence, in 2016 the Russians took the move a step further by insinuating stolen material into the electoral dialogue. Unlike 2012, when scholars and reporters worried that it was difficult to locate and hence analyze micro-targeted campaign content on the web, in 2016, so-called dark ads, visible only to the targeted audience, made ferreting them out impossible.

Although "forewarned is forearmed" is a cliché that has been around since the sixteenth century, when it took the form of the Latin injunction "praemonitus, praemunitus," like many hoary axioms, it conveys a truth. Organizing the existing public data on Russian messaging and hacking into an explanatory framework and drawing together what we can learn from the past about its probable effects are means of issuing a klaxon-like warning. We need to find the wherewithal to translate forewarned into forearmed.

The forms of Russian intrigue at play in the 2016 election would have been just as problematic if directed against a Republican or third-party nominee. In future years, they may be. Reducing the vulnerability of our electorate and electoral systems to marauding hackers and trolls and anticipating the next machinations of web invaders are vital if the US is to prevent a next strike in the cyberwar that caught the country unawares in 2016. In the process of sorting all of this out, we can only hope that, like the trolls of ancient legends, both those who rampaged through our social media structures and their hacking kin will prove unable to survive exposure to sunlight, that the country that gave the world the internet will devise and implement ways to troll- and hacker-proof it, and that our election security experts, media systems, and electorate will find ways to reduce everyone's susceptibility to the evolving weapons of cyberwar.

Evaluations of Clinton and Trump Traits in October

KEN WINNEG, DAN ROMER,
AND KATHLEEN HALL JAMIESON

APPENDIX ONE

Changes in Perceptions of Clinton and Trump in October

Method

The data were collected from three separate cross-sectional, national telephone surveys designed by Kathleen Hall Jamieson and Ken Winneg. The first was fielded beginning on the day following the September 26, 2016, presidential debate from September 27, 2016, through October 2, 2016, among 1,004 adults in the United States. The second was conducted in the days leading up to the third and final presidential debate from October 13, 2016, through October 17, 2016, among 1,013 US adults. The third and final cross-sectional survey was fielded beginning on the day following the October 19, 2016, presidential debate from October 20, 2016, through October 25, 2016, among a sample of 1,008 US adults. Table A.1.1 provides further details on the dual-frame sample, showing the numbers of surveys conducted with respondents on cell phones and landlines, the margins of error, and the response rates. In each crosssection, surveys were also conducted in Spanish. Descriptive results in appendix 1 were weighted to target the US population of adults.

Table A.1.1 Telephone survey field dates and respondent information.

End Date	Field Date	Total N	Total Cell Respondents	Total Landline Respondents	Margin of Sampling Error	Response Rate*
10/25/16	10/20/16–10/25/16	1,008	708	300	+/– 3.64%	11%
10/17/16	10/13/16–10/17/16	1,013	610	403	+/– 3.78%	8%
10/2/16	9/27/16–10/2/16	1,004	704	300	+/– 3.54%	11%

*Based on American Association for Public Opinion Research Response Rate Calculation 3 (AAPOR RR3) response rate calculation.

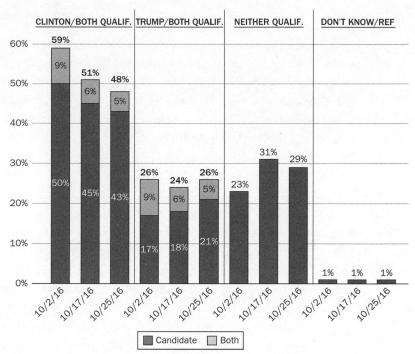

Figure A.1.1 Percentage saying that Clinton/Trump are qualified to be president across the three field periods. Question wording for Figure A.1.1.: Which of the two major party candidates is qualified to be president of the United States: Hillary Clinton, Donald Trump, both, or neither?

Data

(1) Qualified to be president

The results of the surveys show that those who saw Hillary Clinton as qualified to be president declined significantly ($p<.05$) from 59 percent to 48 percent between the first sample, interviewed in early October, and the final sample, interviewed later in the month. Views of whether Donald Trump was qualified to be president did not move significantly during that time (see figure A.1.1).

(2) Traits

Question wording for Figures A.1.2, A.1.3, and A.1.4: *I am going to read you some phrases. For each one, please tell me how well that phrase applies to the following candidates. Please use a scale from 0 to 10, where "zero" means it does not apply at all and "ten" means it applies extremely well. Of course, you can use any number in between. The first candidate is Hillary Clinton. How well does the phrase (INSERT ITEM) apply to Hillary Clinton? The next candidate is Donald Trump. How well does the phrase (INSERT ITEM) apply to Donald Trump? (THE CANDIDATE TRAIT BLOCKS [CLINTON AND TRUMP] WERE ROTATED AND THE TRAITS WERE RANDOMIZED WITHIN BLOCKS.)*

The traits included "has the temperament to be president," "trustworthy," "shares my values," "strong leader," "corrupt," "liar," "mentally unstable," "tax dodger," and "says one thing in public and something else in private." The results presented here show where there were significant changes in traits across the sample periods.

Between early and late October, these survey data show a significant increase in the percent who said the trait, "has the temperament to be president," applies to Donald Trump (26 percent to 31 percent, p<.05). Despite the change, that percentage is below the percentage who said that trait applies to Hillary Clinton. Our results show no significant change in how respondents rated Clinton on this trait during that period (see figure A.1.2).

Perceptions that Trump shared the values of potential voters improved significantly from the first to the third sample period, from 27 percent to 35 percent (p<.05). No change is evident across these samples in the perception of Clinton on the "shares my values" trait (see figure A.1.3).

Perceptions that Trump was "trustworthy" also significantly improved among adults over the three sample periods from 28 percent to 34 percent (p<.05). The change in the difference in percentage among those who said the trait "trustworthy" applied to Clinton was not significant in the period bracketed by the first and third surveys (see figure A.1.4).

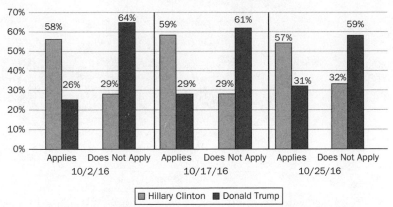

Figure A.1.2 Percentage of respondents who said that trait "has the temperament to be president" applies*/does not apply** to candidate.
* "Applies" = combined ratings of 6 through 10. ** "Does not apply" = combined ratings of 0 through 4 (5 not shown).

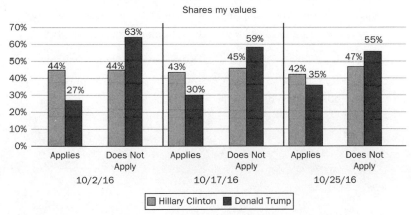

Figure A.1.3 Percentage of respondents who said that trait "shares my values" applies*/does not apply** to candidate. * "Applies" = combined ratings of 6 through 10.
** "Does not apply" = combined ratings of 0 through 4 (5 not shown).

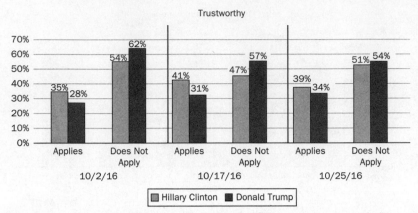

Figure A.1.4 Percentage of respondents who said that trait "trustworthy" applies*/doesn't apply** to candidate. * "Applies" = combined ratings of 6 through 10. ** "Does not apply" = combined ratings of 0 through 4 (5 not shown).

Conclusions

1. By the third Annenberg Public Policy Center survey period, perceptions of Trump had improved among the public on the traits "has the temperament to be president," "shares my values," and "trustworthy."

2. At the same time, there was a decline in the proportion of those who said Clinton was qualified to be president.

APPENDIX TWO

Debate 2 and Debate 3 Exposure Effect on Candidate Trait Evaluations

Method

The results we present in appendix 2 are based on the second and third national cross-sectional telephone surveys. The second was conducted from October 13, 2016, through October 17, 2016, among 1,013 US adults (610 cell phone, 403 landline), beginning a few days following the second presidential debate, leading up to the third and final debate. The margin of error was +/- 3.78 percent and the response rate was 8 percent. The third survey was fielded beginning the day following the third presidential debate from October 20, 2016, through October 25, 2016, among a sample of 1,008 US adults (708 cell phone, 300 landline). The margin of error for total respondents is +/- 3.64 percent, and the response rate was 11 percent. In each crosssection, surveys were also conducted in Spanish.

Dependent Variables: Trait evaluations of Clinton and Trump were assessed on a 0–10-point scale. A "zero" means the trait "does NOT apply at all" and a "ten" means the trait applies "extremely well" (wording for the prefatory statements is in appendix one). Respondents could evaluate candidates using any number from 0 to 10. Traits included "has the temperament to be president," "trustworthy," "shares my values," "strong leader," "corrupt," "liar," "mentally unstable," "tax dodger" (Trump only, for this analysis), and "says one thing in public and something else in private."

Independent Variable: "Viewed debate 2" (from second cross-sectional survey)[1]: Those who said they watched or listened to at least some of the second presidential debate (October 9) (68 percent). "Did not view debate 2": Those who said they did not watch or listen to the second debate (32 percent). "Viewed debate 3" (from third cross-sectional survey)[2]: Those who said they watched or listened to at least some of the third presidential debate (October 19) (64 percent). "Did not view debate 3" (from third cross-sectional survey): Those who said they did not watch or listen to the third debate (36 percent).

Controls: Age (younger to older), gender (female/male), race (black/non-black), education (low to high), party identification (Democrat/non-Democrat), and political ideology (liberal to conservative).

Data

We conducted an OLS linear regression to assess mean differences associated with debate viewing on the trait evaluations. In the presence of statistical controls, after each of the final two debates, debate viewers were significantly more likely than non-viewers to evaluate Clinton as someone who "says one thing in public and something else in private." Viewers also were significantly more likely than non-viewers to say the trait "shares my values" applies to Trump. Following debate 3, debate viewers were significantly less likely to evaluate Trump as someone who would "say one thing in public and something else in private." Additionally, viewers were less likely than non-viewers to say the trait "corrupt" applied to Trump and significantly more likely than non-viewers to say the traits "has the temperament to be president," "trustworthy," "shares my values," and a "strong leader" apply to him (see tables A.2.1 and A.2.2 for the mean scores for viewers and non-viewers).

Conclusions

In summary, the analysis in appendix 2 found the following:

1. In the presence of controls, those who viewed the second or third debate were more likely than those who did not view those debates

Table A.2.1 Mean scores showing differences associated with debate viewing on positive candidate trait evaluations, with controls on age, gender, race, education, party identification, and political ideology. Differences shown are between viewers and non-viewers.

	Clinton Traits				Trump Traits			
	Temperament	Trustworthy	Shares my values	Strong leader	Temperament	Trustworthy	Shares my values	Strong leader
Viewed debate 3	6.04	4.16	4.54	5.45	4.04*	4.69***	4.56***	5.48**
Did not view debate 3	5.57	3.68	4.12	5.08	3.50	3.68	3.53	4.77
N	932	932	932	932	932	932	932	932
Viewed debate 2	6.55	4.77	5.02	5.85	3.42	3.76	3.74**	4.55
Did not view debate 2	5.72	4.22	4.48	5.52	3.56	3.78	3.53	4.91
N	883	883	883	883	883	883	883	883

***p<.001, **p<.01, *p<.05.

Table A.2.2 Mean scores showing differences associated with debate watching on negative candidate trait evaluations, with controls on age, gender, race, education, party identification, and political ideology. Differences shown are between viewers and non-viewers.

	Clinton Traits				Trump Traits				
	Corrupt	Liar	Mentally unstable	Says one thing in public and something else in private	Corrupt	Liar	Tax dodger	Mentally unstable	Says one thing in public and something else in private
Viewed debate 3	5.93	6.18	3.33	6.80*	4.51*	5.32	5.69	4.79	5.12**
Did not view debate 3	6.00	6.39	3.66	6.45	5.10	5.60	6.15	4.83	5.81
N	932	932	932	932	932	932	932	932	932
Viewed debate 2	5.35	5.60	3.27	6.41**	5.06	5.76	5.78*	5.25	5.66
Did not view debate 2	5.58	5.94	3.78	5.95	4.94	5.64	6.15	5.15	5.74
N	883	883	883	883	883	883	883	883	883

**p<.01, *p<.05.

to consider Clinton someone who "says one thing in public and something else in private."

2. After the final debate, in the presence of controls, Trump's ratings on the positive traits (temperament, trustworthy, shares values, strong leader) were significantly higher among debate viewers compared to non-viewers. The debates had no significant effect on Clinton's ratings on the positive traits.

3. Viewers of debate 3 were significantly less likely than non-viewers to ascribe the trait "says one thing in public and something else in private" to Trump, in the presence of controls.

4. In the presence of controls, debate 2 viewers differed from those who did not watch debate 2 and also, separately, debate 3 viewers differed from those who did not view debate three on only one common Clinton trait and on only one common Trump assessment. For Clinton the trait was "says one thing in public and something else in private" (p<.01 in debate 2 and p<.05 in debate 3) (see Table A.2.2). For Trump, it was "shares my values" (p<.01 in debate 2 and p<.001 in debate 3) (Table A.2.1).

5. Recall that when a trait is made more salient by communication the likelihood that it will be used in evaluation of the candidates increases. The finding reported in 4 is not the only indication that debate exposure primed the trait "says one thing in public and something else in private." Of the attributes included in the post debate 3 analysis, "says one thing in public and something else in private" is the only one that elicited significantly different post-viewing (compared to non-viewing) evaluations of both contenders. Viewers were significantly more likely than non-viewers to report that "says one thing in public and something else in private" applied to Clinton (p<.05) and significantly less likely to say that it applied to Trump (p<.01) (see Table A.2.2).

APPENDIX THREE

Association between Perception
Changes and Vote Intentions

Method

In order to test aggregate differences in debate viewers' impressions of Hillary Clinton and Donald Trump from the second debate to the third debate, we merged the second cross-sectional and third cross-sectional survey datasets and defined debate viewing differently. (See appendix 2 for the dates of those surveys.) The combined sample size was 2,021 US adults, with a +/ − 2.60 percent margin of error and a response rate of 10 percent.

Dependent Variables: The dependent variables, the trait evaluations of Clinton and Trump on a 0–10-point scale, are the same as those mentioned in appendix 2. "Zero" means the trait "does NOT apply at all" and "ten" means the trait applies "extremely well" (the question wording for the trait battery can be found in appendix 1). Respondents could evaluate candidates using any number from 0 to 10. Traits included "has the temperament to be president," "trustworthy," "shares my values," "strong leader," "corrupt," "liar," "mentally unstable," "tax dodger" (Trump only, for this analysis), and "says one thing in public and something else in private."

Independent Variable: Our definition of debate viewing changed for this analysis. We created a debate-viewing index for the two debates. Since we asked about prior debate viewing in each of the second and third cross-sectional surveys, we categorized respondents on a three-point index (0, 1, 2):

2- Viewed or listened to both the second and third debates / Viewed or listened to the third debate but not the second. We collapsed those groups because separately, they showed no difference in our analysis of trait ratings.

1- Viewed or listened to the second debate only in the post–debate 3 sample or viewed or listened to the second debate in the post–debate 2 sample

0- Viewed/listened to neither the second nor the third debate

Controls: Age (younger to older), gender (female/male), race (black/nonblack), education (low to high), party identification (Democrat/non-Democrat), and political ideology (liberal to conservative).

Data

Figure A.3.1 presents the findings across both postdebate periods. Those who saw debate 3 posted a significantly higher mean score on the item "says one thing in public, and something else in private" than those who saw or heard debate 2 ONLY ($t = 2.034$, $p<.05$), and those who saw or heard neither debate 2 nor 3 ($t = 2.637$, $p<.01$). The takeaway from this analysis is that those who saw or heard the third debate were more likely to say that Clinton "says one thing in public and something else in private" compared to those exposed only to the second debate or to neither debate.

To rule out other explanatory variables, we ran an OLS linear regression to assess mean differences associated with the "Says one thing in public and something else in private" item and the three-point debate-viewing variable, in the presence of political and demographic controls (age, gender, race, education, party ID, and political ideology). The debate-viewing predictor was still significantly and positively associated with evaluating Clinton

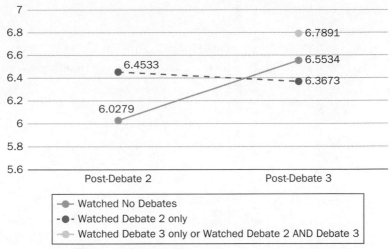

Figure A.3.1 Mean score: Hillary Clinton "says one thing in public and something else in private," by debate viewing.

as saying different things in public than in private (B = .316, S.E. = 0.097, p<.01).

Finally, we reran the OLS linear regression models to determine the effect of debate viewing on the other traits for Clinton and Trump, in the presence of controls. Results showed that viewers or listeners of the final debate were more likely to say the traits "has the temperament to be president," "trust," "shares my values," and "strong leader," applied to Trump, than those who saw or heard debate 2 only or saw or heard neither debates 2 nor 3. Additionally, those who viewed or heard debate 3 were less likely to say the negative traits "corrupt," "liar," and "says one thing in public and something else in private" applied to Trump than those who saw or heard only debate 2 or neither of the final two debates (see tables A.3.1 and A.3.2 for the mean scores for viewers and non-viewers).

Conclusions

In summary, the analysis in appendix 3 found the following:

1. Combining the second (post–debate 2) and third (post–debate 3) cross-sectional surveys reveals results similar to those reported in

Table A.3.1 Mean scores showing impact of debate watching (based on debate-viewing index) on positive candidate trait evaluations, with controls on age, gender, race, education, party identification, and political ideology.

Debate-Viewing Index[†]	Clinton Traits				Trump Traits			
	Temperament	Trustworthy	Shares my values	Strong leader	Temperament	Trustworthy	Shares my values	Strong leader
Viewed debate 3 and debate 2 or debate 3 only (2)	6.22	4.27	4.64	5.53	3.98**	4.60***	4.52***	5.39***
Viewed debate 2 only (1)	6.20	4.45	4.79	5.67	3.52	3.91	3.78	4.78
Viewed neither debates 2 nor 3 (0)	5.75	4.15	4.39	5.36	3.49	3.63	3.51	4.64
N	1,839	1,839	1,839	1,839	1,839	1,839	1,839	1,839

[†] Debate-viewing index defined: 0 = Viewed neither debate 2 nor 3; 1 = Viewed debate 2 only; 2 = Viewed debate 3 AND debate 2 / viewed debate 3 ONLY.

***p<.001, **p<.01

Table A.3.2 Mean scores showing impact of debate viewing (based on debate-viewing index) on negative candidate trait evaluations, with controls on age, gender, race, education, party identification, and political ideology.

Debate-Viewing Index[†]	Clinton Traits				Trump Traits				
	Corrupt	Liar	Mentally unstable	Says one thing in public and something else in private	Corrupt	Liar	Tax dodger	Mentally unstable	Says one thing in public and something else in private
Viewed debate 3 and debate 2 or debate 3 only (2)	5.87	6.09	3.31	6.82**	4.60*	5.37*	5.63	4.85	5.14***
Viewed debate 2 only (1)	5.51	5.81	3.29	6.38	4.96	5.70	5.92	5.13	5.63
Viewed neither debates 2 nor 3 (0)	5.72	6.07	3.81	6.25	5.03	5.58	6.00	4.99	5.81
N	1,839	1,839	1,839	1,839	1,839	1,839	1,839	1,839	1,839

[†] Debate-viewing index defined: 0 = Viewed neither debate 2 nor 3; 1 = Viewed debate 2 only; 2 = Viewed debate 3 AND debate 2 / viewed debate 3 ONLY.

***p<.001, **p<.01, *p<.05.

appendix 2. In the presence of controls, those who viewed the third debate were more likely than those who did not view that debate to consider Clinton as someone who "says one thing in public and something else in private." This difference remained when comparing viewers of debate 3 to those who only viewed debate 2 in either sample.

2. Similar to the results from appendix 2, in the presence of controls, viewing the third debate rather than not viewing it was significantly associated with evaluating Trump positively on "has the temperament to be president," "trustworthy," "shares my values," and "strong leader."

3. In the presence of controls, Trump's ratings on the negative traits "corrupt," "says one thing in public and something else in private," and "liar" were lower among those who viewed debate 3 compared to those who did not. That is, on a 0 to 10 scale, where "zero" means "doesn't apply at all" and "ten" means applies "extremely well," viewers' ratings were closer to zero on the scale than non-viewers.

APPENDIX FOUR

Effect of Traits on Vote Intention

Method

In appendix 4, we examine the effect, if any, that trait evaluations had on intention to vote for Hillary Clinton, regardless of debate viewing. In particular, as our analysis has shown, debate viewers were more likely than nonviewers to evaluate Clinton as someone who says one thing in public and something else in private. Did this negative trait evaluation affect intention to vote for her? For this analysis, we used the second and third cross-sectional data sets (see Appendix 2 for dates and sample sizes).

Dependent Variable: "Intention to vote for Clinton": We created a dichotomous variable based on the survey question *If the 2016 presidential election were being held today and the candidates were Donald Trump and Mike Pence, the Republicans, Hillary Clinton and Tim Kaine, the Democrats, Gary Johnson and William Weld, the Libertarians, and Jill Stein and Ajamu Baraka, the Green Party candidates, for whom would you vote?* Intention to vote for Clinton was recoded as "1" and all others were coded as a "0." Those who refused to answer were coded as missing.

Independent Variables: (1) The trait "says one thing in public and something else in private" coded on a continuous 0–10 scale, where "0" means the trait does not apply at all to Clinton/Trump and a "10" means it applies extremely well to Clinton/Trump. (2) A variable created by calculating the difference in Clinton and Trump evaluations on the "says one thing in public and something else in private" item, which ranged from –10 (Trump more likely than Clinton to be seen as "saying one thing in public and something else in private") to +10 (Clinton more likely than Trump to be seen as "saying one thing in public and something else in private").

Controls: Age (younger to older), gender (female/male), race (black/nonblack), education (low to high), party identification (Democrat/non-Democrat), and political ideology (liberal to conservative).

Data

In the presence of controls, those who were more likely to say Clinton "says one thing in public and something else in private" were less likely to say they were planning to vote for her in the election, among the total samples conducted before and after the final debate. We then compared the mean differences between how respondents rated Clinton and Trump on the "says one thing in public and something else in private" variable in both samples. We found that the differences were significantly greater following the third debate ($t = 2.813$, p<.01). Next, we ran a logistic regression with the post–debate 3 sample, and found that controlling for other predictors of vote choice, the difference we observed after the third debate between Clinton and Trump on the "says one thing in public and something else in private" variable corresponded to a small but significant drop in vote intention for Clinton (odds ratio = .819) (see table A.4.1). The effect persists ($b = -.13$, SE = .03, p<.001) when we added to the model the following positive traits, Trump minus Clinton on "strong leader" ($b = -.12$, SE = .04, p<.01), "shares my values" ($b = -.21$, SE = .04, p<.001), "trustworthy" ($b = -.10$, SE = .04, p<.05), and "has the temperament to be president" ($b = -.08$, SE = .04, p<.05). The result supports the hypothesis that the perception that Clinton "says one thing in public and something else in private" affects vote intention for Clinton.

Table A.4.1 Logistic regression showing effect of item "says one thing in public and something else in private" post–debate 3 as a predictor of an intended vote for Hillary Clinton.

	B (SE)	Exp (B)
Clinton minus Trump: says one thing in private and something else in public (Diff)	−0.200 (0.021)	0.819***
Sex (female)	0.329 (0.198)	1.389
Race (black/nonblack)	1.151 (0.378)	3.160**
Education (low to high)	0.192 (0.042)	1.211***
Party ID (Democrat/non-Democrat)	1.857 (0.220)	6.406***
Ideology (liberal to conservative)	−0.661 (0.092)	0.516***
Age (younger to older)	−0.005 (0.005)	0.995
Constant	−1.568 (0.749)	0.209*
N	890	
Cox & Snell R^2	0.45	

***$p<.001$, **$p<.01$, *$p<.05$.

NOTES

Prologue
1. *Fox News Insider* (2016, December 12) Huckabee: "Have to believe in unicorns" to think Russia changed election results. *Fox News*. Retrieved from http://insider. foxnews.com/2016/12/12/mike-huckabee-unicorns-russian-hacked-us-election-donald-trump-hillary-clinton.
2. Barry, D. (2017, January 1) Dave Barry's Year in Review: Trump and the "hideous monstrosity" that was 2016. *Washington Post*. Retrieved from https://www. washingtonpost.com/lifestyle/magazine/dave-barrys-year-in-review-trump-and-the-hideous-monstrosity-that-was-2016/2016/12/29/17c84a14-b7d6-11e6-b8df-600bd9d38a02_story.html?utm_term=.0850f7c07738.
3. *NBC Nightly News with Lester Holt* (2017, May 11) President Trump: This Russia thing is a made up story. *NBC News*. Retrieved from https://www. nbcnews.com/nightly-news/video/president-trump-this-russia-thing-is-a-made-up-story-941962819745.
4. Fahrenthold, D. A. (2017, June 4) Putin calls US election-meddling charge a "load of nonsense" in Megyn Kelly interview. *Washington Post*. Retrieved from https:// www.washingtonpost.com/politics/putin-calls-election-meddling-charge-a-load-of-nonsense-in-megyn-kelly-interview/2017/06/04/3968c42c-497c-11e7-9669-250d0b15f83b_story.html?utm_term=.5d4751369b21.

5. *Reuters* (2017, September 22) Kremlin: Russia did not use Facebook adverts to sway US election. *Reuters*. Retrieved from https://ca.reuters.com/article/technologyNews/idCAKCN1BX109-OCATC.
6. Twitter user @realDonaldTrump (2017, September 22) The Russia hoax continues, now it's ads on Facebook. Twitter post. Retrieved from https://twitter.com/realDonaldTrump/status/911179462745710593.
7. Hirschfeld Davis, J. (2017, November 11) Trump says Putin "means it" about not meddling. *New York Times*. Retrieved from https://www.nytimes.com/2017/11/11/world/asia/trump-putin-election.html.
8. Hudson, J. (2017, December 8) NO DEAL: How secret talks with Russia to prevent election meddling collapsed. *BuzzFeed*. Retrieved from https://www.buzzfeed.com/johnhudson/no-deal-how-secret-talks-with-russia-to-prevent-election?utm_term=.cxeVnp2aG.
9. Barry, D. (2017, December 29) Dave Barry's 2017 year in review: Did that really happen? *Miami Herald*. Retrieved from http://www.miamiherald.com/living/liv-columns-blogs/dave-barry/article192007484.html.
10. *The Tonight Show Starring Jimmy Fallon* (2018, January 17) Trump's Montreal Cognitive Test answers, Minister for Loneliness—Monologue. YouTube video. Retrieved from https://youtu.be/UgOSM5GbL9I.
11. Bump, P. (2018, February 16) Trump's unfounded insistence that the new indictment proves Russia didn't swing the election. *Washington Post*. Retrieved from https://www.washingtonpost.com/news/politics/wp/2018/02/16/trumps-insistence-that-the-new-indictment-proves-russia-didnt-swing-the-election-is-unfounded/?utm_term=.2ef43f2c0d4a.
12. Smith, A. (2018, March 9) Putin on US election interference: "I couldn't care less." *NBC News*. Retrieved from https://www.nbcnews.com/news/world/putin-u-s-election-interference-i-couldn-t-care-less-n855151.
13. Rucker, P. (2018, March 6) Trump vows to counteract any Russian interference in 2018 elections. *Washington Post*. Retrieved from https://www.washingtonpost.com/politics/trump-vows-to-counteract-any-russian-interference-in-2018-elections/2018/03/06/fde7da52-215a-11e8-94da-ebf9d112159c_story.html.

Introduction

1. Lee, D. (2018, March 2) Reddit dragged into Russian propaganda row. *BBC News*. Retrieved from http://www.bbc.com/news/technology-43255285.
2. Pagliery, J., & O'Sullivan, D. (2018, March 8) Russians released anti-Clinton video game weeks before election. *CNN*. Retrieved from http://money.cnn.com/2018/03/08/technology/hilltendo-russians-anti-clinton-video-game/index.html.
3. Collins, B., & Russell, J. (2018, March 1) Russians used Reddit and Tumblr to troll the 2016 election. *Daily Beast*. Retrieved from https://www.thedailybeast.com/russians-used-reddit-and-tumblr-to-troll-the-2016-election.
4. Riley, M., & Robertson, J. (2017, June 13) Russian cyber hacks on US electoral system far wider than previously known. *Bloomberg Politics*. Retrieved from

https://www.bloomberg.com/news/articles/2017-06-13/russian-breach-of-39-states-threatens-future-u-s-elections.

5. The final tally was 65,844,954 (48.2 percent) for Clinton and 62,979,879 votes (46.1 percent) for Trump. Krieg, G. (2016, December 22) It's official: Clinton swamps Trump in popular vote. *CNN*. Retrieved from https://www.cnn.com/2016/12/21/politics/donald-trump-hillary-clinton-popular-vote-final-count/index.html.

6. US Department of Homeland Security (2016, October 7) Joint statement from the Department of Homeland Security and Office of the Director of National Intelligence on Election Security. Retrieved from https://www.dhs.gov/news/2016/10/07/joint-statement-department-homeland-security-and-office-director-national.

7. Office of the Director of National Intelligence (2017, January 6) Background to "assessing Russian activities and intentions in recent US elections": The analytic process and cyber incident attribution. Retrieved from https://www.dni.gov/files/documents/ICA_2017_01.pdf.

8. *United States v. Internet Research Agency LLC*, 18 U.S.C. §§ 2, 371, 1349, 1028A (D.D.C. 2018) Retrieved from https://www.justice.gov/file/1035477/download.

9. Chen, A. (2016, July 27) The real paranoia-inducing purpose of Russian hacks. *The New Yorker*. Retrieved from https://www.newyorker.com/news/news-desk/the-real-paranoia-inducing-purpose-of-russian-hacks.

10. Wells, G., & Seetharaman, D. (2017, November 1) New Facebook data shows Russians targeted users by race, religion, politics. *Wall Street Journal*. Retrieved from https://www.wsj.com/articles/russian-ads-targeted-facebook-users-by-profile-1509563354.

11. Popken, B. (2017, December 20) Russian trolls went on attack during key election moments. *NBC News*. Retrieved from https://www.nbcnews.com/tech/social-media/russian-trolls-went-attack-during-key-election-moments-n827176?cid=sm_npd_nn_tw_mtp.

12. *United States v. Internet Research Agency LLC*, 18 U.S.C. §§ 2, 371, 1349, 1028A (D.D.C. 2018) Retrieved from https://www.justice.gov/file/1035477/download.

13. Office of the Director of National Intelligence (2017, January 6) Background to "assessing Russian activities and intentions in recent US elections": The analytic process and cyber incident attribution. Retrieved from https://www.dni.gov/files/documents/ICA_2017_01.pdf.

14. Khatchadourian, R. (2010, June 7) No secrets: Julian Assange's mission for total transparency. *The New Yorker*. Retrieved from https://www.newyorker.com/magazine/2010/06/07/no-secrets.

15. Office of the Director of National Intelligence (2017, January 6) Background to "assessing Russian activities and intentions in recent US elections": The analytic process and cyber incident attribution. Retrieved from https://www.dni.gov/files/documents/ICA_2017_01.pdf.

16. Bump, P. (2016, September 6) Donald Trump doesn't have much of an opinion on this new-fangled "cyber" thing. *Washington Post*. Retrieved from

https://www.washingtonpost.com/news/the-fix/wp/2016/09/06/donald-trump-doesnt-have-much-of-an-opinion-on-this-new-fangled-cyber-thing/?utm_term=.5503c1d90743.

17. Clarke, R. A., & Knake, R. K. (2014) *Cyber War: The Next Threat to National Security and What to Do about It* (New York: HarperCollins), 6.

18. *Real Time with Bill Maher* (2017, June 30) Richard A. Clarke: Warnings | *Real Time with Bill Maher* (HBO). YouTube video. Retrieved from https://youtu.be/OCBJSmWY6nE.

19. Barry, R., & Holliday, S. (2018, March 8) Russian trolls tried to torpedo Mitt Romney's shot at Secretary of State. *Wall Street Journal*. Retrieved from https://www.wsj.com/articles/russian-trolls-tried-to-torpedo-mitt-romneys-shot-at-secretary-of-state-1520505000.

20. Kruzel, J. (2018, February 22) How Russian trolls exploited Parkland mass shooting on social media. *PolitiFact*. Retrieved from http://www.politifact.com/truth-o-meter/article/2018/feb/22/how-russian-trolls-exploited-parkland-mass-shootin/.

21. Klimburg, A. (2017) *The Darkening Web: The War for Cyberspace* (New York: Penguin).

22. Page, S., & Icsman, M. (2018, February 26) On Russia, Americans trust special counsel Mueller more than Trump, USA TODAY poll shows. *USA Today*. Retrieved from https://www.usatoday.com/story/news/2018/02/26/russia-americans-trust-special-counsel-mueller-more-than-trump-usa-today-poll-shows/371345002/.

23. Nougayrède, N. (2017, November 4) Beware: This Russian cyber warfare threatens every democracy. *Guardian*. Retrieved from https://www.theguardian.com/commentisfree/2017/nov/04/beware-russian-cyber-warfare-threatens-every-democracy-kremlin.

24. Sengupta, K. (2018, January 22) Cyberwarfare with Russia "now greater threat than terrorism," warns British Army chief. *Independent*. Retrieved from http://www.independent.co.uk/news/uk/home-news/cyberwarfare-russia-terrorism-british-army-general-nick-carter-us-france-nato-a8173136.html.

25. Popken, B. (2018, February 14) Twitter deleted 200,000 Russian trolls' tweets. Read them here. *NBC News*. Retrieved from https://www.nbcnews.com/tech/social-media/now-available-more-200-000-deleted-russian-troll-tweets-n844731.

26. President of Russia (2018, March 10) Interview to American TV channel NBC. Retrieved from http://en.kremlin.ru/events/president/transcripts/57027.

27. Alder, J. (2018, March 9) The cyberwar that never happened: How Obama backed down from a counterstrike against Russia. *Yahoo!* Retrieved from https://www.yahoo.com/news/cyberwar-never-happened-obama-backed-counterstrike-russia-140034672.html.

28. Shane, S. (2018, February 17) Russia isn't the only one meddling in elections. We do it, too. *New York Times*. Retrieved from https://nyti.ms/2C4yLQa.

29. President of Russia (2018, March 10) Interview to American TV channel NBC. Retrieved from http://en.kremlin.ru/events/president/transcripts/57027.

30. The relevant paragraph states: "Il demande donc aux organes de presse, et notamment à leurs sites internet, de ne pas rendre compte du contenu de ces

données, en rappelant que la diffusion de fausses informations est susceptible de tomber sous le coup de la loi, notamment pénale." Commission Nationale de Contrôle de la Campagne Électorale en Vue de l'Élection Présidentielle (2017, May 6) Recommandation aux médias suite à l'attaque informatique dont a été victim l'équipe de campagne de M. Macron [Media recommendation following the hacking which targeted Mr. Macron's campaign]. Retrieved from http://www.cnccep.fr/communiques/cp14.html.

31. Prier, J. (2017) Commanding the trend: Social media as information warfare. *Strategic Studies Quarterly*, Winter 2017: 50–85. Retrieved from http://www.airuniversity.af.mil/Portals/10/SSQ/documents/Volume-11_Issue-4/Prier.pdf.

32. Ferrara, E. (2017) Disinformation and social bot operations in the run up to the 2017 French presidential election. *First Monday, 22*(8). doi: 10.5210/fm.v22i8.8005.

33. Abokhodair, N., Yoo, D., & McDonald, D. W. (2015, February) Dissecting a social botnet: Growth, content and influence in Twitter. In *Proceedings of the 18th ACM Conference on Computer Supported Cooperative Work & Social Computing* (839–851), ACM; Chu, Z., Widjaja, I., & Wang, H. (2012, June) Detecting social spam campaigns on Twitter. In *International Conference on Applied Cryptography and Network Security* (455–472). Springer, Berlin, Heidelberg. My thanks to Douglas Guilbeault for directing me to these sources.

34. The first time I made that argument was in a book titled *Dirty Politics: Deception, Distraction, and Democracy* that was published in 1993.

35. Applebaum, A. (2016, July 25) Connecting the dots: How Russia benefits from the DNC email leak. *Washington Post*. Retrieved from https://www.washingtonpost.com/blogs/post-partisan/wp/2016/07/25/connecting-the-dots-how-russia-benefits-from-the-dnc-email-leak/.

36. *Fox News Insider* (2016, December 12) Huckabee: "have to believe in unicorns" to think Russia changed election results. *Fox News*. Retrieved from http://insider.foxnews.com/2016/12/12/mike-huckabee-unicorns-russian-hacked-us-election-donald-trump-hillary-clinton.

37. Hayden, M. (2017, March 22) Michael Hayden: US intel agencies win big, but Russia intel wins bigger in Comey hearing. *The Hill*. Retrieved from http://thehill.com/blogs/pundits-blog/the-administration/325250-michael-hayden-us-intel-agencies-win-big-but-russia.

38. Statement of Chairman Richard Burr. (2017, November 1) Richard Burr: US Senator for North Carolina. Retrieved from https://www.burr.senate.gov/imo/media/doc/Chairman%27s%20SFR.pdf.

39. Twitter user @realDonaldTrump (2017, January 7) Intelligence stated very strongly there was absolutely no evidence that hacking affected the election results. Twitter post. Retrieved from https://twitter.com/realDonaldTrump/status/817701436096126977.

40. Office of the Director of National Intelligence (2017, January 6) Background to "assessing Russian activities and intentions in recent US elections": The analytic process and cyber incident attribution. Retrieved from https://www.dni.gov/files/documents/ICA_2017_01.pdf.

Part 1

1. Scola, N., & Gold, A. (2017, October 31) Facebook, Twitter: Russian actors sought to undermine Trump after election. *Politico*. Retrieved from https://www.politico. com/story/2017/10/31/facebook-twitter-post-election-russian-meddling-sought-to-undermine-trump-244380.

Chapter 1

1. Hayden, M. (2017, March 22) Michael Hayden: US intel agencies win big, but Russia intel wins bigger in Comey hearing. *The Hill*. Retrieved from http://thehill.com/blogs/pundits-blog/the-administration/325250-michael-hayden-us-intel-agencies-win-big-but-russia.

2. Crowley, M., & Ioffe, J. (2016, July 25) Why Putin hates Hillary. *Politico*. Retrieved from https://www.politico.com/story/2016/07/clinton-putin-226153.

3. Shuster, S. (2016, July 25) Vladimir Putin's bad blood with Hillary Clinton. *TIME Magazine*. Retrieved from http://time.com/4422723/putin-russia-hillary-clinton/.

4. WikiLeaks (n.d.) HRC paid speeches. Attachments: HRC paid speeches flags. Retrieved from https://wikileaks.org/podesta-emails/emailid/927.

5. Fahrenthold, D.A. (2017, June 4) Putin calls US election-meddling charge a "load of nonsense" in Megyn Kelly interview. *Washington Post*. Retrieved from https://www.washingtonpost.com/politics/putin-calls-election-meddling-charge-a-load-of-nonsense-in-megyn-kelly-interview/2017/06/04/3968c42c-497c-11e7-9669-250d0b15f83b_story.html?utm_term=.5d4751369b21.

6. Wilson, S. (2014, March 25) Obama dismisses Russia as "regional power" acting out of weakness. *Washington Post*. Retrieved from https://www.washingtonpost. com/world/national-security/obama-dismisses-russia-as-regional-power-acting-out-of-weakness/2014/03/25/1e5a678e-b439-11e3-b899-20667de76985_story. html?utm_term=.9d68cbdfe745.

7. Remarks by President Obama in Address to the United Nations General Assembly. (2014, September 24) Office of the Press Secretary, White House of President Barack Obama. Retrieved from https://obamawhitehouse.archives.gov/the-press-office/2014/09/24/remarks-president-obama-address-united-nations-general-assembly.

8. RT (2014, September 24) Russia tops ISIS threat, Ebola worst of all? Lavrov puzzled by Obama's UN speech. Retrieved from https://www.rt.com/news/190392-russia-lavrov-obama-threat-speech/.

9. Harding, L. (2016, April 5) What are the Panama Papers? A guide to history's biggest data leak. *Guardian*. Retrieved from https://www.theguardian.com/news/2016/apr/03/what-you-need-to-know-about-the-panama-papers.

10. Jackson, D. (2017, July 12) President Trump on Russia election meddling: Putin told me he didn't do it. *USA Today*. Retrieved from https://www.usatoday.com/story/news/politics/2017/07/12/president-trump-russia-election-meddling-putin-told-me-he-didnt-do/473850001/.

11. Ali, L. (2017, June 4) Megyn Kelly gets outmaneuvered by Vladimir Putin on her NBC premiere "Sunday Night." *Los Angeles Times*. Retrieved from http://www.latimes.com/entertainment/tv/la-et-st-sundays-with-megyn-kelly-review-20170604-story.html.

12. Lipton, E., Sanger, D. E., & Shane, S. (2016, December 13) The perfect weapon: How Russian cyberpower invaded the US. *New York Times*. Retrieved from https://nyti.ms/2jASgpt.

13. *RT* (2017, May 31) Anti-Russia spin pushed by those who lost US election & can't face reality—Putin to *Le Figaro*. Retrieved from https://www.rt.com/news/390253-putin-us-election-trump-russia/.

14. Smith, A. (2017, June 2) Vladimir Putin to Megyn Kelly: Even children could hack an election. *NBC News*. Retrieved from https://www.nbcnews.com/news/world/vladimir-putin-faces-questions-megyn-kelly-st-petersburg-n767481.

15. President of Russia. (2018, March 10) Interview to American TV channel NBC. Retrieved from http://en.kremlin.ru/events/president/transcripts/57027.

16. *RT* (2017, May 31) Anti-Russia spin pushed by those who lost US election & can't face reality—Putin to *Le Figaro*. Retrieved from https://www.rt.com/news/390253-putin-us-election-trump-russia/.

17. Weigel, D. (2017, May 24) The life and death of the Seth Rich conspiracy theory. *Washington Post*. Retrieved from https://www.washingtonpost.com/powerpost/the-life-and-death-of-the-seth-rich-conspiracy-theory/2017/05/23/aba640c4-3ff3-11e7-adba-394ee67a7582_story.html?utm_term=.8689d2ec7b0f.

18. Oremus, W. (2017, May 23) Why Sean Hannity needed the Seth Rich conspiracy. *Slate*. Retrieved from http://www.slate.com/articles/news_and_politics/politics/2017/05/why_sean_hannity_can_t_let_go_of_the_seth_rich_conspiracy.html.

19. Quoted in Weigel, D. (2017, May 24) The life and death of the Seth Rich conspiracy theory. *Washington Post*. Retrieved from https://www.washingtonpost.com/powerpost/the-life-and-death-of-the-seth-rich-conspiracy-theory/2017/05/23/aba640c4-3ff3-11e7-adba-394ee67a7582_story.html?utm_term=.8689d2ec7b0f.

20. Kiely, E. (2017, May 23) Gingrich spreads conspiracy theory. *FactCheck.org*. Retrieved from https://www.factcheck.org/2017/05/gingrich-spreads-conspiracy-theory/.

21. Kiely, E. (2017, May 23) Gingrich spreads conspiracy theory. *FactCheck.org*. Retrieved from https://www.factcheck.org/2017/05/gingrich-spreads-conspiracy-theory/.

22. For an account of both, see Folkenflik, D. (2017, September 19) Fox News fights back on lawsuit filed over Seth Rich story. *NPR*. Retrieved from https://www.npr.org/2017/09/19/552133180/fox-news-fights-back-on-lawsuit-filed-over-seth-rich-story.

23. *RT* (2017, May 29) CrossTalk: "Seth Rich." YouTube video. Retrieved from https://youtu.be/OT9wFXUAjMk.

24. Blinova, E. (2017, February 6) Unresolved murder: Why Seth Rich's case is key to #TrumpRussia investigation. *Sputnik*. Retrieved from https://sputniknews.com/politics/201706021054260081-seth-rich-trump-russia/

25. The video promoted by the @Ten_GOP account: Black Pilled (2017, May 24) Why the Seth Rich "investigation" should terrify everyone. YouTube video. Retrieved from https://www.youtube.com/watch?v=O3GnMx31BJA.

26. Nimmo, B. (2017, October 20) From troll farm to Trump: Assessing the life of Russian troll posing as a far-right American. *Medium.* Retrieved from https://medium.com/dfrlab/from-troll-farm-to-trump-c35667b877fb.

27. Wojcik, N., Hogan, M., & Juang, M. (2017, January 11) Transcript of President-elect Trump's news conference. *CNBC.* Retrieved from https://www.cnbc.com/2017/01/11/transcript-of-president-elect-donald-j-trumps-news-conference.html.

28. Bump, P. (2018, February 16) Trump's unfounded insistence that the new indictment proves Russia didn't swing the election. *Washington Post.* Retrieved from https://www.washingtonpost.com/news/politics/wp/2018/02/16/trumps-insistence-that-the-new-indictment-proves-russia-didnt-swing-the-election-is-unfounded/?utm_term=.2ef43f2c0d4a.

29. Rucker, P. (2018, March 6) Trump vows to counteract any Russian interference in 2018 elections. *Washington Post.* Retrieved from https://www.washingtonpost.com/politics/trump-vows-to-counteract-any-russian-interference-in-2018-elections/2018/03/06/fde7da52-215a-11e8-94da-ebf9d112159c_story.html.

30. Higgins, A. (2017, June 1) Maybe private Russian hackers meddled in election, Putin says. *New York Times.* Retrieved from https://www.nytimes.com/2017/06/01/world/europe/vladimir-putin-donald-trump-hacking.html.

31. President of Russia. (2018, March 10) Interview to American TV channel NBC. Retrieved from http://en.kremlin.ru/events/president/transcripts/57027.

32. *RT* (2017, June 4) Putin to NBC host: "You and I have a much closer relationship than I had with Mr. Flynn." Retrieved from https://www.rt.com/usa/390848-putin-kelly-interview-flynn/.

33. Montanaro, D., & Seipel, A. (2016, December 12) McConnell, differing with Trump, says he has "highest confidence" in intel agencies. *NPR.* Retrieved from https://www.npr.org/2016/12/12/505260062/mcconnell-differing-with-trump-says-he-has-highest-confidence-in-intel-agencies.

34. Smith, A. (2017, June 2) Vladimir Putin to Megyn Kelly: Even children could hack an election. *NBC News.* Retrieved from https://www.nbcnews.com/news/world/vladimir-putin-faces-questions-megyn-kelly-st-petersburg-n767481.

35. Gessen, M. (2017, January 9) Russia, Trump and flawed intelligence. *New York Review of Books.* Retrieved from http://www.nybooks.com/daily/2017/01/09/russia-trump-election-flawed-intelligence/.

36. Lears, J. (2018, January 4) What we don't talk about when we talk about Russian hacking. *London Review of Books.* Retrieved from https://www.lrb.co.uk/v40/n01/jackson-lears/what-we-dont-talk-about-when-we-talk-about-russian-hacking.

37. Priest, D. (2017, November 13) Russia's election meddling is another American intelligence failure. *The New Yorker.* Retrieved from https://www.newyorker.com/news/news-desk/russias-election-meddling-is-another-american-intelligence-failure.

38. Shane, S. (2017, January 6) Russian intervention in American election was no one-off. *New York Times*. Retrieved from https://www.nytimes.com/2017/01/06/us/politics/russian-hacking-election-intelligence.html.

39. House Permanent Select Committee on Intelligence (2018, March 22) Report on Russian active measures. Retrieved from https://docs.house.gov/meetings/IG/IG00/20180322/108023/HRPT-115-1.pdf.

40. Office of the Director of National Intelligence (2017, January 6) Background to "assessing Russian activities and intentions in recent U.S. elections": The analytic process and cyber incident attribution. Retrieved from https://www.dni.gov/files/documents/ICA_2017_01.pdf.

41. Demirjian, K. (2017, October 4) Senate Intelligence Committee leaders: Russia did interfere in 2016 elections. *Washington Post*. Retrieved from https://www.washingtonpost.com/powerpost/senate-intelligence-committee-leaders-russia-did-interfere-in-2016-elections/2017/10/04/1459291c-a91f-11e7-850e-2bdd1236be5d_story.html?utm_term=.459e23de5efc.

42. Fox News (2017, October 26) Nunes: Dems made Russia successful at election interference. Retrieved from http://www.foxnews.com/transcript/2017/10/26/nunes-dems-made-russia-successful-at-election-interference.html.

43. Montanaro, D., & Seipel, A. (2016, December 12) McConnell, differing with Trump, says he has "highest confidence" in intel agencies. *NPR*. Retrieved from https://www.npr.org/2016/12/12/505260062/mcconnell-differing-with-trump-says-he-has-highest-confidence-in-intel-agencies.

44. Demirjian, K. (2018, May 16) Russia favored Trump in 2016, Senate panel says, breaking with House GOP. *Washington Post*. Retrieved from https://www.washingtonpost.com/powerpost/russia-favored-trump-in-2016-senate-panel-says-breaking-with-house-gop/2018/05/16/6cf95a6a-58f6-11e8-8836-a4a123c359ab_story.html?utm_term=.52b6624cb0e1.

45. Andrews, N., & Ballhaus, R. (2017, August 2) Trump signs—and slams—Russia sanctions. *Wall Street Journal*. Retrieved from https://www.wsj.com/articles/president-trump-signs-sanctions-bill-aimed-at-punishing-russia-for-election-meddling-1501685839.

46. Nakashima, E. (2018, March 15) Trump administration hits Russian spies, trolls with sanctions over election interferences, cyberattacks. *Washington Post*. Retrieved from https://www.washingtonpost.com/world/national-security/trump-administration-sanctions-russian-spies-trolls-over-us-election-interference-cyber-attacks/2018/03/15/3eaae186-284c-11e8-b79d-f3d931db7f68_story.html?utm_term=.7ce48bb57389

47. Parks, M. (2017, August 2) Trump signs "seriously flawed" Russia sanctions bill into law amid Putin retaliation. *NPR*. Retrieved from https://www.npr.org/2017/08/02/540660414/hfr-trump-signs-russia-sanctions-into-law-amid-putin-retaliation.

48. Countering America's Adversaries through Sanctions Act, Pub. Law No. 115-44 (2017) Retrieved from https://www.congress.gov/115/plaws/publ44/PLAW-115publ44.pdf.

49. Parenthetically, Putin's observation that US intervention in the elections of other countries would yield an equal and opposite reaction might better have been expressed not as action and reaction but as a "see you and raise you" string bet. Among the US activities that nettled the Russian leader and presumably helped provoke the Russian meddling was US disclosure of information about the assets that his Russian associates had secreted abroad. When the Kremlin responded to this and related intrigue by intervening in the US election, the US Congress responded with sanctions that upped the ante. That response to Moscow-tied hacking and trolling in the US election and aggression in Ukraine legislatively mandated revelations about the finances of Putin and the Russian oligarchs by a date that serendipitously coincided with Putin's 2018 reelection campaign. As this section attests, the legislation's undisguised goal is embarrassing Putin:

> Not later than 180 days after the date of the enactment of this Act [August 2, 2017], the Secretary of the Treasury, in consultation with the Director of National Intelligence and the Secretary of State, shall submit to the appropriate congressional committees a detailed report on the following: (1) Senior foreign political figures and oligarchs in the Russian Federation, including the following: (A) An identification of the most significant senior foreign political figures and oligarchs in the Russian Federation, as determined by their closeness to the Russian regime and their net worth. (B) An assessment of the relationship between individuals identified under subparagraph (A) and President Vladimir Putin or other members of the Russian ruling elite. (C) An identification of any indices of corruption with respect to those individuals. (D) The estimated net worth and known sources of income of those individuals and their family members (including spouses, children, parents, and siblings), including assets, investments, other business interests, and relevant beneficial ownership information. (E) An identification of the non-Russian business affiliations of those individuals.

Since the due date for the Treasury report was January 29, 2018, and Russian voters were scheduled to give the former KGB agent a fourth term on March 18, 2018, it is unsurprising that Kremlin spokesman Dmitry Peskov told journalists on the eve of the release, "We do think that this is a direct and obvious attempt to time some sort of action to coincide with our elections in order to influence them" (Newman, K. [2018, January 29] Russia accuses US of election meddling. *U.S. News & World Report*. Retrieved from https://www.usnews.com/news/world/ articles/2018-01-29/russia-accuses-us-of-election-meddling-with-anticipated-sanctions). That report proved anticlimactic, a cut-and-paste of publicly available data from sources such as the *Forbes* list of the 200 richest businessmen in Russia unaccompanied by new sanctions (Hudson, J. [2018, January 30] Trump administration admits it cribbed from *Forbes* magazine to create "oligarch list." *BuzzFeed*. Retrieved from https://www.buzzfeed.com/johnhudson/trump-administration-admits-it-cribbed-forbes-magazine-to?utm_term=.ooyARvQ96#. vbKXYL9jV). A report more damaging to Putin reportedly created by experts had apparently been shunted aside (Ioffe, J. [2018, January 31] How not to design

Russia sanctions. *The Atlantic*. Retrieved from https://www.theatlantic.com/ international/archive/2018/01/kremlin-report-sanctions-policy/551921/). No new sanctions were needed, declared a state department representative, because "this legislation and its implementation are deterring Russian defense sales" (Blake, A. [2018, January 30] The Trump administration's weird explanation for withholding Russia sanctions. *Washington Post*. Retrieved from https://www.washingtonpost.com/news/the-fix/wp/2018/01/30/the-trump-administrations-weird-explanation-for-withholding-russia-sanctions/?utm_term=.267e43e8b449). The fact that the sanctions were intended to punish went unnoted. And whatever the effect on arms sales, the existing regimen had not deterred ongoing Russian efforts to interfere in US politics, which, of course, forecasts likely activity in the 2018 elections.

50. Weedon, J., Nuland, W., & Stamos, A. (2017, April 27) Information operations and Facebook. Facebook. Retrieved from https://fbnewsroomus.files.wordpress.com/ 2017/04/facebook-and-information-operations-v1.pdf.

51. Scola, N., Dawsey, J., & Watkins, A. (2017, September 21) Facebook's cooperation on Russian ads doesn't stop Democrats' demands. *Politico*. Retrieved from https://www.politico.com/story/2017/09/21/facebook-to-release-russian-purchased-ads-linked-to-2016-election-242982.

52. Parks, M. (2018, February 13) Russian threat to elections to persist through 2018, spy bosses warn Congress. *NPR*. Retrieved from https://www.npr.org/2018/02/13/ 584672450/intelligence-leaders-testify-about-global-threats-in-senate-hearing.

53. *United States v. Internet Research Agency LLC*, 18 U.S.C. §§ 2, 371, 1349, 1028A (D.D.C. 2018) Retrieved from https://www.justice.gov/file/1035477/download.

54. Tatum, S. (2018, February 17) McMaster: Evidence of Russian meddling is "now really incontrovertible." *CNN*. Retrieved from https://www.cnn.com/2018/02/ 17/politics/hr-mcmaster-russia-interference/index.html.

55. *United States v. Viktor Borisovich Netyksho, et al*, 18 U.S.C. §§ 2, 371, 1030, 1028A, 1956, and 3551 et seq. (D.D.C. 2018) Retrieved from https://www.justice.gov/ file/1080281/download; Barrett, D., & Zapotosky, M. (2018, July 13) Mueller probe indicts 12 Russians with hacking of Democrats in 2016. *Washington Post*. Retrieved from https://wapo.st/2uvRLBf?tid=ss_mail&utm_term=. bd4f171f4e2c.

56. Bump, P. (2018, February 16) Trump's unfounded insistence that the new indictment proves Russia didn't swing the election. *Washington Post*. Retrieved from https://www.washingtonpost.com/news/politics/wp/2018/02/16/trumps-insistence-that-the-new-indictment-proves-russia-didnt-swing-the-election-is-unfounded/?utm_term=.2ef43f2c0d4a.

57. Strobel, W., Volz, D., & Landay, J. (2018, February 16) US charges Russians with 2016 US election tampering to boost Trump. *Reuters*. Retrieved from https://www. reuters.com/article/us-usa-trump-russia-indictment/u-s-charges-russians-with-2016-u-s-election-tampering-to-boost-trump-idUSKCN1G022U.

58. Stone, P., & Gordon, G. (2018, January 18) FBI investigating whether Russian money went to NRA to help Trump. *McClatchy*. Retrieved from http://www. mcclatchydc.com/news/nation-world/national/article195231139.html.

59. Cf. Lipton, E., Sanger, D. E., & Shane, S. (2016, December 13) The perfect weapon: How Russian cyberpower invaded the US. *New York Times.* Retrieved from https://nyti.ms/2jASgpt.

60. Fessler, P. (2017, September 22) 10 months after Election Day, feds tell states more about Russian hacking. *NPR.* Retrieved from https://www.npr.org/2017/09/22/552956517/ten-months-after-election-day-feds-tell-states-more-about-russian-hacking; The initial number of states was called into question when some state-level reports argued that it was not the election system that was probed by Russian trolls. See Shepardson, D. (2017, September 28) California, Wisconsin deny election systems targeted by Russian hackers. *Reuters.* Retrieved from https://www.reuters.com/article/us-usa-election/california-wisconsin-deny-election-systems-targeted-by-russian-hackers-idUSKCN1C32SQ.

Chapter 2

1. Jenkins Jr., H. W. (2018, February 20) Mueller focuses on molehills. *Wall Street Journal.* Retrieved from https://www.wsj.com/articles/mueller-focuses-on-molehills-1519169467?mod=e2fb.

2. Tannenbaum, M. B., Hepler, J., Zimmerman, R. S., Saul, L., Jacobs, S., Wilson, K., & Albarracín, D. (2015) Appealing to fear: A meta-analysis of fear appeal effectiveness and theories. *Psychological Bulletin, 141*(6): 1178.

3. The characterization is Mueller's in the February indictment of thirteen Russians: *United States v. Internet Research Agency LLC,* 18 U.S.C. §§ 2, 371, 1349, 1028A (D.D.C. 2018) Retrieved from https://www.justice.gov/file/1035477/download.

4. Edelman, M. (1988) *Constructing the Political Spectacle* (Chicago: University of Chicago Press).

5. Nelson, L. (2017, September 6) Trump hits new low in public opinion—but he's still beating Hillary Clinton. *Politico.* Retrieved from https://www.politico.com/story/2017/09/06/trump-public-opinion-better-than-hillary-clinton-242398.

6. Winneg, K. M., Jamieson, K. H., & Hardy, B. W. (2014) Party identification in the 2012 presidential election. *Presidential Studies Quarterly, 44*(1): 143–156. doi: 10.1111/psq.12091; Winneg, K. M., Jamieson, K. H., & Hardy, B. W. (2010) Party identification in the 2008 election. *Presidential Studies Quarterly, 40*(2): 247–263. doi: 10.1111/j.1741-5705.2010.03757.x; Winneg, K. M., Jamieson, K. H., & Hardy, B. W. (2005) Party identification in the 2004 election. *Presidential Studies Quarterly, 35*(3): 576–589. doi: 10.1111/j.1741-5705.2005.00265.x.

7. Jones, J. M. (2018, January 8) Americans' identification as independents back up in 2017. *Gallup.* Retrieved from http://news.gallup.com/poll/225056/americans-identification-independents-back-2017.aspx.

8. Blake, A. (2016, November 17) How America decided, at the last moment, to elect Donald Trump. *Washington Post.* Retrieved from https://www.washingtonpost.com/news/the-fix/wp/2016/11/17/how-america-decided-at-the-very-last-moment-to-elect-donald-trump/.

9. Fournier, P., Nadeau, R., Blais, A., Gidengil, E., & Nevitte, N. (2004) Time-of-voting decision and susceptibility to campaign effects. *Electoral Studies, 23*(4): 661–681. doi: 10.1016/j.electstud.2003.09.001.

10. Nir, L., & Druckman, J. N. (2008) Campaign mixed-message flows and timing of vote decision. *International Journal of Public Opinion Research, 20*(3): 326–346. doi: 10.1093/ijpor/edn035.

11. Valentino, N. A., Beckmann, M. N., & Buhr, T. A. (2001) A spiral of cynicism for some: The contingent effects of campaign news frames on participation and confidence in government. *Political Communication, 18*(4): 347–367. doi: 10.1080/10584600152647083.

12. Gilbert, C. (2016, November 17) Late deciders loomed large in Trump Wisconsin win. *Journal Sentinel*. Retrieved from https://www.jsonline.com/story/news/blogs/wisconsin-voter/2016/11/17/late-deciders-loomed-large-trump-wisconsin-win/94021250/.

13. Gilbert, C. (2016, November 17) Late deciders loomed large in Trump Wisconsin win. *Journal Sentinel*. Retrieved from https://www.jsonline.com/story/news/blogs/wisconsin-voter/2016/11/17/late-deciders-loomed-large-trump-wisconsin-win/94021250/.

14. Cohen, B. (1963) *The Press and Foreign Policy* (Princeton: Princeton University Press), 13.

15. McCombs, M., & Shaw, D. (1972) The agenda-setting function of mass media. *Public Opinion Quarterly, 36*(2): 176–187.

16. One of the pioneering researchers of this phenomenon, David Weaver, notes that the size of the effect is influenced by factors that include "interest and uncertainty (need for orientation), the obtrusiveness of issues, and the time period" (personal correspondence, March 1, 2018): Tan, Y., & Weaver, D. (2013) Agenda diversity and agenda setting from 1956 to 2004. *Journalism Studies, 14*(6): 773–789. doi: 10.1080/1461670X.2012.748516. Also see McCombs, M. (2014) *Setting the Agenda: The Mass Media and Public Opinion*, 2nd ed. (Malden: Polity Press), 64–74 and 88–92. The .51 reported by the cited study was calculated using a Spearman's Rho non-parametric test that measures the strength of the correlation between two variables. A perfect positive correlation would be expressed as r=1.

17. Page, B. I., Shapiro, R. Y., & Dempsey, G. R. (1987) What moves public opinion? *American Political Science Review, 81*(1): 23–43.

18. Sifry, M. L. (2014, October 31) Facebook wants you to vote on Tuesday. Here's how it messed with your feed in 2012. *Mother Jones*. Retrieved from http://www.motherjones.com/politics/2014/10/can-voting-facebook-button-improve-voter-turnout/; Lind, D. (2014, November 4) Facebook's 'I voted' sticker was a secret experiment on its users. *Vox*. Retrieved from https://www.vox.com/2014/11/4/7154641/midterm-elections-2014-voted-facebook-friends-vote-polls.

19. Prier, J. (2017) Commanding the trend: Social media as information warfare. *Strategic Studies Quarterly, Winter 2017*: 50–85. Retrieved from http://www.airuniversity.af.mil/Portals/10/SSQ/documents/Volume-11_Issue-4/Prier.pdf.

20. Chozick, A. (2016, September 10) Hillary Clinton calls many Trump backers "deplorables," and G.O.P. pounces. *New York Times*. Retrieved from https://www.nytimes.com/2016/09/11/us/politics/hillary-clinton-basket-of-deplorables.html.

21. Prier, J. (2017) Commanding the trend: Social media as information warfare. *Strategic Studies Quarterly, Winter 2017*: 50–85. Retrieved from http://www.airuniversity.af.mil/Portals/10/SSQ/documents/Volume-11_Issue-4/Prier.pdf.

22. Willnat, L., & Weaver, D. H. (2014) The American journalist in the digital age: Key findings. (Bloomington: School of Journalism, Indiana University). Retrieved from http://archive.news.indiana.edu/releases/iu/2014/05/2013-american-journalist-key-findings.pdf.

23. Conway, B. A., Kenski, K., & Wang, D. (2015) The rise of Twitter in the political campaign: Searching for intermedia agenda-setting effects in the presidential primary. *Journal of Computer-Mediated Communication, 20*(4): 363–380. doi: 10.1111/jcc4.12124.

24. Willnat, L., & Weaver, D. H. (2014) The American journalist in the digital age: Key findings. (Bloomington: School of Journalism, Indiana University). Retrieved from http://archive.news.indiana.edu/releases/iu/2014/05/2013-american-journalist-key-findings.pdf.

25. Nelson, T. E., Clawson, R. A., & Oxley, Z. M. (1997) Media framing of a civil liberties conflict and its effect on tolerance. *American Political Science Review, 91*(3): 567–583. doi: 10.2307/2952075. For perspectives on framing, see Cappella, J. N., & Jamieson, K. H. (1997) *Spiral of Cynicism: The Press and the Public Good* (New York: Oxford University Press); Reese, S. D., Gandy Jr., O. H., & Grant, A. E. (Eds.) (1974) *Framing Public Life: Perspectives on Media and Our Frame Analysis: An Essay on the Organization of Experience* (Cambridge: Harvard University Press); and Gamson, W. A., & Modigliani, A. (1989) Media discourse and public opinion on nuclear power: A constructionist approach. *American Journal of Sociology, 95*(1): 1–37.

26. Scheufele, D. A., & Tewksbury, D. (2006) Framing, agenda setting, and priming: The evolution of three media effects models. *Journal of Communication, 57*(1): 9–20. doi: 10.1111/j.0021-9916.2007.00326.x.

27. Price, V., Tewksbury, D., & Powers, E. (1997) Switching trains of thought: The impact of news frames on readers' cognitive responses. *Communication Research, 24*(5): 481–506.

28. Price, V., & Tewksbury, D. (1997) News values and public opinion: A theoretical account of media priming and framing. In G. A. Barnett & E. J. Boster (Eds.), *Progress in Communication Sciences: Advances in Persuasion*, vol. 13 (Greenwich: Ablex), 173–212.

29. Nelson, T. E., Oxley, Z. M., & Clawson, R. A. (1997) Toward a psychology of framing effects. *Political Behavior, 19*(3): 221–246; Gamson W. A., & Lasch, K. E. (1983) The political culture of social welfare policy. In S. E. Spiro & E. Yuchtman-Yaar (Eds.), *Evaluating the Welfare State* (New York: Academic Press), 397–415.

30. Rozin, P., & Royzman, E. B. (2001) Negativity bias, negativity dominance, and contagion. *Personality and Social Psychology Review,* 5(4): 296–320.

31. Scheufele, D. A., & Iyengar, S. (2012) The state of framing research: A call for new directions. In K. Kenski & K. H. Jamieson (Eds.), *The Oxford Handbook of Political Communication Theories* (New York: Oxford University Press).

32. Iyengar, S., & Kinder, D. (1987) *News That Matters: Television and American Opinion* (Chicago: University of Chicago Press), 4.

33. Johnston, R., Hagen, M. G., & Jamieson, K. H. (2004) *The 2000 Presidential Election and the Foundations of Party Politics* (New York: Cambridge University Press).

34. Kenski, K., Hardy, B. W., & Jamieson, K. H. (2010) *The Obama Victory: How Media, Money, and Message Shaped the 2008 Election* (New York: Oxford University Press).

35. Iyengar, S., & Kinder, D. R. (2010) *News That Matters: Television and American Opinion* (Chicago: University of Chicago Press).

36. Schaffner, B. F., & Sellers, P. J. (Eds.) (2009) *Winning with Words: The Origins and Impact of Political Framing* (New York: Routledge).

37. Bryan, C. J., Walton, G. M., Rogers, T., & Dweck, C. S. (2011) Motivating voter turnout by invoking the self. *PNAS,* 108(31): 12653–12656. doi: 10.1073/pnas.1103343108.

38. Pearson, M. R. (2010) How "undocumented workers" and "illegal aliens" affect prejudice toward Mexican immigrants. *Social Influence,* 5(2): 118–132. doi: 10.1080/15534511003593679.

39. Igartua, J. J., & Cheng, L. (2009) Moderating effect of group cue while processing news on immigration: Is the framing effect a heuristic process? *Journal of Communication,* 59(4): 726–749. doi: 10.1111/j.1460-2466.2009.01454.x.

40. Monge, P. R., & Contractor, N. S. (2003) *Theories of Communication Networks* (New York: Oxford University Press).

41. Kramer, A. D. I., Guillory, J., & Hancock, J. T. (2014) Experimental evidence of massive-scale emotional contagion through social networks. *PNAS,* 111(24): 8788–8790. doi: 10.1073/pnas.1320040111.

42. Rozin, P., & Royzman, E. B. (2001) Negativity bias, negativity dominance, and contagion. *Personality and Social Psychology Review,* 5(4): 296–320. doi: 10.1207/S15327957PSPR0504_2.

43. Dwoskin, E. (2018, January 22) Facebook thought it was more powerful than a nation-state. Then that became a liability. *Washington Post.* Retrieved from https://www.washingtonpost.com/business/economy/inside-facebooks-year-of-reckoning/2018/01/22/cfd7307c-f4c3-11e7-beb6-c8d48830c54d_story.html?utm_term=.36cdc6ea6fd3.

44. Milkman, K. L., & Berger, J. (2014) The science of sharing and the sharing of science. *PNAS,* 111(Supplement 4): 13642–13649. doi: 10.1073/pnas.1317511111.

45. Berger, J., & Milkman, K. L. (2012) What makes online content viral? *Journal of Marketing Research,* 49(2): 195–205. doi: 10.1509/jmr.10.0353.

46. Milkman, K. L., & Berger, J. (2014) The science of sharing and the sharing of science. *PNAS,* 111(Supplement 4): 13642–13649. doi: 10.1073/pnas.1317511111.

47. Lazarsfeld, P., Berelson, B., & Gaudet, H. (1944) *The People's Choice: How the Voter Makes Up His Mind in a Presidential Campaign* (New York: Duell, Sloan and Pearce); Berelson, B., Lazarsfeld, P., & McPhee, W. (1954) *Voting: A Study of Opinion Formation in a Political Campaign* (Chicago: University of Chicago Press); Katz, E., & Lazarsfeld, P. (1955) *Personal Influence: The Part Played by People in the Flow of Mass Communication*, 2nd ed. (New Brunswick: Transaction).

48. Lazarsfeld, P., Berelson, B., & Gaudet, H. (1944) *The People's Choice: How the Voter Makes Up His Mind in a Presidential Campaign* (New York: Duell, Sloan and Pearce), 151.

49. Arndt, J. (1968) A test of the two-step flow in diffusion of a new product. *Journalism Quarterly, 45*(3): 457–465.

50. Troldahl, V. C. (1966) A field test of a modified "two-step flow of communication" model. *Public Opinion Quarterly, 30*(4): 609–623.

51. Feldman, L., Maibach, E. W., Roser-Renouf, C., & Leiserowitz, A. (2012) Climate on cable: The nature and impact of global warming coverage on Fox News, CNN, and MSNBC. *International Journal of Press/Politics, 17*(1): 3–31. doi: 10.1177/1940161211425410.

52. Druckman, J. N., Levendusky, M. S., & McLain, A. (2018) No need to watch: How the effects of partisan media can spread via interpersonal discussions. *American Journal of Political Science, 62*(1): 99–112. doi: 10.1111/ajps.12325.

53. Bond, R. M., Fariss, C. J., Jones, J. J., Karmer, A. D. I., Marlow, C., Settle, J. E., & Fowler, J. H. (2012) A 61-million-person experiment in social influence and political mobilization. *Nature, 489*: 295–298. doi: 10.1038/nature11421.

54. Lazarsfeld, P., Berelson, B., & Gaudet, H. (1944) *The People's Choice: How the Voter Makes Up His Mind in a Presidential Campaign* (New York: Duell, Sloan and Pearce), 102.

55. Lazarsfeld, P., Berelson, B., & Gaudet, H. (1944) *The People's Choice: How the Voter Makes Up His Mind in a Presidential Campaign* (New York: Duell, Sloan and Pearce), 102.

56. Becker, L., McCombs, M., & McLeod, J. M. (1975) The development of political cognition. In S. Chaffee (Ed.), *Political Communication: Issues and Strategies for Research* (Beverly Hills: Sage), 21–63.

57. Jamieson, K. H., & Cappella, J. N. (2008) *Echo Chamber: Rush Limbaugh and the Conservative Media Establishment* (New York: Oxford University Press).

58. DellaVigna, S., & Kaplan, E. (2007) The Fox News effect: Media bias and voting. *Quarterly Journal of Economics, 122*(3): 1187–1234. doi: 10.1162/qjec.122.3.1187.

59. DellaVigna, S., & Kaplan, E. (2007) The Fox News effect: Media bias and voting. *Quarterly Journal of Economics, 122*(3): 1187–1234. doi: 10.1162/qjec.122.3.1187.

60. Shaw, D. R. (1999) The effect of TV ads and candidate appearances on statewide presidential votes, 1988–96. *American Political Science Review, 93*(2): 345–361. doi: 10.2307/2585400.

61. Gerber, A. S., Gimpel, J. G., Green, D. P., & Shaw, D. R. (2011) How large and long-lasting are the persuasive effects of televised campaign ads? Results from a

randomized field experiment. *American Political Science Review, 105*(1): 135–150. doi: 10.1017/S000305541000047X.

62. Huber, G. A., & Arceneaux, K. (2007) Identifying the persuasive effects of presidential advertising. *American Journal of Political Science, 51*(4): 957–977. doi: 10.1111/j.1540-5907.2007.00291.x. Specifically, "increasing Bush's advertising above the average by 1.57 GRPs/1000 is associated with a 9.1% increase in the predicted probability of supporting Bush (95% confidence interval .5 to 18.2%) and a 7.8% decrease in the probability of supporting Gore (95% confidence interval −17.3 to −.3%). The same increase in Gore's advertising is predicted to increase the probability of supporting Gore by 6.6% (95% confidence interval −.2 to 15.4%) and decrease the probability of supporting Bush by 6.6% (95% confidence interval −15.2 to 0.3%)."

63. Sears, D. O., Freedman, J. L., & O'Connor, E. F. (1964) The effects of anticipated debate and commitment on the polarization of audience opinion. *Public Opinion Quarterly, 28*(4): 615–627. doi: 10.1086/267285; Sears, D., & Chaffee, S. (1979) Uses and effects of the 1976 debates: An overview of empirical studies. In Sidney Kraus (Ed.), *The Great Debates: Carter vs. Ford, 1976* (Bloomington: Indiana University Press), 223–261; Sigelman, L., & Sigelman, C. K. (1984) Judgments of the Carter-Reagan debate: The eyes of the beholders. *Public Opinion Quarterly, 48*(3): 624–628. doi: 10.1086/268863; Cho, J., & Ha, Y. (2012) On the communicative underpinnings of campaign effects: Presidential debates, citizen communication, and polarization in evaluations of candidates. *Political Communication, 29*(2): 184–204. doi: 10.1080/10584609.2012.671233.

64. Silver, N. (2012, October 3) First debate often helps challenger in polls. *FiveThirtyEight.* Retrieved from https://fivethirtyeight.com/features/first-debate-often-helps-challenger-in-polls/.

65. Chaffee, S. H. (1978) Presidential debates—Are they helpful to voters? *Communication Monographs, 45*: 330–346. doi: 10.1080/03637757809375978.

66. Cf. McKinney, M., & Carlin, D. (2004) Political campaign debates. In L. Lee Kaid (Ed.), *Handbook of Political Communication Research* (Mahwah: Lawrence Erlbaum), 211.

67. Shaw, D. R. (1999) The effect of TV ads and candidate appearances on statewide presidential votes, 1988–96. *American Political Science Review, 93*(2): 345–361. doi: 10.2307/2585400.

68. Hill, S. J., Lo, J., Vavreck, L., & Zaller, J. (2013) How quickly we forget: The duration of persuasion effects from mass communication. *Political Communication, 30*(4): 521–547. doi: 10.1080/10584609.2013.828143.

69. Jamieson, K. H., & Waldman, P. (2003) *The Press Effect: Politicians, Journalists, and the Stories That Shape the Political World* (New York: Oxford University Press), 56.

70. Johnston, R., Hagen, M. G., & Jamieson, K. H. (2004) *The 2000 Presidential Election and the Foundations of Party Politics* (New York: Cambridge University Press), 127.

71. Johnston, R., Hagen, M. G., & Jamieson, K. H. (2004) *The 2000 Presidential Election and the Foundations of Party Politics* (New York: Cambridge University Press), 129.

72. Although for most it remains constant, political identity can shift within and across elections. The rolling cross-sectional survey called the National Annenberg

Election Survey (NAES), which my policy center ran in 2000, 2004, and 2008 and our cross-sectional surveys in 2012 all show slight changes in the partisan configuration of the voting population. The change between elections can also be noteworthy. The Democratic edge over the Republicans grew from nearly 4 points in the 2004 NAES to almost 9 points in the 2008 one.

73. Cf. Berelson, B., Lazarsfeld, P., & McPhee, W. (1954) *Voting: A Study of Opinion Formation in a Political Campaign* (Chicago: University of Chicago Press).

74. Johnston, R., Hagen, M. G., & Jamieson, K. H. (2004) *The 2000 Presidential Election and the Foundations of Party Politics* (New York: Cambridge University Press), 6.

75. Conover, P. J., & Feldman, S. (1989) Candidate perceptions in an ambiguous world: Campaigns, cues, and inference processes. *American Journal of Political Science*, 33(4): 141–154.

76. Finkel, S. E. (1993) Reexamining the "minimal effects" model in recent presidential campaigns. *Journal of Politics*, 55(1): 1–21.

77. Zaller, J. (1996) The myth of massive media effects revived: Empirical support for a discredited idea. In D. Mutz, P. Sniderman, & R. Brody (Eds.), *Political Persuasion and Attitude Change* (Ann Arbor: University of Michigan Press), 20.

78. Bartels, L. M. (2008) *Unequal Democracy: The Political Economy of the New Gilded Age* (Princeton: Princeton University Press), 120–123.

79. Johnston, R., Hagen, M. G., & Jamieson, K. H. (2004) *The 2000 Presidential Election and the Foundations of Party Politics* (New York: Cambridge University Press).

80. Kenski, K., Hardy, B. W., & Jamieson, K. H. (2010) *The Obama Victory: How Media, Money, and Message Shaped the 2008 Election* (New York: Oxford University Press), 274.

81. Kenski, K., Hardy, B. W., & Jamieson, K. H. (2010) *The Obama Victory: How Media, Money, and Message Shaped the 2008 Election* (New York: Oxford University Press).

82. Spartz, J. T., Su, L. Y. F., Griffin, R., Brossard, D., & Dunwoody, S. (2017) YouTube, social norms and perceived salience of climate change in the American mind. *Environmental Communication*, 11(1): 1–16. doi: 10.1080/17524032.2015.1047887.

83. Noelle-Neumann, E. (1974) The spiral of silence: A theory of public opinion. *Journal of Communication*, 24(2): 43–51. doi: 10.1111/j.1460-2466.1974.tb00367.x.

84. Gearhart, S., & Zhang, W. (2015) "Was it something I said?" "No, it was something you posted!" A study of the spiral of silence theory in social media contexts. *Cyberpsychology, Behavior, and Social Networking*, 18(4): 208–213. doi: 10.1089/cyber.2014.0443.

85. Fazio, L. K., Brashier, N. M., Payne, B. K., & Marsh, E. J. (2015) Knowledge does not protect against illusory truth. *Journal of Experimental Psychology: General*, 144(5): 993–1002. doi: 10.1037/xge0000098.

Chapter 3

1. Techonomy (2016, November 17) In conversation with Mark Zuckerberg. Techonomy 16 Conference Report. Retrieved from https://techonomy.com/conf/te16/videos-conversations-with-2/in-conversation-with-mark-zuckerberg/.

2. Stone, P., & Gordon, G. (2017, July 12) Trump-Russia investigators probe Jared Kushner-run digital operation. *McClatchy*. Retrieved from http://www.mcclatchydc.com/news/nation-world/national/article160803619.html.

3. Pierson, D. (2018, February 2) YouTube will start labeling videos that receive government funding. *Los Angeles Times*. Retrieved from http://www.latimes.com/business/technology/la-fi-tn-youtube-news-20180202-story.html.

4. Gold, H. (2018, February 3) YouTube to start labeling videos posted by state-funded media. *CNN*. Retrieved from http://money.cnn.com/2018/02/02/media/youtube-state-funded-media-label/index.html.

5. *RT* (2016, November 4) "Clinton and ISIS funded by same money"—Assange interview with John Pilger (Courtesy Darthmouth Films). YouTube video. Retrieved from https://youtu.be/k9xbokQO4M0.

6. *RT* (2016, September 13) US media accused of burying concerns over Clinton health. YouTube video. Retrieved from https://youtu.be/hjATqbDcvFY.

7. Friedman, U. (2017, July 24) 5 ways to interfere in American elections—without breaking the law. *The Atlantic*. Retrieved from https://www.theatlantic.com/international/archive/2017/07/legal-ways-interfere-election/534057/.

8. Wakabayashi, D., & Confessore, N. (2017, October 23) Russia's favored outlet is an online news giant. YouTube helped. *New York Times*. Retrieved from https://nyti.ms/2zxqO0G.

9. Timberg, C. (2018, February 15) Russia used mainstream media to manipulate American voters. *Washington Post*. Retrieved from https://www.washingtonpost.com/business/technology/russia-used-mainstream-media-to-manipulate-american-voters/2018/02/15/85f7914e-11a7-11e8-9065-e55346f6de81_story.html?utm_term=.36034ce56e96.

10. Schleifer, T. (2016, September 9) On Russian TV, Trump says it's "unlikely" Putin trying to sway election. *CNN*. Retrieved from https://www.cnn.com/2016/09/08/politics/russia-television-donald-trump-interview/index.html.

11. President of Russia (2018, March 10) Interview to American TV channel NBC. Retrieved from http://en.kremlin.ru/events/president/transcripts/57027.

12. Office of the Director of National Intelligence (2017, January 6) Assessing Russian activities and intentions in recent US elections. Retrieved from https://www.dni.gov/files/documents/ICA_2017_01.pdf.

13. Ruffini, P. (2017, November 3) Why Russia's Facebook ad campaign wasn't such a success. *Washington Post*. Retrieved from https://www.washingtonpost.com/outlook/why-russias-facebook-ad-campaign-wasnt-such-a-success/2017/11/03/b8efacca-bffa-11e7-8444-a0d4f04b89eb_story.html.

14. Weise, E. (2017, October 30) Russian fake accounts showed posts to 126 million Facebook users. *USA Today*. Retrieved from https://www.usatoday.com/story/tech/2017/10/30/russian-fake-accounts-showed-posts-126-million-facebook-users/815342001/.

15. Romm, T., & Molla, R. (2017, November 4) Here's a longer list of news organizations that cited Russia-linked Twitter accounts. *Recode*. Retrieved from https://www.recode.net/2017/11/4/16606188/twitter-russia-troll-news-citation-list.

16. Seetharaman, D. (2017, October 30) Russian-backed Facebook accounts staged events around divisive issues. *Wall Street Journal.* Retrieved from https://www.wsj. com/articles/russian-backed-facebook-accounts-organized-events-on-all-sides-of-polarizing-issues-1509355801.

17. Bump, P. (2017, December 28) There's still little evidence that Russia's 2016 social media efforts did much of anything. *Washington Post.* Retrieved from https:// www.washingtonpost.com/news/politics/wp/2017/12/28/theres-still-little-evidence-that-russias-2016-social-media-efforts-did-much-of-anything/?utm_term=.72a144596f5f.

18. Guynn, J. (2018, January 19) Twitter: There were more Russian trolls than we thought. *USA Today.* Retrieved from https://www.usatoday.com/story/tech/news/2018/01/19/twitter-there-were-more-russian-trolls-than-we-thought/1050091001/. See also Twitter Public Policy (2018, January 18) Update on Twitter's review of the 2016 US election. *Twitter.* Updated on January 31, 2018. Retrieved from https://blog. twitter.com/official/en_us/topics/company/2018/2016-election-update.html.

19. De Vynck, G., & Wang, S. (2018, January 29) Russian bots retweeted Trump's Twitter 470,000 times. *Bloomberg.* Retrieved from https://www.bloomberg.com/news/articles/2018-01-26/twitter-says-russian-linked-bots-retweeted-trump-470-000-times. For the full report, see Twitter, Inc. (January 19, 2018) Edgett appendix to responses: Update on results of retrospective review of Russian-related election activity. United States Senate Committee on the Judiciary, Subcommittee on Crime and Terrorism. Retrieved from https://www.judiciary.senate.gov/imo/media/doc/Edgett%20Appendix%20to%20Responses.pdf.

20. Twitter Public Policy (2018, January 19) Update on Twitter's review of the 2016 US election. *Twitter.* Updated on January 31, 2018. Retrieved from https://blog. twitter.com/official/en_us/topics/company/2018/2016-election-update.html.

21. Parlapiano, A., & Lee, J. C. (2018, February 16) The propaganda tools used by Russians to influence the 2016 election. *New York Times.* Retrieved from https:// nyti.ms/2C7mFpE.

22. Timberg, C. (2017, October 5) Russian propaganda may have been shared hundreds of millions of times, new research says. *Washington Post.* Retrieved from https://www.washingtonpost.com/news/the-switch/wp/2017/10/05/russian-propaganda-may-have-been-shared-hundreds-of-millions-of-times-new-research-says/?utm_term=.04cbfb1335ec.

23. Frenkel, S. (2017, December 17) For Russian "trolls," Instagram's pictures can spread wider than words. *New York Times.* Retrieved from https://www.nytimes. com/2017/12/17/technology/instagram-russian-trolls.html.

24. Silverman, C. (2018, February 6) Russian trolls ran wild on Tumblr and the company refuses to say anything about it. *BuzzFeed.* Retrieved from https:// www.buzzfeed.com/craigsilverman/russian-trolls-ran-wild-on-tumblr-and-the-company-refuses?utm_term=.amMP05JdR.

25. Persily, N. (2017) The 2016 US election: Can democracy survive the internet? *Journal of Democracy, 28*(2): 63–76. Retrieved from https://www.journalofdemocracy.org/article/can-democracy-survive-the-internet.

26. Guilbeault, D., & Woolley, S. (2016, November 1) How Twitter bots are shaping the election. *The Atlantic.* Retrieved from https://www.theatlantic.com/technology/archive/2016/11/election-bots/506072/.

27. Bertrand, N. (2018, January 19) Russia-leaked Twitter accounts are working overtime to help Devin Nunes and WikiLeaks. *Business Insider.* Retrieved from http://www.businessinsider.com/release-the-memo-campaign-russia-linked-twitter-accounts-2018-1.

28. Persily, N. (2017) The 2016 US election: Can democracy survive the internet? *Journal of Democracy, 28*(2): 63–76. Retrieved from https://www.journalofdemocracy.org/article/can-democracy-survive-the-internet.

29. See more from the Computational Propaganda Project, University of Oxford, http://comprop.oii.ox.ac.uk/; Kollanyi, B., Howard, P. N., & Woolley, S. C. (2016) Bots and automation over Twitter during the US election. Computational Propaganda Project, University of Oxford. Data memo. Retrieved from http://comprop.oii.ox.ac.uk/research/working-papers/bots-and-automation-over-twitter-during-the-u-s-election/.

30. Markoff, J. (2016, November 17) Automated pro-Trump bots overwhelmed pro-Clinton messages, researchers say. *New York Times.* Retrieved from https://nyti.ms/2k22soF.

31. Twitter Public Policy (2018, January 18) Update on Twitter's review of the 2016 US election. *Twitter.* Updated on January 31, 2018. Retrieved from https://blog.twitter.com/official/en_us/topics/company/2018/2016-election-update.html.

32. Ferrara, E., Varol, O., Davis, C., Menczer, F., & Flammini, A. (2016, July) The rise of social bots. *Communications of the ACM, 59*(7): 98–104. doi: 10.1145/2818717.

33. Burke, S. (2017, June 17) How many social followers does Trump actually have? *CNN.* Retrieved from http://money.cnn.com/2017/06/17/technology/trump-social-media-followers/index.html.

34. Greenwood, S., Perrin, A., & Duggan, M. (2016, November 11) Social media update 2016. *Pew Research Center.* Retrieved from http://www.pewinternet.org/2016/11/11/social-media-update-2016/.

35. *United States v. Internet Research Agency LLC,* 18 U.S.C. §§ 2, 371, 1349, 1028A (D.D.C. 2018) Retrieved from https://www.justice.gov/file/1035477/download.

36. Seetharaman, D. (2017, October 30) Russian-backed Facebook accounts staged events around divisive issues. *Wall Street Journal.* Retrieved from https://www.wsj.com/articles/russian-backed-facebook-accounts-organized-events-on-all-sides-of-polarizing-issues-1509355801.

37. Timberg, C., & Dwoskin, E. (2018, January 25) Russians got tens of thousands of Americans to RSVP for their phony political events on Facebook. *Washington Post.* Retrieved from https://www.washingtonpost.com/news/the-switch/wp/2018/01/25/russians-got-tens-of-thousands-of-americans-to-rsvp-for-their-phony-political-events-on-facebook/?utm_term=.099676080c22.

38. Timberg, C., & Dwoskin, E. (2018, January 25) Russians got tens of thousands of Americans to RSVP for their phony political events on Facebook. *Washington Post.* Retrieved from https://www.washingtonpost.com/news/the-switch/wp/2018/

01/25/russians-got-tens-of-thousands-of-americans-to-rsvp-for-their-phony-political-events-on-facebook/?utm_term=.099676080c22.

39. Satter, R., Donn, J., & Day, C. (2017, November 3) Inside story: How Russians hacked the Democrats' emails. *Associated Press*. Retrieved from https://www.bloomberg.com/news/articles/2017-11-03/inside-story-how-russians-hacked-the-democrats-emails.

40. Satter, R., Donn, J., & Day, C. (2017, November 3) Inside story: How Russians hacked the Democrats' emails. *Associated Press*. Retrieved from https://www.bloomberg.com/news/articles/2017-11-03/inside-story-how-russians-hacked-the-democrats-emails.

41. Satter, R., Donn, J., & Day, C. (2017, November 3) Inside story: How Russians hacked the Democrats' emails. *Associated Press*. Retrieved from https://www.bloomberg.com/news/articles/2017-11-03/inside-story-how-russians-hacked-the-democrats-emails.

Chapter 4

1. Cox, D., Lienesch, R., & Jones, R. P. (2017, May 9) Beyond economics: Fears of cultural displacement pushed the white working class to Trump. Public Religion Research Institute. Retrieved from https://www.prri.org/research/white-working-class-attitudes-economy-trade-immigration-election-donald-trump/.

2. Green, E. (2017, May 9) It was cultural anxiety that drove white, working-class voters to Trump. *The Atlantic*. Retrieved from https://www.theatlantic.com/politics/archive/2017/05/white-working-class-trump-cultural-anxiety/525771/.

3. Mutz, D. C. (2018) Status threat, not economic hardship, explains the 2016 presidential vote. *PNAS* 201718155. doi: 10.1073/pnas.1718155115.

4. Tavernise, S., & Gebeloff, R. (2018, May 4) They voted for Obama, then went for Trump. Can Democrats win them back? *New York Times*. Retrieved from https://nyti.ms/2KBdsH1.

5. Kolko, J. (2016, November 10) Trump was stronger where the economy is weaker. *FiveThirtyEight*. Retrieved from https://fivethirtyeight.com/features/trump-was-stronger-where-the-economy-is-weaker/.

6. Cherlin, A. J. (2018, May 6) You can't separate money from culture. *New York Times*. Retrieved from https://nyti.ms/2KF9PzX.

7. Griffin, R., & Teixeira, R. (2017, June) The story of Trump's appeal: A portrait of Trump voters. *Democracy Fund Voter Study Group*. Retrieved from https://www.voterstudygroup.org/publications/2016-elections/story-of-trumps-appeal.

8. Harding, L. (2017) *Collusion: Secret Meetings, Dirty Money, and How Russia Helped Donald Trump Win* (New York: Vintage), 11–12.

9. Isaac, M., & Shane, S. (2017, October 2) Facebook's Russia-linked ads came in many disguises. *New York Times*. Retrieved from https://nyti.ms/2fLiHcR.

10. Facebook user Patriototus (2016, April 3) "The Second Amendment to our Constitution is clear. The right of the people to keep and bear Arms shall not be infringed upon. Period."—Donald J. Trump. Facebook post. Archived by Jonathan Albright (Tableau user d1gi). Retrieved from https://public.tableau.com/shared/S7XT4NKGM?:display_count=yes.

11. Facebook user Secured.Borders (2016, September 12) Our government spends billions of dollars on illegal aliens, while our brave Veterans are dying waiting for

help. Facebook post. Archived by Jonathan Albright (Tableau user d1gi). Retrieved from https://public.tableau.com/shared/NG66HH7GD?:display_count=no.

12. Newport, F., & Dugan, A. (2016, July 12) One in four Americans dislike both presidential candidates. *Gallup News*. Retrieved from http://news.gallup.com/opinion/polling-matters/187652/one-four-americans-dislike-presidential-candidates.aspx.

13. Jamieson, K. H., & Taussig, D. (2017) Disruption, demonization, deliverance, and norm destruction: The rhetorical signature of Donald J. Trump. *Political Science Quarterly, 132*(4): 619–650.

14. Twitter PublicPolicy (2018, January 18) Update on Twitter's review of the 2016 US election. *Twitter*. Updated on January 31, 2018. Retrieved from https://blog.twitter.com/official/en_us/topics/company/2018/2016-election-update.html.

15. Both high-ranking Republicans and representatives of the social media platforms have implied that more so than securing a specific electoral outcome, the goal of the Russian IRA's St. Petersburg–based trolls was sowing division in the United States. So, for example, Senator Chuck Grassley (R-IA), chair of the Senate Judiciary Committee, supposed the campaign was intended "to divide us and discredit our democracy." (Kang, C., Fandos, N., & Isaac, M. [2017, October 31] Tech executives are contrite about election meddling, but make few promises on Capitol Hill. *New York Times*. Retrieved from https://www.nytimes.com/2017/10/31/us/politics/facebook-twitter-google-hearings-congress.html.) Facebook's general counsel, Colin Stretch, described it as "an insidious attempt to drive people apart." (Isaac, M., & Wakabayashi, D. [2017, October 30] Russian influence reached 126 million through Facebook alone. *New York Times*. Retrieved from https://www.nytimes.com/2017/10/30/technology/facebook-google-russia.html.) Facebook CEO Zuckerberg stated that he was upset that "Russians used our tools to sow mistrust." (Kang, C., Fandos, N., & Isaac, M. [2017, November 1] Russia-financed ad linked Clinton and Satan. *New York Times*. Retrieved from https://www.nytimes.com/2017/11/01/us/politics/facebook-google-twitter-russian-interference-hearings.html.) After the February 2018 release of the Mueller troll indictment, the vice president of Facebook Ads, Rob Goldman, tweeted, "Most of the coverage of Russian meddling involves their attempt to effect [*sic*] the outcome of the 2016 US election. I have seen all of the Russian ads and I can say very definitively that swaying the election was *NOT* the main goal." (Roose, K. [2018, February 19] On Russia, Facebook sends a message it wishes it hadn't. *New York Times*. Retrieved from https://nyti.ms/2BDkIQI.) Goldman then added, "The majority of the Russian ad spend [*sic*] happened AFTER the election. We shared that fact, but very few outlets have covered it because it doesn't align with the main media narrative of Trump and the election." In a follow-up tweet, Goldman conceded that "the Russian campaign was certainly in favor of Trump." (Quito, A. [2018, February 17] Facebook's answer to Russian election meddling: postcards. *Quartz*. Retrieved from https://qz.com/1210286/facebooks-rob-goldman-and-the-postcard-solution-to-russian-election-meddling/.)

Obviously any effort can have multiple goals. Aspirations also can evolve or change. Because one is compatible with the other, casting the Russian objective as either magnifying discord or defeating Hillary Clinton creates a false dichotomy. Just because the trolls were both trying to widen tears in the US social fabric and engaging in messaging before Trump's announcement of his presidential bid and after his election does not alter the fact, confirmed by the February 2018 Mueller grand jury indictment, that by February 2016 these minions were supporting Trump and opposing Clinton. And importantly, even before the New York builder-and-brand-broker announced his candidacy, their activities, whatever the motive, were likely ultimately to redound against Clinton.

Because the bulk of the Russian messaging reportedly did not explicitly mention the candidates, voting, or the election, some suggest that we should infer that it did not influence any of the three. Among those inviting that inference was Alex Stamos, chief security officer for Facebook, who reported in early September 2017 that "[t]he vast majority of ads run by these [Russian Facebook] accounts didn't specifically reference the U.S. presidential election, voting or a particular candidate. Rather, the ads and accounts appeared to focus on amplifying divisive social and political messages across the ideological spectrum." (Stamos, A. [2017, September 6] An update on information operations on Facebook.) Facebook Newsroom. *Facebook.* Retrieved from https://newsroom.fb.com/news/2017/09/information-operations-update/.) Nonetheless, as I noted in chapter 2, since increasing our awareness of some issues over others (or, in the jargon of psychologists, "increasing their cognitive accessibility") can prioritize them in voters' assessments of candidates (Iyengar, S., & Kinder, D. R. [2010] *News That Matters: Television and American Opinion* [Chicago: University of Chicago Press]), a disinformation campaign that focuses the news and campaign agenda on topics congenial to one contender or uncongenial to the other can affect ballots.

Still, a caveat noted by Senate Intelligence Committee chairman Richard Burr (R-NC) is of value here. In his opening statement at the fall 2017 hearings on Russian content in social media, the North Carolina Republican noted, "A lot of folks, including many in the media, have tried to reduce this entire conversation to one premise: foreign actors conducted a surgical executed covert operation to help elect a United States president. . . . I'm here to tell you, this story does not simplify that easily." (Shepherd, T. [2017, November 1] Richard Burr tries to burst the narrative of Russia's meddling in the 2016 election. *Washington Examiner.* Retrieved from http://www.washingtonexaminer.com/richard-burr-tries-to-burst-the-narrative-of-russias-meddling-in-the-2016-election/article/2639231.) Senator Burr is correct for a number of reasons, among them the one expressed by Florida senator Marco Rubio (R): the efforts were in existence before Trump secured the nomination and persisted after he had secured election.

The notion that the incumbent Democratic president was a troll target is validated by a January 6, 2016, post that read "Obama should stop treating military veterans like garbage! Millions of American soldiers who were deployed in Iraq and Afghanistan struggle with the difficulties they face when they return back home. Despite the fact that Obama prefers to keep the problems hidden, our veterans cannot afford the level of medical care they need. The Government simply doesn't care for them!" (Facebook user Patriototus [2016, January 6] Obama should stop treating military veterans like garbage! Facebook post. Archived by Jonathan Albright (Tableau user d1gi). Retrieved from https://public.tableau.com/shared/ 347Y66QNR?:display_count=yes.) In a like vein, a February 5th Russian missive falsely declared, "In 2013, the government released 36,007 convicted criminal aliens responsible for homicides, sexual assaults, kidnapping, and other serious crimes. Meanwhile, ranchers along the southern border are victimized with impunity by drug cartels exploiting the open border. Is it not time to close our Southern border?" (Facebook user Patriototus [2016, February 5] In 2013, the government released 36,007 convicted criminal aliens responsible for homicides, sexual assaults, kidnapping, and other serious crimes. Facebook post. Archived by Jonathan Albright (Tableau user d1gi). Retrieved from https://public.tableau.com/shared/ ZG79X4WRM?:display_count=yes.) Another troll message, this one a retweet, asked, "Obama trying to start WWIII to avoid a Trump presidency?" Its link was to a tweet by the Associated Press "about Syrian government allegations of a U.S. strike on forces there." (Timberg, C. [2018, February 15] Russia used mainstream media to manipulate American voters. *Washington Post*. Retrieved from https:// www.washingtonpost.com/business/technology/russia-used-mainstream-media-to-manipulate-american-voters/2018/02/15/85f7914e-11a7-11e8-9065-e55346f6de81_story.html?utm_term=.36034ce56e96.)

Nor does the notion that Russian machinations persisted after Trump's election establish that, *during* the 2016 campaign, undermining Clinton was not a central Kremlin objective. However, once Trump was elected, representatives of both Facebook and Twitter, as well as Senate Judiciary Committee member Senator Lindsey Graham (R-SC), have asserted that "Russian-tied groups and organizations [tried] to undermine President Trump's legitimacy." (Scola, N., & Gold, A. [2017, October 31] Facebook, Twitter: Russian actors sought to undermine Trump after election. *Politico*. Retrieved from https://www.politico.com/story/ 2017/10/31/facebook-twitter-post-election-russian-meddling-sought-to-undermine-trump-244380.) A desire to defeat Clinton is, of course, not incompatible with later undermining a Trump presidency for the sheer propaganda value of making the United States look bad or in response to evidence that it might prove less congenial than anticipated to Russian interests. Until all of the postelection messaging is analyzed, we won't know how much of it was consistent with complicating the administration of the new incumbent and how much rallied support for his causes.

Some clearly did perform that latter role. As reported by the *Wall Street Journal*, one postelection tweet from a Russian account using the name Chelsey Jones and the handle @cheelsyJoTRs said on October 14, 2017, "BUSTED! Two Obama 'Dreamers' Arrested For Smuggling in Illegals!" (Wells, G., & Seetharaman, D. [2017, November 1] New Facebook data shows Russians targeted users by race, religion, politics. *Wall Street Journal*. Retrieved from https://www.wsj.com/articles/russian-ads-targeted-facebook-users-by-profile-1509563354.) The account's profile included #MAGA, the acronym for Trump's "Make America Great Again" slogan. And, consistent with an agenda hostile to Democrats and hospitable to

Trump, an examination of seventy-eight articles that were among the top URLs shared by Kremlin-oriented accounts on Twitter (November 18–30, 2017) found that "[j]ust under 40% of the top URLs featured attacks on Democrats, with the Clintons the subject of roughly half of those attacks. Sexual misconduct remained a top topic: 18 percent of the examined URLs focused on allegations against prominent figures (there was roughly a 50-50 split between articles defending [Republican Senate candidate] Roy Moore and those attacking other men, particularly [Democrats] Al Franken and John Conyers)." (Hamilton 68 & Alliance for Securing Democracy [2017, December 8] Dashboard: Tracking Russian influence operations on Twitter. *German Marshall Fund of the United States*. Retrieved from http://dashboard.securingdemocracy.org/.)

16. Lizza, R. (2017, November 2) How Trump helps Russian trolls. *The New Yorker*. Retrieved from https://www.newyorker.com/news/our-columnists/how-trump-helps-russian-trolls.

17. Sullivan, K. (2017, July 23) The rise of black nationalist groups that captivated killers in Dallas, Baton Rouge. *Washington Post*. Retrieved from https://www.washingtonpost.com/national/inside-the-black-nationalist-groups-that-captivated-killers-in-dallas-baton-rouge/2016/07/23/e53aef66-4f89-11e6-a422-83ab49ed5e6a_story.html.

18. Facebook user Blacktivists (2016, February 16) The Black Panthers were originally created to help black community to survive in a racist country. Facebook post. Archived by Jonathan Albright (Tableau user d1gi). Retrieved from https://public.tableau.com/shared/YPJN4DZ9D?:display_count=no.

19. Facebook user Blacktivists (2016, February 23) Trust me, underneath those KKK robes are cops, teachers, lawyers, judges, politicians, banker, etc. Facebook post. Archived by Jonathan Albright (Tableau user d1gi). Retrieved from https://public.tableau.com/shared/JBTGXGH6F?:display_count=no.

20. Facebook user Blacktivists (2016, May 18) If Black Panthers, Malcolm X, Martin Luther King could stand up to cops back then, why can't we get together and do it again together? Archived by Jonathan Albright (Tableau user d1gi). Retrieved from https://public.tableau.com/shared/5T7FQG9TW?:display_count=no.

21. Facebook user Blacktivists (2016, June 27) The KKK employed violence to obtain their objectives, in fact, this racial hate group was committed to maintain the status of white supremacy and suppress the activities of people of color. Archived by Jonathan Albright (Tableau user d1gi). Retrieved from https://public.tableau.com/shared/J67J9BCJS?:display_count=no.

22. Facebook user Blacktivists (2016, July 11) Today, KKK wear suits and blue uniform with a license to kill. Archived by Jonathan Albright (Tableau user d1gi). Retrieved from https://public.tableau.com/shared/2XB7YHWJ9?:display_count=yes.

23. Facebook user Blacktivists (2016, October 10) Blank Panthers were dismantled by U.S. government because they were black men and women standing up for justice and equality. Archived by Jonathan Albright (Tableau user d1gi). Retrieved from https://public.tableau.com/shared/HKDP5MZZR?:display_count=yes.

24. O'Sullivan, D., & Byers, D. (2017, October 13) Exclusive: Even Pokémon Go used by extensive Russian-linked meddling effort. *CNN*. Retrieved from http://money. cnn.com/2017/10/12/media/dont-shoot-us-russia-pokemon-go/index.html.

25. Collins, B., Resnick, G., Poulsen, K., & Ackerman, S. (2017, September 20) Exclusive: Russians appear to use Facebook to push Trump rallies in 17 US cities. *Daily Beast*. Retrieved from https://www.thedailybeast.com/ russians-appear-to-use-facebook-to-push-pro-trump-flash-mobs-in-florida.

26. Facebook user Blacktivists (2016, February 12) Whites actually brought their children to watch planned lynching as a form of twisted entertainment. Facebook post. Archived by Jonathan Albright (Tableau user d1gi). Retrieved from https://public. tableau.com/shared/CQXKDSD8N?:display_count=yes.

27. Twitter Public Policy (2018, January 19) Update on Twitter's review of the 2016 US election. *Twitter*. Updated on January 31, 2018. Retrieved from https://blog. twitter.com/official/en_us/topics/company/2018/2016-election-update.html.

28. *Fox News* (2016, August 30) Trump calls Kaepernick's refusal to stand for national anthem "terrible." Retrieved from http://www.foxnews.com/politics/2016/08/ 30/trump-calls-kaepernicks-refusal-to-stand-for-national-anthem-terrible.html.

29. Ross, B., Mosk, M., Kreider, R., Park, C., & Hosenball, A. (2017, October 18) Russian internet trolls sought to co-opt unwitting American activists. *ABC News*. Retrieved from http://abcnews.go.com/Politics/russian-internet-trolls-sought-opt-unwitting-american-activists/story?id=50570832.

30. Ross, B., Mosk, M., Kreider, R., Park, C., & Hosenball, A. (2017, October 18) Russian internet trolls sought to co-opt unwitting American activists. *ABC News*. Retrieved from http://abcnews.go.com/Politics/russian-internet-trolls-sought-opt-unwitting-american-activists/story?id=50570832.

31. *United States v. Internet Research Agency LLC*, 18 U.S.C. §§ 2, 371, 1349, 1028A (D.D.C. 2018) Retrieved from https://www.justice.gov/file/1035477/download.

32. Poulsen, K. (2017, November 7) Exclusive: Russia activated Twitter sleeper cells for 2016 Election Day blitz. *Daily Beast*. Retrieved from https://www.thedailybeast. com/exclusive-russia-activated-twitter-sleeper-cells-for-election-day-blitz.

33. Stelter, B. (2016, November 3) Here are the ads Clinton and Trump bought in Game 7. *CNN*. Retrieved from http://money.cnn.com/2016/11/02/media/ clinton-trump-world-series-ads/index.html.

34. Dolan, K. (2013) Gender stereotypes, candidate evaluations, and voting for women candidates: What really matters? *Political Research Quarterly, 67*(1): 96–107. doi: 10.1177/1065912913487949.

35. Barnes, T. D., & Beaulieu, E. (2014) Gender stereotypes and corruption: How candidates affect perceptions of election fraud. *Politics & Gender, 10*(3): 365–391. doi: 10.1017/S1743923X14000221.

36. Abramowitz, A. I., & Webster, S. (2016) The rise of negative partisanship and the nationalization of US elections in the 21st century. *Electoral Studies, 41*: 12–22.

37. Fetzer, J. (2016, June 4) Killary: The Clinton body-count. Retrieved from http:// jamesfetzer.blogspot.com/2016/06/killary-clinton-body-count.html.

38. Rivero, M. (2016) The Clinton body-count. *What Really Happened*. Retrieved from http://www.whatreallyhappened.com/RANCHO/POLITICS/BODIES. php#axzz4AcbphGca.

39. The Truth Factory (2017, July 19) Killary Clinton body count song. YouTube video. Retrieved from https://youtu.be/BJTURA1_SLY.

40. The Truth Factory (n.d.) Twitter account. Retrieved from https://twitter.com/ truthfactorycat.

41. WITW Staff (2017, July 26) Vendors sell "Killary Rotten Clinton" shooting targets at Trump rally in Ohio. *Women in the World*. Retrieved from https:// womenintheworld.com/2017/07/26/vendors-sell-killary-rotten-clinton-shooting-targets-at-trump-rally-in-ohio/.

42. Michel, C. (2017, October 6) These are the Facebook posts Russia used to undermine Hillary Clinton's campaign. *ThinkProgress*. Retrieved from https:// thinkprogress.org/russia-facebook-clinton-campaign-d6d76b2a2e82/.

43. Shane, S. (2018, February 18) How unwitting Americans encountered Russian operatives online. *New York Times*. Retrieved from https://nyti.ms/2BCzNSH.

44. Koff, S. (2015, December 14) 'Killary Clinton' PAC creates trouble for Ohio high school students. *Cleveland.com*. Retrieved from http://www.cleveland.com/open/ index.ssf/2015/12/killary_clinton_pac_creates_trouble_for_ohio_high_ school_students.html.

45. Facebook user Heart of Texas (2016, October 26) Fellow Texans! It's time to say a strong NO to the establishment robbers. Facebook post. Archived by US House Permanent Select.Committee on Intelligence. Ad ID 724. Retrieved from https:// democrats-intelligence.house.gov/facebook-ads/social-media-advertisements.htm.

46. Instagram user american.veterans (2016, August 17) Killary Clinton will never understand what it feels like to lose the person you love for the sake of your country. Instagram post. Archived by US House Permanent Select Committee on Intelligence. Ad ID 1840. Retrieved from https://democrats-intelligence.house. gov/facebook-ads/social-media-advertisements.htm.

47. Twitter user @christinawilkie (2016, August 9) One guy just yelled "Kill her! Kill her!" at the Trump rally in NC. Twitter post. Retrieved from https://twitter.com/ christinawilkie/status/763076960121556992.

48. Twitter user @realDonaldTrump (2016, October 22) WikiLeaks: Clinton-Kaine even lied about timing of veep pick. Twitter post. Retrieved from https://twitter. com/realDonaldTrump/status/790016528011890688.

49. Twitter user @realDonaldTrump (2016, October 27) WikiLeaks drip-drop releases prove one thing: There's no Nov. 8 deadline on Clinton's dishonesty and scandals. Twitter post. Retrieved from https://twitter.com/realDonaldTrump/ status/791642669256769536.

50. Twitter user @realDonaldTrump (2016, July 23) The Wikileaks e-mail release today was so bad to Sanders that it will make it impossible for him to support her unless he is a fraud! Twitter post. Retrieved from https://twitter.com/realDonaldTrump/ status/756962332228612096.

51. Twitter user @realDonaldTrump (2016, July 23) Leaked e-mails of DNC show plans to destroy Bernie Sanders. Twitter post. Retrieved from https://twitter.com/realDonaldTrump/status/756804886038192128.

52. Twitter user @realDonaldTrump (2016, November 1) So terrible that Crooked didn't report she got the debate questions from Donna Brazile, if that were me it would have been front page news! Twitter post. Retrieved from https://twitter.com/realDonaldTrump/status/793456094198759424.

53. Twitter user @realDonaldTrump (2016, October 21) WikiLeaks reveals Clinton camp's work with "VERY friendly and malleable reporters." Twitter post. Retrieved from https://twitter.com/realDonaldTrump/status/789598795315150853.

54. Twitter user @realDonaldTrump (2016, October 12) Very little pick-up by the dishonest media of incredible information provided by WikiLeaks. Twitter post. Retrieved from https://twitter.com/realDonaldTrump/status/786201435486781440.

55. Facebook user Patriototus (2016, April 1) How ironic, Hillary accuses another candidate of lies! Facebook post. Archived by Jonathan Albright (Tableau user d1gi). Retrieved from https://public.tableau.com/shared/Y7RHXJFHB?:display_count=yes.

56. Twitter user @TEN_GOP (2016, June 18) Once a liar always a liar! Twitter post. Archived on TweetSave.com. Retrieved from https://tweetsave.com/ten_gop/status/744306225261666305.

57. Nimmo, B. (2017, November 14) How a Russian troll fooled America. *Medium*. Retrieved from https://medium.com/dfrlab/how-a-russian-troll-fooled-america-80452a4806d1.

58. Shane, S. (2018, February 18) How unwitting Americans encountered Russian operatives online. *New York Times*. Retrieved from https://nyti.ms/2BCzNSH.

Chapter 5

1. Gronke, P., Galanes-Rosenbaum, E., & Miller, P. A. (2007) Early voting and turnout. *PS: Political Science & Politics, 40*(4): 639–645. doi: 10.1017/S1049096507071028.

2. Gronke, P., Galanes-Rosenbaum, E., Miller, P. A., & Toffey, D. (2008) Convenience voting. *Annual Review of Political Science, 11*: 437–455. doi: 10.1146/annurev.polisci.11.053006.190912.

3. Gomez, B. T., Hansford, T. G., & Krause, G. A. (2007) The Republicans should pray for rain: Weather, turnout, and voting in US presidential elections. *Journal of Politics, 69*(3): 649–663.

4. Gerber, A. S., Green, D. P., & Larimer, C. W. (2008) Social pressure and voter turnout: Evidence from a large-scale field experiment. *American Political Science Review, 102*(1): 33–48. doi: 10.1017/S000305540808009X.

5. Gerber, A. S., & Green, D. P. (2000) The effects of canvassing, telephone calls, and direct mail on voter turnout: A field experiment. *American Political Science Review, 94*(3): 653–663. doi: 10.2307/2585837.

6. Cohn, N. (2016, December 23) How the Obama coalition crumbled, leaving an opening for Trump. *New York Times*. Retrieved from https://nyti.ms/2jAiqIZ.

7. Ruffini, P. (2017, November 3) Why Russia's Facebook ad campaign wasn't such a success. *Washington Post*. Retrieved from https://www.washingtonpost.com/outlook/why-russias-facebook-ad-campaign-wasnt-such-a-success/2017/11/03/b8efacca-bffa-11e7-8444-a0d4f04b89eb_story.html.

8. Gottfried, J., & Shearer, E. (2016, May 26) News use across social media platforms 2016. Pew Research Center. Retrieved from http://www.journalism.org/2016/05/26/news-use-across-social-media-platforms-2016/.

9. Finn, M. (2016, April 5) Flag-stomping protesters fueling tensions at Trump, other events. *Fox News*. Retrieved from http://www.foxnews.com/politics/2016/04/05/flag-stomping-protesters-fueling-tensions-at-trump-other-events.html.

10. Datoc, C. (2016, April 4) "F**k this flag. F**k this country'—BLM protesters spit and stomp on American flag [VIDEO]. *Daily Caller*. Retrieved from http://dailycaller.com/2016/04/04/fk-this-flag-fk-this-country-blm-protesters-spit-and-stomp-on-american-flag-video/.

11. Facebook user Patriototus (2016, April 5) Trump's rally in West Allis this Sunday faced a protest from BLM riots. Facebook post. Archived by Jonathan Albright (Tableau user d1gi). Retrieved from https://public.tableau.com/shared/HZKXQBJKY?:display_count=yes.

12. Tversky, A., & Kahneman, D. (1973) Availability: A heuristic for judging frequency and probability. *Cognitive Psychology, 5*(2): 207–232.

13. BBC News (2017, November 1) Social-media images shown as evidence of "Russian trolls." Retrieved from http://www.bbc.com/news/technology-41829537.

14. RT America (2016, August 17) How 100% of the Clintons' 2015 "charity" went to . . . themselves. Facebook video. Retrieved from https://www.facebook.com/RTAmerica/videos/10153703671361366/.

15. Office of the Director of National Intelligence (2017, January 6) Background to "Assessing Russian Activities and Intentions in Recent US Elections": The analytic process and cyber incident attribution. Retrieved from https://www.dni.gov/files/documents/ICA_2017_01.pdf.

16. Fox News (2016, October 12) Clinton campaign spokeswoman takes shots at Catholics, evangelicals in leaked email exchange. Retrieved from http://www.foxnews.com/politics/2016/10/12/clinton-campaign-spokeswoman-takes-shots-at-catholics-evangelicals-in-leaked-email-exchange.html.

17. Weber, P. (2016, October 17) Something stinks about Hillary Clinton's "anti-Catholic" scandal. *The Week*. Retrieved from http://theweek.com/articles/655175/something-stinks-about-hillary-clintons-anticatholic-scandal.

18. Farley, H. (2016, October 12) Leaked emails reveal top Clinton aide mocked evangelicals and Catholics. *Christian Today*. Retrieved from https://www.christiantoday.com/article/leaked-emails-reveal-top-clinton-aide-mocked-evangelicals-and-catholics/97763.htm.

19. Easley, J. (2016, October 12) Catholic group demands top Clinton aide resign over leaked emails. *The Hill*. Retrieved from http://thehill.com/blogs/ballot-box/presidential-races/300543-catholic-group-demands-top-clinton-aide-resign-over.

20. Dias, E. (2016, October 12) Hillary Clinton campaign pushes back on "anti-Catholic" charge. *TIME Magazine*. Retrieved from http://time.com/4528532/hillary-clinton-campaign-pushes-back-on-anti-catholic-charge/.

21. Twitter user @realDonaldTrump (2016, October 24) Why has nobody asked Kaine about the horrible views emanated on WikiLeaks about Catholics? Twitter post. Retrieved from https://twitter.com/realDonaldTrump/status/790539740118446080.

22. Pew Research Center (2016, January 27) Faith and the 2016 campaign. Retrieved from http://www.pewforum.org/2016/01/27/faith-and-the-2016-campaign/.

23. Pew Research Center (2016, July 13) Evangelicals rally to Trump, religious 'nones' back Clinton. Retrieved from http://www.pewforum.org/2016/07/13/evangelicals-rally-to-trump-religious-nones-back-clinton/.

24. Smith, G. A., & Martínez, J. (2016, November 9) How the faithful voted: A preliminary 2016 analysis. Pew Research Center. Retrieved from http://www.pewresearch.org/fact-tank/2016/11/09/how-the-faithful-voted-a-preliminary-2016-analysis/.

25. Cox, D. (2016, November 9) White Christians side with Trump. Public Religion Research Institute (PRRI). Retrieved from https://www.prri.org/spotlight/religion-vote-presidential-election-2004-2016/.

26. Heroes at Home Act of 2006, S.3517, 109th Congress (2006). Retrieved from https://www.congress.gov/bill/109th-congress/senate-bill/3517.

27. Facebook user Patriototus (2016, September 8) At least 50,000 homeless veterans are starving dying in the streets, but liberals want to invite 620,000 refugees and settle them among us. Facebook post. Archived by Jonathan Albright (Tableau user d1gi). Retrieved from https://public.tableau.com/profile/d1gi#!/vizhome/FB4/TableofFullTextPosts.

28. Facebook user Secured.Borders (2016, September 12) Our government spends billions of dollars on illegal aliens, while our brave veterans are dying waiting for help. Facebook post. Archived by Jonathan Albright (Tableau user d1gi). Retrieved from https://public.tableau.com/profile/d1gi#!/vizhome/FB4/TableofFullTextPosts.

29. Wells, G., & Seetharaman, D. (2017, November 1) New Facebook data shows Russians targeted users by race, religion, politics. *Wall Street Journal*. Retrieved from https://www.wsj.com/articles/russian-ads-targeted-facebook-users-by-profile-1509563354.

30. Wagner, K. (2017, October 31) These are some of the tweets and Facebook ads Russia used to try and influence the 2016 presidential election. *Recode*. Retrieved from https://www.recode.net/2017/10/31/16587174/fake-ads-news-propaganda-congress-facebook-twitter-google-tech-hearing.

31. Brzozowski, M. J., Sandholm, T., & Hogg, T. (2009) Effects of feedback and peer pressure on contributions to enterprise social media. Hewlett-Packard Laboratories. Retrieved from https://dl.acm.org/citation.cfm?id=1531684; Van de Bongardt, D., Reitz, E., Sandfort, T., & Deković, M. (2015) A meta-analysis of the relations between three types of peer norms and adolescent sexual

behavior. *Personality and Social Psychology Review, 19*(3): 203–234. doi: 10.1177/ 1088868314544223; Tropp, L. R., O'Brien, T. C., & Migacheva, K. (2014) How peer norms of inclusion and exclusion predict children's interest in cross-ethnic friendships. *Journal of Social Issues, 70*(1): 151–166. doi: 10.1111/josi.12052.

32. Michel, C. (2017, October 6) These are the Facebook posts Russia used to undermine Hillary Clinton's campaign. *ThinkProgress.* Retrieved from https:// thinkprogress.org/russia-facebook-clinton-campaign-d6d76b2a2e82/.

33. Hartig, H., Lapinski, J., & Psyllos, S. (2016, August 16) Poll: Trump leads Clinton among military households. *NBC News.* Retrieved from https://www.nbcnews.com/politics/2016-election/poll-trump-leads-clinton-among-military-households-n632106.

34. Clement, S. (2014, November 11) Veterans are voting Republican. And that's not likely to change. *Washington Post.* Retrieved from https://www.washingtonpost. com/news/the-fix/wp/2014/11/11/veterans-are-voting-republican-and-thats-not-likely-to-change/.

35. *CNN* (2016, November 23) Exit polls. Retrieved from http://www.cnn.com/election/results/exit-polls/national/president.

36. Byers, D. (2017, September 28) Exclusive: Russian-bought Black Lives Matter ad on Facebook targeted Baltimore and Ferguson. *CNN.* Retrieved from http:// money.cnn.com/2017/09/27/media/facebook-black-lives-matter-targeting/ index.html.

37. *United States v. Internet Research Agency LLC*, 18 U.S.C. §§ 2, 371, 1349, 1028A (D.D.C. 2018) Retrieved from https://www.justice.gov/file/1035477/download.

38. Facebook user Woke Blacks (2016, October 18) Staying Woke, building-up our Black communities, uplifting Black people. Facebook post. Archived by US House Permanent Select Committee on Intelligence. Ad ID 2815. Retrieved from https:// democrats-intelligence.house.gov/facebook-ads/social-media-advertisements. htm.

39. Facebook user Blacktivist (2016, November 3) What this heart-piercing story about a racial bias that might cause law enforcement officers to shoot innocent and unarmed black people. Facebook post. Archived by US House Permanent Select Committee on Intelligence. Ad ID 1028. Retrieved from https:// democrats-intelligence.house.gov/facebook-ads/social-media-advertisements. htm.

40. Tynes, T. (2016, February 24) Black Lives Matter activists interrupt Hillary Clinton at private event in South Carolina. *Huffington Post.* Retrieved from https:// www.huffingtonpost.com/entry/clinton-black-lives-matter-south-carolina_us_ 56ce53b1e4b03260bf7580ca?section=politics.

41. Capehart, J. (2016, February 25) Hillary Clinton on "superpredator" remarks: "I shouldn't have used those words." *Washington Post.* Retrieved from https://www. washingtonpost.com/blogs/post-partisan/wp/2016/02/25/hillary-clinton-responds-to-activist-who-demanded-apology-for-superpredator-remarks/?utm_ term=.9eb05ddf33ca.

42. Graves, A. (2016, August 28) Did Hillary Clinton call African-American youth "superpredators"? *PolitiFact*. Retrieved from http://www.politifact.com/truth-o-meter/statements/2016/aug/28/reince-priebus/did-hillary-clinton-call-african-american-youth-su/.

43. Alexander, M. (2016, February 10) Why Hillary Clinton doesn't deserve the black vote. *The Nation*. Retrieved from https://www.thenation.com/article/hillary-clinton-does-not-deserve-black-peoples-votes/.

44. Facebook user Blacktivist (2016, May 21) Black people should wake up as soon as possible. Facebook post. Archived by Jonathan Albright (Tableau user d1gi). Retrieved from https://public.tableau.com/profile/d1gi#!/vizhome/FB4/TableofFullTextPosts.

45. Facebook user Blacktivist (2016, June 9) US prisons now hold more black men than slavery ever did. Facebook post. Archived by Jonathan Albright (Tableau user d1gi). Retrieved from https://public.tableau.com/profile/d1gi#!/vizhome/FB4/TableofFullTextPosts.

46. Facebook user Blacktivist (2016, July 15) Black people continue to make up more than 30 percent of the people dying from police misconduct, though we make up only 13 percent of nation's population. Facebook post. Archived by Jonathan Albright (Tableau user d1gi). Retrieved from https://public.tableau.com/profile/d1gi#!/vizhome/FB4/TableofFullTextPosts.

47. Silverman, C. (2018, February 6) Russian trolls ran wild on Tumblr and the company refuses to say anything about it. *BuzzFeed News*. Retrieved from https://www.buzzfeed.com/craigsilverman/russian-trolls-ran-wild-on-tumblr-and-the-company-refuses?utm_term=.amMP05JdR.

48. Collins, B. (2018, March 7) The Russian troll Tumblr post so stupid it went viral. *Daily Beast*. Retrieved from https://www.thedailybeast.com/the-russian-troll-tumblr-post-so-stupid-it-went-viral.

49. Green, J., & Issenberg, S. (2016, October 27) Inside the Trump bunker, with days to go. *Bloomberg Businessweek*. Retrieved from https://www.bloomberg.com/news/articles/2016-10-27/inside-the-trump-bunker-with-12-days-to-go.

50. Winston, J. (2016, November 16) How the Trump campaign built an identity database and used Facebook ads to win the election. *Medium*. Retrieved from https://medium.com/startup-grind/how-the-trump-campaign-built-an-identity-database-and-used-facebook-ads-to-win-the-election-4ff7d24269ac.

51. Winston, J. (2016, November 16) How the Trump campaign built an identity database and used Facebook ads to win the election. *Medium*. Retrieved from https://medium.com/startup-grind/how-the-trump-campaign-built-an-identity-database-and-used-facebook-ads-to-win-the-election-4ff7d24269ac.

52. Green, J., & Issenberg, S. (2016, October 27) Inside the Trump bunker, with days to go. *Bloomberg Businessweek*. Retrieved from https://www.bloomberg.com/news/articles/2016-10-27/inside-the-trump-bunker-with-12-days-to-go.

53. Institute of Politics, Harvard Kennedy School (2017) *Campaign for President: The Managers Look at 2016* (Lanham: Rowman and Littlefield), 228.

54. Modell, J. (2017, November 2) Russian hackers used a secret weapon: Aziz Ansari. *AV Club*. Retrieved from https://www.avclub.com/russian-hackers-used-a-secret-weapon-aziz-ansari-1820076677.

55. Caldwell, D. (2016, November 3) Vote from home. *Know Your Meme*. Retrieved from http://knowyourmeme.com/memes/vote-from-home.

56. Seetharaman, D., Wells, G., & Tau, B. (2018, May 10) Release of thousands of Russia-linked Facebook ads shows how propaganda sharpened. *Wall Street Journal*. Retrieved from https://www.wsj.com/articles/full-stock-of-russia-linked-facebook-ads-shows-how-propaganda-sharpened-1525960804.

57. Nakashima, R., & Ortutay, B. (2017, November 10) AP exclusive: Russia Twitter trolls deflected Trump bad news. *Associated Press*. Retrieved from https://apnews.com/fc9ab2b0bbc34f11bc10714100318ae1.

58. Ross, B., Mosk, M., Kreider, R., Park, C., & Hosenball, A. (2017, October 18) Russian internet trolls sought to co-opt unwitting American activists. *ABC News*. Retrieved from http://abcnews.go.com/Politics/russian-internet-trolls-sought-opt-unwitting-american-activists/story?id=50570832.

59. Silverman, C. (2018, February 6) Russian trolls ran wild on Tumblr and the company refuses to say anything about it. *BuzzFeed News*. Retrieved from https://www.buzzfeed.com/craigsilverman/russian-trolls-ran-wild-on-tumblr-and-the-company-refuses?utm_term=.amMP05JdR.

60. Collins, B., & Russell, J. (2018, March 1) Russians used Reddit and Tumblr to troll the 2016 election. *Daily Beast*. Retrieved from https://www.thedailybeast.com/russians-used-reddit-and-tumblr-to-troll-the-2016-election.

61. Lee, T. (2016, October 10) Watch: Actress walks off set of pro–Hillary Clinton ad. *Breitbart*. Retrieved from http://www.breitbart.com/big-government/2016/10/10/hold-kahn-clever-anti-hillary-ad-slays-making-viewers-think-pro-clinton/.

62. Elliott, P. (2016, October 9) Exclusive: Anti-Clinton PAC adding TV commercials. *TIME Magazine*. Retrieved from http://time.com/4524276/defeat-crooked-hillary-ads/.

63. Defeat Crooked Hillary (2016, October 9) Cut. YouTube video. Retrieved from https://youtu.be/ZdbupFQEaWc.

64. Elliott, P. (2016, October 9) Exclusive: Anti-Clinton PAC adding TV commercials. *TIME Magazine*. Retrieved from http://time.com/4524276/defeat-crooked-hillary-ads/.

65. Lee, T. (2016, October 10) Watch: Actress walks off set of pro–Hillary Clinton ad. *Breitbart*. Retrieved from http://www.breitbart.com/big-government/2016/10/10/hold-kahn-clever-anti-hillary-ad-slays-making-viewers-think-pro-clinton/.

66. *United States v. Internet Research Agency LLC*, 18 U.S.C. §§ 2, 371, 1349, 1028A (D.D.C. 2018) Retrieved from https://www.justice.gov/file/1035477/download.

67. *United States v. Internet Research Agency LLC*, 18 U.S.C. §§ 2, 371, 1349, 1028A (D.D.C. 2018) Retrieved from https://www.justice.gov/file/1035477/download.

68. Wagner, J., & Schuster, S. (2016, December 9) Trump says blacks who stayed home were "almost as good" as those who voted for him. *Washington Post*. Retrieved

from https://www.washingtonpost.com/news/post-politics/wp/2016/12/09/
trump-says-blacks-who-stayed-home-were-almost-as-good-as-those-who-voted-
for-him/.

69. File, T. (2017, May 10) Voting in America: A look at the 2016 presidential election. United States Census Bureau. Retrieved from https://www.census.gov/news-
room/blogs/random-samplings/2017/05/voting_in_america.html.

70. Krogstad, J. M., & Lopez, M. H. (2017, May 12) Black voter turnout fell in 2016,
even as a record number of Americans cast ballots. Pew Research Center. Retrieved
from http://www.pewresearch.org/fact-tank/2017/05/12/black-voter-turnout-
fell-in-2016-even-as-a-record-number-of-americans-cast-ballots/.

71. Politico Staff (2016, July 21) Full text: Donald Trump 2016 RNC draft speech
transcript. *Politico*. Retrieved from https://www.politico.com/story/2016/07/
full-transcript-donald-trump-nomination-acceptance-speech-at-rnc-225974.

72. Trump intelligence allegations (2017, January 10) Posted by Mark Schoofs,
Buzzfeed on DocumentCloud. Retrieved from https://www.documentcloud.org/
documents/3259984-Trump-Intelligence-Allegations.html#document/p17.

73. Stein, J. (2016, July 24) Why DNC chair Debbie Wasserman Schultz won't speak
at her own party's convention. *Vox*. Retrieved from https://www.vox.com/2016/7/
24/12265380/dnc-chair-wasserman-schultz-email-leaks.

74. Twitter user @wikileaks (2016, July 22) Release: 19,252 emails from the US
Democratic National Committee. Twitter post. Retrieved from https://twitter.
com/wikileaks/status/756501723305414656.

75. Brazile, D. (2017) *Hacks: The Inside Story of the Break-ins and Breakdowns That Put
Donald Trump in the White House* (New York: Hachette), 8.

76. Brazile, D. (2017) *Hacks: The Inside Story of the Break-ins and Breakdowns That Put
Donald Trump in the White House* (New York: Hachette), 8.

77. Fox News (2016, July 23) Wikileaks dump appears to show DNC favored Clinton
campaign. Retrieved from http://www.foxnews.com/politics/2016/07/23/
wikileaks-dump-appears-to-show-dnc-favored-clinton-campaign.html.

78. Twitter user @realDonaldTrump (2016, July 23) The Wikileaks e-mail release today was so bad to Sanders that it will make it impossible for him to support her unless he is a fraud! Twitter post. Retrieved from https://twitter.com/
realDonaldTrump/status/756962332228612096.

79. Twitter user @realDonaldTrump (2016, July 23) Leaked e-mails of DNC show
plans to destroy Bernie Sanders. Twitter post. Retrieved from https://twitter.com/
realDonaldTrump/status/756804886038192128.

80. Twitter user @realDonaldTrump (2016, July 25) How much BAD JUDGEMENT
was on display by the people in DNC in writing those really dumb e-mails, using
even religion, against Bernie! Twitter post. Retrieved from https://twitter.com/
realDonaldTrump/status/757545252026712064.

81. Twitter user @realDonaldTrump (2016, October 19) Bernie Sanders on HRC: Bad
judgement. John Podesta on HRC: Bad instincts. Twitter post. Retrieved from
https://twitter.com/realDonaldTrump/status/788927558288969729.

82. Stein, J. (2016, July 24) Why DNC chair Debbie Wasserman Schultz won't speak at her own party's convention. *Vox*. Retrieved from https://www.vox.com/2016/7/24/12265380/dnc-chair-wasserman-schultz-email-leaks.

83. Bokhari, A. (2016, October 7) October surprise: WikiLeaks releases 2,050 emails from Clinton campaign chairman John Podesta. *Breitbart*. Retrieved from http://www.breitbart.com/tech/2016/10/07/wikileaks-releases-2050-emails-clinton-campaign-chief-john-podesta/.

84. Borger, J. (2017, July 5) Investigators explore if Russia colluded with pro-Trump sites during US election. *Guardian*. Retrieved from https://www.theguardian.com/us-news/2017/jul/05/donald-trump-russia-investigation-fake-news-hillary-clinton.

85. Silverman, C. (2018, February 6) Russian trolls ran wild on Tumblr and the company refuses to say anything about it. *BuzzFeed News*. Retrieved from https://www.buzzfeed.com/craigsilverman/russian-trolls-ran-wild-on-tumblr-and-the-company-refuses?utm_term=.amMP05JdR.

86. Le Miere, J. (2017, August 23) Bernie Sanders voters helped Trump win and here's proof. *Newsweek*. Retrieved from http://www.newsweek.com/bernie-sanders-trump-2016-election-654320.

87. Henderson, M., Hillygus, D. S., & Tompson, T. (2010) "Sour grapes" or rational voting? Voter decision making among thwarted primary voters in 2008. *Public Opinion Quarterly*, 74(31): 499–529. doi: 10.1093/poq/nfq008.

88. Sides, J. (2017, August 24) Did enough Bernie Sanders supporters vote for Trump to cost Clinton the election? *Washington Post*. Retrieved from https://www.washingtonpost.com/news/monkey-cage/wp/2017/08/24/did-enough-bernie-sanders-supporters-vote-for-trump-to-cost-clinton-the-election/.

89. Enten, H. (2017, January 5) Registered voters who stayed home probably cost Clinton the election. *FiveThirtyEight*. Retrieved from https://fivethirtyeight.com/features/registered-voters-who-stayed-home-probably-cost-clinton-the-election/.

90. Enten, H. (2017, January 5) Registered voters who stayed home probably cost Clinton the election. *FiveThirtyEight*. Retrieved from https://fivethirtyeight.com/features/registered-voters-who-stayed-home-probably-cost-clinton-the-election/.

91. Bacon, P., Jr. (2016, May 28) Huge split between older and younger blacks in the Democratic Party. *NBC News*. Retrieved from https://www.nbcnews.com/news/nbcblk/huge-split-between-older-younger-blacks-democratic-primary-n580996.

92. Facebook user Blacktivist (2016, November 3) Choose peace and vote for Jill Stein. Facebook post. Archived by US House Permanent Select Committee on Intelligence. Ad ID 1183. Retrieved from https://democrats-intelligence.house.gov/facebook-ads/social-media-advertisements.htm.

93. Tracy, A. (2017, December 19) Washington's Russia circus comes for Jill Stein. *Vanity Fair*. Retrieved from https://www.vanityfair.com/news/2017/12/senate-intelligence-committee-jill-stein-russia.

94. Jalonick, M. C. (2017, December 19) Stein says she is cooperating with Russia collusion probe. *Associated Press*. Available via *Mercury News*. Retrieved from https://www.mercurynews.com/2017/12/19/stein-says-she-is-cooperating-with-russia-collusion-probe/.

95. Clinton, H. R. (2017) *What Happened* (New York: Simon and Schuster), 411–412.
96. Windrem, R. (2017, December 20) Senate Russia investigators are interested in Jill Stein. *NBC News*. Retrieved from https://www.nbcnews.com/news/us-news/why-are-senate-russia-investigators-interested-jill-stein-n831261.
97. 2012 presidential election: Popular vote totals (n.d.) National Archives and Records Administration: US Electoral College. Retrieved from https://www.archives.gov/federal-register/electoral-college/2012/popular-vote.html.
98. Office of the Governor, State of Wisconsin (2016, December 12) Certificate of ascertainment for president, vice president and presidential electors: General election—November 8, 2016. Retrieved from https://www.archives.gov/federal-register/electoral-college/2016-certificates/pdfs/ascertainment-wisconsin.pdf.
99. Office of the Governor, State of Wisconsin (2016, December 12) Certificate of ascertainment for president, vice president and presidential electors: General election—November 8, 2016. Retrieved from https://www.archives.gov/federal-register/electoral-college/2016-certificates/pdfs/ascertainment-wisconsin.pdf.
100. 2012 presidential election: Popular vote totals (n.d.) National Archives and Records Administration: US Electoral College. Retrieved from https://www.archives.gov/federal-register/electoral-college/2012/popular-vote.html.
101. State of Michigan, Executive Office (2016, December 2) Certificate of ascertainment of the electors of the president and vice president of the United States of America. Retrieved from https://www.archives.gov/federal-register/electoral-college/2016-certificates/pdfs/ascertainment-michigan.pdf.
102. State of Michigan, Executive Office (2016, December 2) Certificate of ascertainment of the electors of the president and vice president of the United States of America. Retrieved from https://www.archives.gov/federal-register/electoral-college/2016-certificates/pdfs/ascertainment-michigan.pdf.
103. 2012 presidential election: Popular vote totals (n.d.) National Archives and Records Administration: US Electoral College. Retrieved from https://www.archives.gov/federal-register/electoral-college/2012/popular-vote.html.
104. Commonwealth of Pennsylvania (2016, December 12) Certificate of ascertainment of presidential electors. Retrieved from https://www.archives.gov/federal-register/electoral-college/2016-certificates/pdfs/ascertainment-pennsylvania.pdf.
105. Commonwealth of Pennsylvania (2016, December 12) Certificate of ascertainment of presidential electors. Retrieved from https://www.archives.gov/federal-register/electoral-college/2016-certificates/pdfs/ascertainment-pennsylvania.pdf.
106. McElwee, S., Rhodes, J. H., Schaffner, B. F., & Fraga, B. L. (2018, March 10) The missing Obama millions. *New York Times*. Retrieved from https://nyti.ms/2GeDy0V.

Chapter 6

1. Timberg, C. (2017, October 5) Russian propaganda may have been shared hundreds of millions of times, new research says. *Washington Post*. Retrieved from https://www.washingtonpost.com/news/the-switch/wp/2017/10/05/russian-propaganda-may-have-been-shared-hundreds-of-millions-of-times-new-research-says/?utm_term=.04cbfb1335ec; Albright, J. (Tableau user d1gi) (2017,

October 5) Itemized posts and historical engagement - 6 now-closed FB pages. Tableau. Retrieved from https://public.tableau.com/profile/d1gi#!/vizhome/FB4/TotalReachbyPage.

2. Harris, D. (2017, November 1) Former employees expose inner workings of Russian troll farm. *ABC News.* Retrieved from http://abcnews.go.com/International/employees-expose-workings-russian-troll-farm/story?id=50866368.

3. LaBan, C. (2009, July 2) Photo oop: Kerry eats a cheesesteak hoagie . . . with Swiss. *Philadelphia Inquirer.* Retrieved from http://www.philly.com/philly/food/restaurants/Photo_oop_Kerry_eats_a_cheesesteak_hoagie__with_Swiss.html.

4. LaBan, C. (2009, July 2) Photo oop: Kerry eats a cheesesteak hoagie . . . with Swiss. *Philadelphia Inquirer.* Retrieved from http://www.philly.com/philly/food/restaurants/Photo_oop_Kerry_eats_a_cheesesteak_hoagie__with_Swiss.html.

5. Bunch, W. (2017, September 28) The crazy fake Russian "Miners for Trump" rally in Philly—and why it matters. *Philadelphia Inquirer.* Retrieved from http://www.philly.com/philly/columnists/will_bunch/the-crazy-fake-russian-miners-for-trump-rally-in-philly-and-why-it-matters-will-bunch-20170928.html.

6. Poulsen, K. (2017, November 7) Exclusive: Russia activated Twitter sleeper cells for 2016 Election Day blitz. *Daily Beast.* Retrieved from https://www.thedailybeast.com/exclusive-russia-activated-twitter-sleeper-cells-for-election-day-blitz.

7. Woodruff, B., Collins, B., Poulsen, K., & Ackerman, S. (2017, October 18) Trump campaign staffers pushed Russian propaganda days before the election. *Daily Beast.* Retrieved from https://www.thedailybeast.com/trump-campaign-staffers-pushed-russian-propaganda-days-before-the-election.

8. Robb, A. (2017, November 16) Anatomy of a fake news scandal. *Rolling Stone.* Retrieved from http://www.rollingstone.com/politics/news/pizzagate-anatomy-of-a-fake-news-scandal-w511904.

9. Nimmo, B. (2017, November 14) How a Russian troll fooled America. *Medium.* Retrieved from https://medium.com/dfrlab/how-a-russian-troll-fooled-america-80452a4806d1.

10. Timberg, C., & Dwoskin, E. (2018, January 25) Russians got tens of thousands of Americans to RSVP for their phony political events on Facebook. *Washington Post.* Retrieved from https://www.washingtonpost.com/news/the-switch/wp/2018/01/25/russians-got-tens-of-thousands-of-americans-to-rsvp-for-their-phony-political-events-on-facebook/?utm_term=.099676080c22.

11. Howard, P., Kollanyi, B., Bradshaw, S., & Neudert, L.-M. (2017) Social media, news and political information during the US election: Was polarizing content concentrated in swing states? Data memo. Project on Computational Propaganda. Retrieved from http://comprop.oii.ox.ac.uk/publishing/working-papers/social-media-news-and-political-information-during-the-us-election-was-polarizing-content-concentrated-in-swing-states/.

12. O'Connor, G., & Schneider, A. (2017, April 3) How Russian Twitter bots pumped out fake news during the 2016 election. *NPR.* Retrieved from https://www.npr.org/sections/alltechconsidered/2017/04/03/522503844/how-russian-twitter-bots-pumped-out-fake-news-during-the-2016-election.

13. Shane, S. (2017, September 7) The fake Americans Russia created to influence the election. *New York Times*. Retrieved from https://www.nytimes.com/2017/09/07/us/politics/russia-facebook-twitter-election.html.

14. Shane, S. (2017, September 7) The fake Americans Russia created to influence the election. *New York Times*. Retrieved from https://www.nytimes.com/2017/09/07/us/politics/russia-facebook-twitter-election.html.

15. Metzger, M. J., Flanagin, A. J., & Medders, R. B. (2010) Social and heuristic approaches to credibility evaluation online. *Journal of Communication, 60*(3): 413–439. doi: 10.1111/j.1460-2466.2010.01488.x.

16. US House of Representatives Permanent Select Committee on Intelligence—Democrats (n.d.) Stop A.I.: Like and share if you want Burqa banned in America. Screenshot of Facebook post. Retrieved from https://democrats-intelligence.house.gov/uploadedfiles/stop_ai_burqa.pdf.

17. Byers, D. (2017, October 31) Facebook estimates 126 million people were served content from Russia-linked pages. *CNN*. Retrieved from http://money.cnn.com/2017/10/30/media/russia-facebook-126-million-users/index.html.

18. Youyou, W., Kosinski, M., & Stillwell, D. (2015) Computer-based personality judgments are more accurate than those made by humans. *PNAS, 112*(4): 1036–1040. doi: 10.1073/pnas.1418680112.

19. Bump, P. (2017, September 6) The key question about Facebook political ads: Who's seeing them? *Washington Post*. Retrieved from https://www.washingtonpost.com/news/politics/wp/2017/09/06/the-key-question-in-facebook-political-ads-whos-seeing-them/?utm_term=.22da003741c9.

20. Raju, M., Byers, D., & Bash, D. (2017, October 4) Exclusive: Russian-linked Facebook ads targeted Michigan and Wisconsin. *CNN*. Retrieved from https://www.cnn.com/2017/10/03/politics/russian-facebook-ads-michigan-wisconsin/index.html.

21. Confessore, N., & Wakabayashi, D. (2017, October 9) How Russia harvested American rage to reshape US politics. *New York Times*. Retrieved from https://nyti.ms/2yTN6cF.

22. Potter, M. C., Wyble, B., Hagmann, C. E., & McCourt, E. S. (2014) Detecting meaning in RSVP at 13 ms per picture. *Attention, Perception, & Psychophysics, 76*(2): 270–279. doi: 10.3758/s13414-013-0605-z.

23. Stieglitz, S., & Dang-Xuan, L. (2013) Emotions and information diffusion in social media—sentiment of microblogs and sharing behavior. *Journal of Management Information Systems, 29*(4): 217–248. doi: 10.2753/MIS0742-1222290408.

24. Schultz, M. (2017, November 1) These were the Russian-bought political Facebook ads. *New York Post*. Retrieved from http://nypost.com/2017/11/01/these-were-the-russian-bought-political-facebook-ads/.

25. *United States v. Internet Research Agency LLC*, 18 U.S.C. §§ 2, 371, 1349, 1028A (D.D.C. 2018) Retrieved from https://www.justice.gov/file/1035477/download.

26. *United States v. Internet Research Agency LLC*, 18 U.S.C. §§ 2, 371, 1349, 1028A (D.D.C. 2018) Retrieved from https://www.justice.gov/file/1035477/download.

27. Popken, B. (2017, November 30) Russian trolls pushed graphic, racist tweets to American voters. *NBC News*. Retrieved from https://www.nbcnews.com/tech/

social-media/russian-trolls-pushed-graphic-racist-tweets-american-voters-n823001.

28. Twitter user @seanhannity (2016, November 4) LEAKED EMAIL appears to link Clinton Campaign Chairman to bizarre occult ritual. Twitter post. Retrieved from https://twitter.com/seanhannity/status/794612729852166144.

29. Triest, V., & Grim, R. (2017, April 26) Bernie-backing Albanian fake news site proprietor closes up shop. *Huffington Post*. Retrieved from https://www.huffingtonpost. com/entry/2016-election-fake-news-sites_us_58efb05be4b0b9e9848a3520.

30. Frankovic, K. (2016, December 27) Belief in conspiracies largely depends on political identity. *YouGov*. Retrieved from https://today.yougov.com/news/2016/12/ 27/belief-conspiracies-largely-depends-political-iden/.

31. Frankovic, K. (2016, December 27) Belief in conspiracies largely depends on political identity. *YouGov*. Retrieved from https://today.yougov.com/news/2016/12/ 27/belief-conspiracies-largely-depends-political-iden/.

32. Lippman, J. R. (2015) I did it because I never stopped loving you: The effects of media portrayals of persistent pursuit on beliefs about stalking. *Communication Research*, 45(3): 394–421. doi: 10.1177/0093650215570653.

33. Bursztyn, L., Egorov, G., & Fiorin, S. (2017) From extreme to mainstream: How social norms unravel. National Bureau of Economic Research. Working Paper 23415. Retrieved from http://www.nber.org/papers/w23415.

Chapter 7

1. Weedon, J., Nuland, W., & Stamos, A. (2017, April 27) Information operations and Facebook. Facebook Newsroom. *Facebook*. Retrieved from https://fbnewsroomus. files.wordpress.com/2017/04/facebook-and-information-operations-v1.pdf.

2. Twitter Public Policy (2018, January 18) Update on Twitter's review of the 2016 US election. *Twitter*. Updated on January 31, 2018. Retrieved from https:// blog.twitter.com/official/en_us/topics/company/2018/2016-election-update.html.

3. President of Russia (2018, March 10) Interview to American TV channel NBC. Retrieved from http://en.kremlin.ru/events/president/transcripts/57027.

4. Stamos, A. (2017, September 6) An update on information operations on Facebook. Facebook Newsroom. *Facebook*. Retrieved from https://newsroom.fb.com/news/ 2017/09/information-operations-update/.

5. Shepherd, T. (2017, November 1) Richard Burr tries to burst the narrative of Russia's meddling in the 2016 election. *Washington Examiner*. Retrieved from http://www.washingtonexaminer.com/richard-burr-tries-to-burst-the-narrative-of-russias-meddling-in-the-2016-election/article/2639231.

6. Statement of Chairman Richard Burr (2017, November 1) Richard Burr: US Senator for North Carolina. Retrieved from https://www.burr.senate.gov/imo/ media/doc/Chairman%27s%20SFR.pdf.

7. Ruffini, P. (2017, November 3) Why Russia's Facebook ad campaign wasn't such a success. *Washington Post*. Retrieved from https://www.washingtonpost.com/

outlook/why-russias-facebook-ad-campaign-wasnt-such-a-success/2017/11/03/ b8efacca-bffa-11e7-8444-a0d4f04b89eb_story.html.

8. Attention to the Lone Star state, the second most populous in the nation, (World Population Review [n.d.] State populations 2017. Retrieved from http:// worldpopulationreview.com/states/) may reveal Russian ignorance about Article 2, Section 1, of the Constitution, which mandates selection of the president by vote of the Electoral College. Underscoring the possibility that the trolls just didn't get how the US system actually works is the obliviousness evident in their assertion that, should Clinton be elected, "the American army should be withdrawn from Hillary's control according to the amendments to the Constitution."

9. Byers, D. (2017, September 28) Exclusive: Russian-bought Black Lives Matter ad on Facebook targeted Baltimore and Ferguson. *CNN*. Retrieved from http://money. cnn.com/2017/09/27/media/facebook-black-lives-matter-targeting/index.html.

10. Popken, B. (2017, November 30) Russian trolls pushed graphic, racist tweets to American voters. *NBC News*. Retrieved from https://www.nbcnews.com/tech/ social-media/russian-trolls-pushed-graphic-racist-tweets-american-voters- n823001.

11. Collins, B., Resnick, G., Poulsen, K., & Ackerman, S. (2017, September 20) Exclusive: Russians appear to use Facebook to push Trump rallies in 17 US cities. *Daily Beast*. Retrieved from https://www.thedailybeast.com/ russians-appear-to-use-facebook-to-push-pro-trump-flash-mobs-in-florida.

12. Cloud, D. S. (2017, November 1) Lawmakers slam social media giants for failing to block Russian ads and posts during 2016 campaign. *Los Angeles Times*. Retrieved from http://www.latimes.com/nation/la-na-social-media-russia-20171101-story.html.

13. Glenn, M. (2016, May 21) Dozens turn out to support Houston Muslims. *Houston Chronicle*. Retrieved from http://www.chron.com/news/houston-texas/houston/ article/Dozens-turnout-to-support-Houston-Muslims-7926843.php.

14. Collins, B., Resnick, G., Poulsen, K., & Ackerman, S. (2017, September 20) Exclusive: Russians appear to use Facebook to push Trump rallies in 17 US cities. *Daily Beast*. Retrieved from https://www.thedailybeast.com/ russians-appear-to-use-facebook-to-push-pro-trump-flash-mobs-in-florida.

15. Facebook user Being Patriotic (2016, September 23) America has always been hinged on hard-working people. Facebook post. Archived by US House Permanent Select Committee on Intelligence. Ad ID 470. Retrieved from https://democrats- intelligence.house.gov/facebook-ads/social-media-advertisements.htm.

16. Seetharaman, D., Wells, G., & Tau, B. (2018, May 10) Release of thousands of Russia-linked Facebook ads shows how propaganda sharpened. *Wall Street Journal*. Retrieved from https://www.wsj.com/articles/full-stock-of-russia-linked- facebook-ads-shows-how-propaganda-sharpened-1525960804.

17. Seetharaman, D. (2017, October 30) Russian-backed Facebook accounts staged events around divisive issues. *Wall Street Journal*. Retrieved from https://www.wsj. com/articles/russian-backed-facebook-accounts-organized-events-on-all-sides- of-polarizing-issues-1509355801.

18. Furst, R. (2017, November 1) Did Russian hackers organize Philando Castile protest? Activists say no. *Star Tribune*. Retrieved from http://www.startribune. com/local-organizers-doubt-reports-of-russian-ties-to-castile-protest/ 454368633/.

19. Collins, B., Resnick, G., Poulsen, K., & Ackerman, S. (2017, September 20) Exclusive: Russians appear to use Facebook to push Trump rallies in 17 US cities. *Daily Beast*. Retrieved from https://www.thedailybeast.com/ russians-appear-to-use-facebook-to-push-pro-trump-flash-mobs-in-florida.

20. Ng, A. (2018, May 10) Congress releases all 3,000-plus Facebook ads bought by Russians. *CBS News*. Retrieved from https://www.cbsnews.com/news/congress- releases-all-3000-plus-facebook-ads-bought-by-russians/.

21. *United States v. Internet Research Agency LLC*, 18 U.S.C. §§ 2, 371, 1349, 1028A (D.D.C. 2018) Retrieved from https://www.justice.gov/file/1035477/download.

22. Savidge, M. (2016, August 9) Florida: The swingiest swing state. *CNN*. Retrieved from https://www.cnn.com/2016/08/09/politics/election-2016-donald-trump- hillary-clinton-florida/index.html.

23. Wasserman, D. (2016, May 17) Why Pennsylvania could decide the 2016 election. *FiveThirtyEight*. Retrieved from https://fivethirtyeight.com/features/ pennsylvania-could-be-an-electoral-tipping-point/.

24. Patterson, T. E. (2016, December 7) News coverage of the 2016 general election: How the press failed the voters. Shorenstein Center. Retrieved from https:// shorensteincenter.org/news-coverage-2016-general-election/.

25. *United States v. Internet Research Agency LLC*, 18 U.S.C. §§ 2, 371, 1349, 1028A (D.D.C. 2018) Retrieved from https://www.justice.gov/file/1035477/ download.

26. *United States v. Internet Research Agency LLC*, 18 U.S.C. §§ 2, 371, 1349, 1028A (D.D.C. 2018) Retrieved from https://www.justice.gov/file/1035477/download.

27. *United States v. Internet Research Agency LLC*, 18 U.S.C. §§ 2, 371, 1349, 1028A (D.D.C. 2018) Retrieved from https://www.justice.gov/file/1035477/download.

28. Stone, P., & Gordon, G. (2017, July 12) Trump-Russia investigators probe Jared Kushner–run digital operation. *McClatchy*. Retrieved from http://www. mcclatchydc.com/news/nation-world/national/article160803619.html.

29. Brazile, D. (2017) *Hacks: The Inside Story of the Break-ins and Breakdowns That Put Donald Trump in the White House* (New York: Hachette), 85.

30. Gallagher, S. (2017, May 25) Florida GOP consultant admits he worked with Guccifer 2.0, analyzing hacked data. *Ars Technica*. Retrieved from https:// arstechnica.com/tech-policy/2017/05/florida-gop-consultant-admits-he-worked- with-guccifer-2-0-analyzing-hacked-data/.

31. Hello FLA (2016, September 8) **Exclusive** Democrats turnout model. Retrieved from http://hellofla.com/2016/09/08/exclusive-democrats-turnout-model/.

32. Riley, M., & Robertson, J. (2017, June 13) Russian cyberhacks on US electoral system far wider than previously known. *Bloomberg*. Retrieved from https://www. bloomberg.com/news/articles/2017-06-13/russian-breach-of-39-states-threatens- future-u-s-elections.

33. Politico Staff (2017, November 1) The social media ads Russia wanted Americans to see. *Politico*. Retrieved from https://www.politico.com/story/2017/11/01/social-media-ads-russia-wanted-americans-to-see-244423.

34. Dwoskin, E., Entous, A., & Demirjian, K. (2017, September 28) Twitter finds hundreds of accounts tied to Russian operatives. *Washington Post*. Retrieved from https://www.washingtonpost.com/business/economy/twitter-finds-hundreds-of-accounts-tied-to-russian-operatives/2017/09/28/6cf26f7e-a484-11e7-ade1-76d061d56efa_story.html?utm_term=.d6029ec3aae8.

35. Albright, J. (2017, November 8) Instagram, meme seeding, and the truth about Facebook manipulation, pt. 1. *Medium*. Retrieved from https://medium.com/berkman-klein-center/instagram-meme-seeding-and-the-truth-about-facebook-manipulation-pt-1-dae4d0b61db5.

36. Tufekci, Z. (2018, March 19) Facebook's surveillance machine. *New York Times*. Retrieved from https://www.nytimes.com/2018/03/19/opinion/facebook-cambridge-analytica.html?smprod=nytcore-ipad&smid=nytcore-ipad-share

37. Edgerton, A., & Frier, S. (2018, May 10) Lawmakers release trove of more than 3,500 Russian-backed Facebook ads. *Bloomberg*. Retrieved from https://www.bloomberg.com/news/articles/2018-05-10/trove-of-russian-backed-facebook-ads-show-2016-strategy-at-work.

38. Politico Staff (2017, November 1) The social media ads Russia wanted Americans to see. *Politico*. Retrieved from https://www.politico.com/story/2017/11/01/social-media-ads-russia-wanted-americans-to-see-244423.

39. *United States v. Internet Research Agency LLC*, 18 U.S.C. §§ 2, 371, 1349, 1028A (D.D.C. 2018) Retrieved from https://www.justice.gov/file/1035477/download.

40. Halpern, S. (2017, July 19) Hacking the vote: Who helped whom? *New York Review of Books*. Retrieved from http://www.nybooks.com/daily/2017/07/19/hacking-the-vote-trump-russia-who-helped-whom/.

41. Cadwalladr, C. (2017, February 26) Robert Mercer: The big data billionaire waging war on mainstream media. *Guardian*. Retrieved from https://www.theguardian.com/politics/2017/feb/26/robert-mercer-breitbart-war-on-media-steve-bannon-donald-trump-nigel-farage.

42. Kosinski, M., Stillwell, D., & Graepel, T. (2013) Private traits and attributes are predictable from digital records of human behavior. *Proceedings of the National Academy of Sciences, 110*(15): 5802–5805. doi: 10.1073/pnas.1218772110.

43. Lewandowski, C. R., & Bossie, D. N. (2017) *Let Trump Be Trump: The Inside Story of His Rise to the Presidency* (New York: Hachette), 178.

44. Rosenberg, M., Confessore, N., & Cadwalladr, C. (2018, March 17) How Trump consultants exploited the Facebook data of millions. Retrieved from https://www.nytimes.com/2018/03/17/us/politics/cambridge-analytica-trump-campaign.html.

45. Timberg, C., & Dwoskin, E. (2018, January 25) Russians got tens of thousands of Americans to RSVP for their phony political events on Facebook. *Washington Post*. Retrieved from https://www.washingtonpost.com/news/the-switch/wp/2018/01/25/russians-got-tens-of-thousands-of-americans-to-rsvp-for-their-phony-political-events-on-facebook/?utm_term=.099676080c22.

46. Frier, S., & Dennis, S. T. (2018, January 25) Facebook says "insignificant" overlap between Russia ads, Trump. *Bloomberg*. Retrieved from https://www. bloomberg.com/news/articles/2018-01-25/facebook-says-insignificant-overlap-between-russia-ads-trump.

47. Helderman, R. S., Troianovski, A., & Hamburger, T. (2017, December 7) Russian social media executive sought to help Trump campaign in 2016, emails show. *Washington Post*. Retrieved from https://www.washingtonpost.com/politics/russian-social-media-executive-sought-to-help-trump-campaign-in-2016-emails-show/2017/12/07/31ec8d90-db9a-11e7-b859-fb0995360725_story.html?utm_term=.855bfa19dc12.

48. Rothfeld, M., & Palazzolo, J. (2018, January 12) Trump lawyer arranged $130,000 payment for adult-film star's silence. *Wall Street Journal*. Retrieved from https://www.wsj.com/articles/trump-lawyer-arranged-130-000-payment-for-adult-film-stars-silence-1515787678.

49. Hartmann, M. (2016, November 5) *National Enquirer* paid to suppress story of Donald Trump cheating on Melania: Report. *New York Magazine*. Retrieved from http://nymag.com/daily/intelligencer/2016/11/national-enquirer-paid-to-kill-trump-affair-story-report.html.

50. Zaller, J. (1992) *The Nature and Origins of Mass Opinion* (New York: Cambridge University Press).

Part 3

1. Harrington, R., & Gould, S. (2016, December 21) Americans beat one voter turnout record—here's how 2016 compares with past elections. *Business Insider*. Retrieved from https://amp.businessinsider.com/trump-voter-turnout-records-history-obama-clinton-2016-11.

   Early voting expert Michael McDonald estimated that just under 430,000 voted before October 9th. (McDonald, M. [n.d.] 2016 November general election early voting. *United States Election Project*. Retrieved from http://www.electproject. org/early_2016.) In total, 46 million voted early. Hence my estimate that in the October 7th to November 7th period, 45.5 million early votes were cast.

2. Office of the Director of National Intelligence (2017, January 6) Background to "Assessing Russian Activities and Intentions in Recent US Elections": The analytic process and cyber incident attribution. Retrieved from https://www.dni.gov/files/documents/ICA_2017_01.pdf.

3. Healy, G. (2017, April 21) Did Trump really mention WikiLeaks over 160 times in the last month of the election cycle? *PolitiFact*. Retrieved from http://www.politifact.com/truth-o-meter/statements/2017/apr/21/jackie-speier/did-trump-really-mention-wikileaks-over-160-times-/.

4. Ioffe, J. (2017, November 13) The secret correspondence between Donald Trump Jr. and WikiLeaks. *The Atlantic*. Retrieved from https://www.theatlantic.com/politics/archive/2017/11/the-secret-correspondence-between-donald-trump-jr-and-wikileaks/545738/.

5. Twitter user @DonaldJTrumpJr (2016, October 14) For those who have the time to read about all the corruption and hypocrisy all the @wikileaks emails are right here. Twitter post. Retrieved from https://twitter.com/DonaldJTrumpJr/status/786923210512142336.

6. Weedon, J., Nuland, W., & Stamos, A. (2017, April 27) Information operations and Facebook. Facebook. Retrieved from https://fbnewsroomus.files.wordpress.com/2017/04/facebook-and-information-operations-v1.pdf.

Chapter 8

1. Nakashima, R., & Ortutay, B. (2017, November 10) AP exclusive: Russia Twitter trolls deflected Trump bad news. *Associated Press*. Retrieved from https://apnews.com/fc9ab2b0bbc34f11bc10714100318ae1.

2. Nakashima, R., & Ortutay, B. (2017, November 10) AP exclusive: Russia Twitter trolls deflected Trump bad news. *Associated Press*. Retrieved from https://apnews.com/fc9ab2b0bbc34f11bc10714100318ae1.

3. US Department of Homeland Security (2016, October 7) Joint statement from the Department of Homeland Security and Office of the Director of National Intelligence on Election Security. Retrieved from https://www.dhs.gov/news/2016/10/07/joint-statement-department-homeland-security-and-office-director-national.

4. Yahoo! News Staff (2017, October 6) 64 hours in October: How one weekend blew up the rules of American politics. *Yahoo!* Retrieved from https://www.yahoo.com/news/64-hours-october-one-weekend-blew-rules-american-politics-2-162827162.html.

5. The Aspen Institute (2017, July 20) Active measures: The Kremlin plan to beat the west without firing a shot. Transcript. Aspen Security Forum. Retrieved from http://aspensecurityforum.org/wp-content/uploads/2017/07/Active-Measures_The-Kremlin-Plan-to-Beat-the-West-without-Firing-a-Shot.pdf.

6. Fahrenthold, D. A. (2016, October 6) Trump recorded having extremely lewd conversation about women in 2005. *Washington Post*. Retrieved from https://www.washingtonpost.com/politics/trump-recorded-having-extremely-lewd-conversation-about-women-in-2005/2016/10/07/3b9ce776-8cb4-11e6-bf8a-3d26847eeed4_story.html?utm_term=.2f527a2cf467.

7. Yahoo! News Staff (2017, October 6) 64 hours in October: How one weekend blew up the rules of American politics. *Yahoo!* Retrieved from https://www.yahoo.com/news/64-hours-october-one-weekend-blew-rules-american-politics-2-162827162.html.

8. I am relying on the timeline created by *Yahoo!* authors. See Yahoo! News Staff (2017, October 6) 64 hours in October: How one weekend blew up the rules of American politics. *Yahoo!* Retrieved from https://www.yahoo.com/news/64-hours-october-one-weekend-blew-rules-american-politics-2-162827162.html.

9. Twitter user @johnpodesta (2016, October 7) 2. . . . . I'm not happy about being hacked by the Russians in their quest to throw the election to Donald Trump. Twitter post. Retrieved from https://twitter.com/johnpodesta/status/

784539455453560833; Twitter user @johnpodesta (2016, October 7) 3. Don't have time to figure out which docs are real and which are faked.... Twitter post. Retrieved from https://twitter.com/johnpodesta/status/784539553281355776.

10. Office of the Director of National Intelligence (2017, January 6) Assessing Russian activities and intentions in recent US Elections. Retrieved from https://www.dni. gov/files/documents/ICA_2017_01.pdf.

11. Nakashima, R., & Ortutay, B. (2017, November 10) AP exclusive: Russia Twitter trolls deflected Trump bad news. *Associated Press*. Retrieved from https://apnews. com/fc9ab2b0bbc34f11bc10714100318ae1.

12. Nakashima, R., & Ortutay, B. (2017, November 10) AP exclusive: Russia Twitter trolls deflected Trump bad news. *Associated Press*. Retrieved from https://apnews. com/fc9ab2b0bbc34f11bc10714100318ae1.

13. Timberg, C. (2018, February 15) Russia used mainstream media to manipulate American voters. *Washington Post*. Retrieved from https://www.washingtonpost. com/business/technology/russia-used-mainstream-media-to-manipulate-american-voters/2018/02/15/85f7914e-11a7-11e8-9065-e55346f6de81_story. html?utm_term=.36034ce56e96.

14. Faris, R. M., Roberts, H., Etling, B., Bourassa, N., Zuckerman, E., & Benkler, Y. (2017, August) Partisanship, propaganda, and disinformation: Online media and the 2016 US presidential election. Berkman Klein Center for Internet & Society at Harvard University. Retrieved from https://cyber.harvard.edu/publications/ 2017/08/mediacloud.

15. Weise, E. (2017, October 30) Russian fake accounts showed posts to 126 million Facebook users. *USA Today*. Retrieved from https://www.usatoday.com/story/ tech/2017/10/30/russian-fake-accounts-showed-posts-126-million-facebook-users/815342001/.

16. Lipton, E., Sanger, D. E., & Shane, S. (2016, December 13) The perfect weapon: How Russian cyberpower invaded the US. *New York Times*. Retrieved from https://nyti. ms/2jASgpt.

17. House Permanent Select Committee on Intelligence (2018, March 26) Minority Views to the Majority-produced "Report on Russian Active Measures, March 22, 2018." Retrieved from https://docs.house.gov/meetings/IG/IG00/20180322/ 108023/HRPT-115-2.pdf.

18. Enten, H. (2016, December 23) How much did WikiLeaks hurt Hillary Clinton? *FiveThirtyEight*. Retrieved from https://fivethirtyeight.com/features/wikileaks-hillary-clinton/.

19. Plantz, K. (2016, September 18) Donald Trump's deplorables: A reclamation of the name. *InsideSources*. Retrieved from http://insidesources.staging.wpengine.com/ donald-trumps-deplorables-a-reclamation-of-the-name/.

20. *Meet the Press* (2016, October 9) *Meet the Press*—October 9, 2016. *NBC News*. Retrieved from https://www.nbcnews.com/meet-the-press/meet-press-october-9-2016-n662746.

21. Tom Patterson's study of the 2016 campaign cited elsewhere documents that this was the dominant focus on 2016. In *Spiral of Cynicism: The Press and the Public Good*,

Joe Cappella and I show that the press focus on tactical or strategic considerations in campaign coverage activates cynicism and depresses learning.

22. Cappella, J. N., & Jamieson, K. H. (1997) *Spiral of Cynicism: The Press and the Public Good* (New York: Oxford University Press).

23. *Face the Nation* (2016, October 9) *Face the Nation* transcript, October 9, 2016: Giuliani, Mook, Schieffer, O'Donnell, Cordes, Garrett. *CBS News*. Retrieved from https://www.cbsnews.com/news/face-the-nation-transcript-october-9-2016-giuliani-mook/.

24. McCarthy, M. (2016, October 9) Republican voters remain loyal to Trump in first national poll after video. *Morning Consult*. Retrieved from https://morningconsult.com/2016/10/09/republican-voters-remain-loyal-trump-first-national-poll-video/.

25. *Fox News Sunday* (2016, October 9) Giuliani addresses Trump's treatment of women; John Podesta speaks out after his email is hacked. *Fox News*. Retrieved from http://www.foxnews.com/transcript/2016/10/09/giuliani-addresses-trump-treatment-women-john-podesta-speaks-out-after-his.html.

26. *Face the Nation* (2016, October 9) *Face the Nation* transcript, October 9, 2016: Giuliani, Mook, Schieffer, O'Donnell, Cordes, Garrett. *CBS News*. Retrieved from https://www.cbsnews.com/news/face-the-nation-transcript-october-9-2016-giuliani-mook/.

27. *This Week*, ABC News (2016, October 9) *This Week* transcript: Rudy Giuliani and Donna Brazile. *ABC News*. Retrieved from http://abcnews.go.com/Politics/week-transcript-rudy-giuliani-donna-brazile/story?id=42670926.

28. Paul Waldman and I showed how this occurred in 2000 when the Sunday interview show moderators adopted the Republican assumptions about the nature of the recount of the Florida vote. See Jamieson, K. H., & Waldman, P. (2004) *The Press Effect: Politicians, Journalists, and the Stories That Shape the Political World* (New York: Oxford University Press).

29. *Face the Nation* (2016, October 9) *Face the Nation* transcript, October 9, 2016: Giuliani, Mook, Schieffer, O'Donnell, Cordes, Garrett. *CBS News*. Retrieved from https://www.cbsnews.com/news/face-the-nation-transcript-october-9-2016-giuliani-mook/.

30. *Meet the Press* (2016, October 9) *Meet the Press*—October 9, 2016. *NBC News*. Retrieved from https://www.nbcnews.com/meet-the-press/meet-press-october-9-2016-n662746.

31. *This Week*, ABC News (2016, October 9) *This Week* transcript: Rudy Giuliani and Donna Brazile. *ABC News*. Retrieved from http://abcnews.go.com/Politics/week-transcript-rudy-giuliani-donna-brazile/story?id=42670926.

32. *Fox News Sunday* (2016, October 9) Giuliani addresses Trump's treatment of women; John Podesta speaks out after his email is hacked. *Fox News*. Retrieved from http://www.foxnews.com/transcript/2016/10/09/giuliani-addresses-trump-treatment-women-john-podesta-speaks-out-after-his.html.

33. State of the Union (2016, October 9) Dump Trump?; heat on Trump in second debate; interview with vice presidential candidate Tim Kaine; interview with former

New York mayor Rudy Giuliani; Donald Trump's sexually aggressive comments caught on tape. *CNN.* Retrieved from http://www.cnn.com/TRANSCRIPTS/ 1610/09/sotu.01.html.

34. WikiLeaks (n.d.) HRC paid speeches. Retrieved from https://wikileaks.org/ podesta-emails/emailid/927.

35. House Permanent Select Committee on Intelligence (2018, March 26) Minority Views to the Majority-produced "Report on Russian Active Measures, March 22, 2018." Retrieved from https://docs.house.gov/meetings/IG/IG00/20180322/ 108023/HRPT-115-2.pdf.

36. WikiLeaks (n.d.) HRC paid speeches. Retrieved from https://wikileaks.org/ podesta-emails/emailid/927.

37. Watts, D. J., & Rothschild, D. M. (2017, December 5) Don't blame the election on fake news. Blame it on the media. *Columbia Journalism Review.* Retrieved from https://www.cjr.org/analysis/fake-news-media-election-trump.php.

38. Watts, D. J., & Rothschild, D. M. (2017, December 5) Don't blame the election on fake news. Blame it on the media. *Columbia Journalism Review.* Retrieved from https://www.cjr.org/analysis/fake-news-media-election-trump.php.

39. Yahoo! News Staff (2017, October 6) 64 hours in October: How one weekend blew up the rules of American politics. *Yahoo!* Retrieved from https://www.yahoo. com/news/64-hours-october-one-weekend-blew-rules-american-politics-2- 162827162.html.

40. Hayward, J. (2016, October 13) The most explosive WikiLeaks Clinton revelations (so far). *Breitbart.* Retrieved from http://www.breitbart.com/big-government/ 2016/10/13/the-most-explosive-wikileaks-clinton-revelations-so-far/.

41. Malone, C. (2016, August 18) Trump made Breitbart great again. *FiveThirtyEight.* Retrieved from https://fivethirtyeight.com/features/trump-made-breitbart-great-again/.

42. Faris, R. M., Roberts, H., Etling, B., Bourassa, N., Zuckerman, E., & Benkler, Y. (2017, August) Partisanship, propaganda, and disinformation: Online media and the 2016 US presidential election. Berkman Klein Center for Internet & Society at Harvard University. Retrieved from https://cyber.harvard.edu/publications/ 2017/08/mediacloud.

43. Breitbart News (2016, November 7) Breitbart News hits record 240+ million pageviews, 37 million uniques in October. *Breitbart.* Retrieved from http://www. breitbart.com/big-journalism/2016/11/07/breitbart-news-hits-record-240- million-pageviews-37-million-uniques-in-october/.

44. Swan, J., & Fischer, S. (2017, February 6) Breitbart's online stats outpacing main-stream rivals. *Axios.* Retrieved from https://www.axios.com/breitbart-grows-its-reach-2243435087.html.

45. Stranahan, L. (2016, October 14) WikiLeaks reveals long list of media canoodling with Hillary Clinton. *Breitbart.* Retrieved from http://www.breitbart.com/ wikileaks/2016/10/14/wikileaks-reveals-long-list-clinton-media-canoodling/.

46. Dulis, E. (2016, October 17) WikiLeaks: Journalists dined at top Clinton staffers' homes days before Hillary's campaign launch. *Breitbart.* Retrieved from http://

www.breitbart.com/big-journalism/2016/10/17/wikileaks-journalists-clinton-staff-homes-before-hillarys-campaign-launch/.

47. Blake, A. (2016, November 17) How America decided, at the last moment, to elect Donald Trump. *Washington Post.* Retrieved from https://www.washingtonpost. com/news/the-fix/wp/2016/11/17/how-america-decided-at-the-very-last-moment-to-elect-donald-trump/.

48. Enten, H. (2016, December 23) How much did WikiLeaks hurt Hillary Clinton? *FiveThirtyEight.* Retrieved from https://fivethirtyeight.com/features/wikileaks-hillary-clinton/.

49. Howard, P., Kollanyi, B., Bradshaw, S., & Neudert, L-M. (2017) Social media, news and political information during the US election: Was polarizing content concentrated in swing states? Data memo. Project on Computational Propaganda. Retrieved from http://comprop.oii.ox.ac.uk/publishing/working-papers/social-media-news-and-political-information-during-the-us-election-was-polarizing-content-concentrated-in-swing-states/.

Chapter 9

1. Cheney, K. (2016, October 12) Hacked 80-page roundup of paid speeches shows Clinton "praising Wall Street." *Politico.* Retrieved from https://www.politico.com/story/2016/10/hillary-clinton-wall-street-speeches-podesta-emails-229689.

2. Vogel, K. P. (2016, October 11) Chelsea flagged "serious concerns" about Clinton Foundation conflicts. *Politico.* Retrieved from https://www.politico.com/story/2016/10/chelsea-clinton-foundation-conflicts-emails-229605.

3. As a side note, although viewers did not know it, Raddatz had abstracted the question from the context into which its author had set it. Taken as a whole, the awkward phrasing of the total submission hinted that "Tu E. from VA," whom Raddatz identified only as Tu, was not a native speaker of English. It read: "The 10/07 Wikileaks email dump highlights a particularly important conversation exchange where it is said, 'You need both a public and a private position'. Is it okay for politicians to be two-faced?" (Open Debate Coalition [2016, October 7] Is it acceptable for a politican to have 'private' stance on issues? Retrieved from https://presidentialopenquestions.com/questions/17099/vote/).

4. Fernholz, T. (2016, October 9) The leaked email behind Hillary Clinton's mid-debate reference to Steven Spielberg's Abraham Lincoln biopic. *Quartz.* Retrieved from https://qz.com/805005/the-leaked-email-behind-hillary-clintons-mid-debate-reference-to-steven-spielbergs-abraham-lincoln-biopic/.

5. Littleton, C., & Schwindt, O. (2016, October 10) Trump-Clinton second debate ratings fall 21% with 66.5 million viewers. *Variety.* Retrieved from http://variety.com/2016/tv/news/trump-clinton-debate-2-ratings-drop-1201883637/.

6. Katz, A. J. (2016, October 22) The presidential debates set ratings records in 2016. *Adweek.* Retrieved from http://www.adweek.com/tv-video/presidential-debates-set-ratings-records-2016-does-format-need-change-174205/#/.

7. WikiLeaks (n.d.) HRC paid speeches. Retrieved from https://wikileaks.org/podesta-emails/emailid/927.

8. Montanaro, D. (2016, August 19) Watch: Donald Trump releases first campaign ad, to air in 4 states. *NPR*. Retrieved from https://www.npr.org/2016/08/19/490609443/watch-donald-trump-releases-first-campaign-ad-to-air-in-4-states.
9. Blake, A. (2016, October 11) Donald Trump, unplugged as ever. *Washington Post*. Retrieved from https://www.washingtonpost.com/news/the-fix/wp/2016/10/11/donald-trump-unplugged-as-ever/?utm_term=.47ac0a2f240d.
10. Gore, D., Kiely, E., Jackson, B., Robertson, L., Farley, R., Schipani, V., Gross, Z., Wang, J., & Wallace, C. (2016, October 20) FactChecking the final presidential debate. *FactCheck.org*. Retrieved from https://www.factcheck.org/2016/10/factchecking-the-final-presidential-debate-2/.
11. WikiLeaks (n.d.) HRC paid speeches. Attachments: HRC paid speeches flags. Retrieved from https://wikileaks.org/podesta-emails/emailid/927.
12. Twitter user @realDonaldTrump (2016, October 19) Moderator: Hillary paid $225000 by a Brazilian bank for a speech that called for "open borders." Twitter post. Retrieved from https://twitter.com/realDonaldTrump/status/788914975779663872.

Chapter 10

1. Nixon Library and Museum (n.d.) Memoirs v. tapes: President Nixon and the December bombings. Retrieved from https://www.nixonlibrary.gov/exhibits/decbomb/chapter-ii.html.
2. USA Today (2016, November 6) Read the full text of James Comey's letter on the new Clinton emails. Retrieved from https://www.usatoday.com/story/news/politics/onpolitics/2016/11/06/read-full-text-comeys-letter-new-clinton-emails/93398304/.
3. Diamond, J. (2016, October 28) Trump reinvigorated by FBI Clinton probe. *CNN*. Retrieved from https://www.cnn.com/2016/10/28/politics/donald-trump-reacts-to-fbi-clinton-probe/index.html.
4. Silver, N. (2017, May 3) The Comey letter probably cost Clinton the election. *FiveThirtyEight*. Retrieved from https://fivethirtyeight.com/features/the-comey-letter-probably-cost-clinton-the-election/.
5. Watts, D. J., & Rothschild, D. M. (2017, December 5) Don't blame the election on fake news. Blame it on the media. *Columbia Journalism Review*. Retrieved from https://www.cjr.org/analysis/fake-news-media-election-trump.php.
6. Patterson, T. E. (2016, December 7) News coverage of the 2016 general election: How the press failed the voters. *Shorenstein Center on Media, Politics and Public Policy*. Harvard Kennedy School. Retrieved from https://shorensteincenter.org/news-coverage-2016-general-election/.
7. Patterson, T. E. (2018, March 8) Personal correspondence.
8. Silver, N. (2017, May 3) The Comey letter probably cost Clinton the election. *FiveThirtyEight*. Retrieved from https://fivethirtyeight.com/features/the-comey-letter-probably-cost-clinton-the-election/.
9. Wang, S. (2016, December 10) The Comey effect. *Princeton Election Consortium*. Retrieved from http://election.princeton.edu/2016/12/10/the-comey-effect/.

10. *Washington Post* Staff (2017, May 3) Read the full testimony of FBI Director James Comey in which he discusses Clinton email investigation. *Washington Post*. Retrieved from https://www.washingtonpost.com/news/post-politics/wp/2017/05/03/read-the-full-testimony-of-fbi-director-james-comey-in-which-he-discusses-clinton-email-investigation/?utm_term=.cd8ad6c5b7ae.

11. Comey, J. (2018) *A Higher Loyalty* (New York: Flatiron Books), 178.

12. *Washington Post* Staff (2017, May 3) Read the full testimony of FBI Director James Comey in which he discusses Clinton email investigation. *Washington Post*. Retrieved from https://www.washingtonpost.com/news/post-politics/wp/2017/05/03/read-the-full-testimony-of-fbi-director-james-comey-in-which-he-discusses-clinton-email-investigation/?utm_term=.cd8ad6c5b7ae.

13. Golshan, T. (2017, June 8) The Comey testimony included a big reveal about the 2016 election. *Vox*. Retrieved from https://www.vox.com/2017/6/8/15762140/comey-testimony-2016-election-clinton-lynch.

14. Apuzzo, M., Schmidt, M.S., Goldman, A., & Lichtblau, E. (2017, April 22) Comey tried to shield the F.B.I. from politics. Then he shaped an election. *The New York Times*. Retrieved from https://www.nytimes.com/2017/04/22/us/politics/james-comey-election.html.

15. Demirjian, K., & Barrett, D. (2017, May 24) How a dubious Russian document influenced the FBI's handling of the Clinton probe. *Washington Post*. Retrieved from https://www.washingtonpost.com/world/national-security/how-a-dubious-russian-document-influenced-the-fbis-handling-of-the-clinton-probe/2017/05/24/f375c07c-3a95-11e7-9e48-c4f199710b69_story.html?utm_term=.28075c1f0a89.

16. Comey, J. (2018) *A Higher Loyalty* (New York: Flatiron Books), 171.

17. Comey, J. (2018) *A Higher Loyalty* (New York: Flatiron Books).

18. Bash, D., Prokupecz, S., & Borger, G. (2017, May 26) Sources: Comey acted on Russian intelligence he knew was fake. *CNN*. Retrieved from https://amp.cnn.com/cnn/2017/05/26/politics/james-comey-fbi-investigation-fake-russian-intelligence/index.html.

19. Demirjian, K., & Barrett, D. (2017, May 24) How a dubious Russian document influenced the FBI's handling of the Clinton probe. *Washington Post*. Retrieved from https://www.washingtonpost.com/world/national-security/how-a-dubious-russian-document-influenced-the-fbis-handling-of-the-clinton-probe/2017/05/24/f375c07c-3a95-11e7-9e48-c4f199710b69_story.html?utm_term=.023a5abadb52.

20. Woodruff, J., Summers, E., & Guray, G.L. (2018, May 1) On Clinton email revelations, 'there was no good option' for FBI, says James Comey. *PBS NewsHour*. Retrieved from https://www.pbs.org/newshour/show/james-comey-on-clinton-email-probe-no-win-situation.

21. *Face the Nation* (2017, June 11) Transcript: Sen. Lindsey Graham on *Face the Nation*, June 11, 2017. *CBS News*. Retrieved from https://www.cbsnews.com/news/transcript-senator-lindsey-graham-on-face-the-nation-june-11-2017/.

22. Apuzzo, M., Schmidt, M.S., Goldman, A., & Lichtblau, E. (2017, April 22) Comey tried to shield the F.B.I. from politics. Then he shaped an election. *The New York*

Times. Retrieved from https://www.nytimes.com/2017/04/22/us/politics/james-comey-election.html.

23. McArdle, M. (2018, April 18) Loretta Lynch claps back at James Comey. *National Review.* Retrieved from https://www.nationalreview.com/news/loretta-lynch-claps-back-at-james-comey/.

24. Jenkins, H.W. (2018, April 17) The Comey coverup. *The Wall Street Journal.* Retrieved from https://www.wsj.com/amp/articles/the-comey-coverup-1524004580.

25. Comey, J. (2018) *A Higher Loyalty* (New York: Flatiron Books), 177.

26. Jenkins, H.W. (2018, April 17) The Comey coverup. *The Wall Street Journal.* Retrieved from https://www.wsj.com/amp/articles/the-comey-coverup-1524004580.

27. Lipton, E., Sanger, D. E., & Shane, S. (2016, December 13) The perfect weapon: How Russian cyberpower invaded the US. *New York Times.* Retrieved from https://nyti.ms/2jASgpt.

28. *Washington Post* Staff (2017, May 3) Read the full testimony of FBI Director James Comey in which he discusses Clinton email investigation. *Washington Post.* Retrieved from https://www.washingtonpost.com/news/post-politics/wp/2017/05/03/read-the-full-testimony-of-fbi-director-james-comey-in-which-he-discusses-clinton-email-investigation/?utm_term=.cd8ad6c5b7ae.

29. *Washington Post* Staff (2017, May 3) Read the full testimony of FBI Director James Comey in which he discusses Clinton email investigation. *Washington Post.* Retrieved from https://www.washingtonpost.com/news/post-politics/wp/2017/05/03/read-the-full-testimony-of-fbi-director-james-comey-in-which-he-discusses-clinton-email-investigation/?utm_term=.cd8ad6c5b7ae.

30. Comey, J. (2018) *A Higher Loyalty* (New York: Flatiron Books), 204.

31. Schultheis, E. (2016, November 6) FBI director to Congress: Still no charges recommended after latest Clinton emails reviewed. *CBS News.* Retrieved from https://www.cbsnews.com/news/fbi-director-comey-congress-new-letter-hillary-clinton-emails-still-no-charges/.

32. Schouten, F., Johnson, K., & Przybyla, H. (2016, November 6) FBI declares it is finally done investigating Hillary Clinton's email. Retrieved from https://www.usatoday.com/story/news/politics/elections/2016/2016/11/06/fbi-not-recommending-charges-over-new-clinton-emails/93395808/

33. Barrett, D. (2016, October 30) FBI in internal feud over Hillary Clinton probe. *Wall Street Journal.* Retrieved from https://www.wsj.com/articles/laptop-may-include-thousands-of-emails-linked-to-hillary-clintons-private-server-1477854957.

34. Editorial Board (2018, April 14) McCabe and a lower loyalty. *Wall Street Journal.* Retrieved from https://www.wsj.com/articles/mccabe-and-a-lower-loyalty-1523660629.

35. Lichtblau, E. & Myers, S. L. (2016, October 31) Investigating Donald Trump, F.B.I. sees no clear link to Russia. *New York Times.* Retrieved from https://www.nytimes.com/2016/11/01/us/politics/fbi-russia-election-donald-trump.html.

36. Comey, J. (2018) *A Higher Loyalty* (New York: Flatiron Books), 191.

37. Lichtblau, E. & Myers, S. L. (2016, October 31) Investigating Donald Trump, F.B.I. sees no clear link to Russia. *New York Times.* Retrieved from https://www. nytimes.com/2016/11/01/us/politics/fbi-russia-election-donald-trump.html.

38. Twitter Public Policy (2018, January 18) Update on Twitter's review of the 2016 US election. *Twitter.* Updated on January 31, 2018. Retrieved from https://blog. twitter.com/official/en_us/topics/company/2018/2016-election-update.html.

39. Festinger, L. (1962) *A Theory of Cognitive Dissonance,* vol. 2 (Stanford: Stanford University Press); Jarcho, J. M., Berkman, E. T., & Lieberman, M. D. (2010) The neural basis of rationalization: Cognitive dissonance reduction during decision-making. *Social Cognitive and Affective Neuroscience,* 6(4): 460–467. doi: 10.1093/scan/nsq054.

40. Chan, M.P.S., Jones, C.R., Jamieson, K.H., & Albarracín, D. (2017) Debunking: a meta-analysis of the psychological efficacy of messages countering misinforma-tion. *Psychological Science,* 28(11): 1531–1546. doi: 10.1177/0956797617714579.

41. McDonald, M. (n.d.) 2016 November general election early voting. United States Election Project. Retrieved from http://www.electproject.org/early_2016.

Part 4

1. Smith, S. B. (2007) *For Love of Politics: Bill and Hillary Clinton: The White House Years* (New York: Random House).

2. Pramuk, J. (2016, November 9) Trump spent about half of what Clinton did on his way to the presidency. *CNBC.* Retrieved from https://www.cnbc.com/2016/11/09/trump-spent-about-half-of-what-clinton-did-on-his-way-to-the-presidency.html.

3. Lynch, J. (2016, November 2) Donald Trump and Hillary Clinton have been spending the most money on these ads. *Adweek.* Retrieved from http://www.adweek.com/tv-video/donald-trump-and-hillary-clinton-have-been-wooing-voters-these-ads-174396/.

4. Associated Press in Washington (2016, December 9) Donald Trump and Hillary Clinton's final campaign spending revealed. *Guardian.* Retrieved from https://www.theguardian.com/us-news/2016/dec/09/trump-and-clintons-final-campaign-spending-revealed.

5. Associated Press in Washington (2016, December 9) Donald Trump and Hillary Clinton's final campaign spending revealed. *Guardian.* Retrieved from https://www.theguardian.com/us-news/2016/dec/09/trump-and-clintons-final-campaign-spending-revealed.

6. Kenski, K., Hardy, B. W., & Jamieson, K. H. (2010) *The Obama Victory: How Media, Money, and Message Shaped the 2008 Election* (New York: Oxford University Press); Hill, S. J., Lo, J., Vavreck, L., & Zaller, J. (2013) How quickly we forget: The du-ration of persuasion effects from mass communication. *Political Communication,* 30(4): 521–547.

7. We summarize this literature and make this case from 2008 data in *The Obama Victory*: Kenski, K., Hardy, B. W., & Jamieson, K. H. (2010) *The Obama Victory: How*

Media, Money, and Message Shaped the 2008 Election (New York: Oxford University Press).

8. Associated Press in Washington (2016, December 9) Donald Trump and Hillary Clinton's final campaign spending revealed. *Guardian*. Retrieved from https://www.theguardian.com/us-news/2016/dec/09/trump-and-clintons-final-campaign-spending-revealed.

9. Sides, J. (2017, June) *Race, Religion, and Immigration in 2016: How the Debate over American Identity Shaped the Election and What It Means for a Trump Presidency*. Democracy Fund Voter Study Group. Retrieved from https://www.voterstudy group.org/publications/2016-elections/race-religion-immigration-2016.

10. For an alternative point of view, see Gessen, M. (2017, November 3) Russian interference in the 2016 election: A cacophony, not a conspiracy. *The New Yorker*. Retrieved from https://www.newyorker.com/news/our-columnists/russian-interference-in-the-2016-election-a-cacophony-not-a-conspiracy.

11. Taylor, S. E. (1991) Asymmetrical effects of positive and negative events: The mobilization-minimization hypothesis. *Psychological Bulletin, 110*(1): 67.

12. CNN (2016, November 23) Exit polls. Retrieved from http://www.cnn.com/election/results/exit-polls/national/president.

Afterword

1. Gerstein, J., & Cheney, K. (2018, February 13) Intelligence officials say Russia intent on disrupting US elections. *Politico*. Retrieved from https://www.politico.com/story/2018/02/13/russia-us-elections-intelligence-officials-407253.

2. Halper, E., & Megerian, C. (2018, February 14) As foreign hackers plot next attack, Washington struggles to shore up vulnerable voting systems. *Los Angeles Times*. Retrieved from http://www.latimes.com/politics/la-na-pol-elections-security-20180213-story.html.

3. Dilanian, K. (2018, February 13) US intel agencies predict Russia to escalate election meddling efforts. *NBC News*. Retrieved from https://www.nbcnews.com/politics/national-security/u-s-intel-agencies-expect-russia-escalate-election-meddling-efforts-n847551.

4. Leonhardt, D. (2017, May 9) A French lesson for the American media. *New York Times*. Retrieved from https://nyti.ms/2pq5Jjn.

5. Chozick, A. (2018) *Chasing Hillary* (New York: Harper), Kindle Loc 5237 of 6078.

6. Lipton, E., Sanger, D. E., & Shane, S. (2016, December 13) The perfect weapon: How Russian cyberpower invaded the US. *New York Times*. Retrieved from https://nyti.ms/2jASgpt.

7. Facebook Newsroom (2018, May 10) Russian ads released by Congress. *Facebook*. Retrieved from https://newsroom.fb.com/news/2018/05/russian-ads-released-by-congress/.

8. Twitter Public Policy (2018, Janury 31) Update on Twitter's review of the 2016 U.S. election. *Twitter*. Retrieved from https://blog.twitter.com/official/en_us/topics/company/2018/2016-election-update.html.

9. Glaser, A. (2017, December 17) Political ads on Facebook now need to say who paid for them. *Slate*. Retrieved from http://www.slate.com/blogs/future_tense/2017/12/18/political_ads_on_facebook_now_need_to_say_who_paid_for_them.html.

10. Facebook Newsroom (2018, May 10) Russian ads released by Congress. *Facebook*. Retrieved from https://newsroom.fb.com/news/2018/05/russian-ads-released-by-congress/.

11. Statt, N. (2018, March 28) Facebook will no longer allow third-party data for targeting ads. *The Verge*. Retrieved from https://www.theverge.com/2018/3/28/17174854/facebook-shutting-down-partner-categories-ad-targeting-cambridge-analytica.

12. Guess, A., Nyhan, B., & Reifler, J. (2018) Selective exposure to misinformation: Evidence from the consumption of fake news during the 2016 US presidential campaign. Retrieved from https://www.dartmouth.edu/~nyhan/fake-news-2016.pdf.

13. Silverman, C. (2016, November 16) This analysis shows how fake election news stories outperformed real news on Facebook. *BuzzFeed*. Retrieved from https://www.buzzfeed.com/craigsilverman/viral-fake-election-news-outperformed-real-news-on-facebook?utm_term=.wwJkPPmPn#.ne3dKK1KM

14. Allcott, H., & Gentzkow, M. (2017) Social media and fake news in the 2016 election. *Journal of Economic Perspectives, 31*(2): 211–236. doi: 10.3386/w23089.

15. Iyengar, S., Sood, G. & Lelkes, Y. (2012) Affect, not ideology: A social identity perspective on polarization. *Public Opinion Quarterly, 76*(3): 405-431. doi: 10.1093/poq/nfs038.

16. Vavreck, L. (2017, January 31) A measure of identity: Are you wedded to your party? *New York Times*. Retrieved from https://nyti.ms/2jOITm3.

17. Lau, R., Andersen, D., Ditonto, T., Kleinberg, M. & Redlawsk, D. (2017) How negative ads from diverse right-wing media makes conservative voters dislike Democratic candidates even more. *USAPP – American Politics and Policy*. United States Centre, London School of Economics. Retrieved from http://blogs.lse.ac.uk/usappblog/about-usapp/.

18. Hetherington, M. J. & Rudolph, T. J. (2015) *Why Washington Won't Work: Polarization, Political Trust, and the Governing Crisis* (Chicago: University of Chicago Press).

Appendix 2

1. Full question wording Debate 2: *Did you happen to watch or listen to the town hall style presidential debate between Donald Trump and Hillary Clinton on Sunday, October 9? IF YES: Did you watch or listen to all, most, or just some of the debate?*

2. Full question wording Debate 3: *Did you watch or listen to Wednesday's (October 19) presidential debate between Donald Trump and Hillary Clinton? IF YES: Did you watch or listen to all, most, or just some of the debate?*

INDEX